Memory in Literature

Memory in Literature

From Rousseau to Neuroscience

Suzanne Nalbantian

First published 2003 by
PALGRAVE MACMILLAN
Houndmills, Basingstoke, Hampshire RG21 6XS and
175 Fifth Avenue, New York, N.Y. 10010
Companies and representatives throughout the world

PALGRAVE MACMILLAN is the global academic imprint of the Palgrave
Macmillan division of St. Martin's Press, LLC and of Palgrave Macmillan Ltd.
Macmillan® is a registered trademark in the United States, United Kingdom
and other countries. Palgrave is a registered trademark in the European
Union and other countries.

ISBN 1-4039-6687-7

This book is printed on paper suitable for recycling and made from fully
managed and sustained forest sources.

A catalogue record for this book is available from the British Library.

Library of Congress Cataloging-in-Publication Data
Nalbantian, Suzanne
  Memory in literature : from Rousseau to neuroscience / Suzanne Nalbantian.
      p.   cm.
  Includes bibliographical references and index.
  ISBN 0–333–74065–3 (cloth)
  ISBN 1-4039-6687-7 (paperback)

  1. Memory in literature.   2. Literature, Modern—History and criticism.
  I. Title.
PN56.M44 N35 2002
809'.93353—dc21

                                                            2002026749

Printed and bound in Great Britain by
Antony Rowe Ltd, Chippenham and Eastbourne

To my husband, David S. Reynolds

Contents

List of Plates

Acknowledgments

This book was contracted in London, gestated in Paris, and was written in New York. The project grew from my previous book, *Aesthetic Autobiography*, when I realized that memory events intrinsic to autobiographical writings could be approached with objective, extrinsic scrutiny.

My utmost gratitude goes to my scholar-husband, David S. Reynolds, who was a constant source of encouragement and support to me as I took my lone journey down unexplored interdisciplinary pathways. I also wish to thank my devoted economist brother, Haig R. Nalbantian, whose scientific, critical eye examined the manuscript. I appreciate greatly the insights I gained from my discussions of modern science with my physicist friend William Wallace. I have also profited from collegial dialogues with Professors André Topia, Jean Bessière, and Pascal Michon. I am grateful to the indefatigable librarian Louis Pisha of Long Island University, who made available to me research materials from across the United States. My appreciation goes to Tim Farmiloe, the former Director of Macmillan Publishers, who sustained faith in my work over two decades of publishing books with his firm. His successor, Josie Dixon, and her colleagues Emily Rosser and Becky Mashayekh at Palgrave have ably seen the publication through to completion.

My year-long sabbatical from Long Island University, at the turn of the century, enabled me to spend a productive research year in Paris, where I doggedly mined the collections of the Sorbonne, the Salpêtrière Hospital, the Bibliothèque interuniversitaire de Médecine, and the Bibliothèque Nationale, and was stimulated by lectures at the Collège de France and scholarly exchanges at the Pasteur Institute. This time, I had to forgo Paris's cafés for its libraries, which provided me with other kinds of sustenance.

Bridgehampton, Long Island
May 2002

Note on the Text

In quotations from French texts, passages that are in the original French followed by an English translation are my own translated versions except where otherwise indicated. Where only English appears, the translation are those of others.

Introduction

A remembering human subject stands out in Western literature that would catch some neuroscientists by surprise. It is the case of the artist figure Lily Briscoe in Virginia Woolf's *To the Lighthouse* whose whole task over a ten-year period is to transfer her recollections of her friend Mrs Ramsay into a painting which would preserve her memory forever. The novel takes place on a distant Scottish island in the Hebrides. Lily had first contemplated Mrs Ramsay as her model sitting in front of a window which looked out at a lighthouse. As Lily tries to plot out the abstract design of her painting, she has a moment of insight as she moves a salt cellar across a patterned tablecloth at the last dinner over which Mrs Ramsay presides at the summer house with her family and friends. Ten years pass for a period of retention and consolidation. When Lily returns to the abandoned house, left vacant after the death of Mrs Ramsay during the Great War, she finds herself sitting alone at the table, aged and wistful, susceptible to be awakened by environmental cues. With an eye on the lighthouse which had been associated with the nurturing Mrs Ramsay figure and with a glance at the pattern on the tablecloth that she had contemplated ten years before, her memory is triggered, enabling her to complete what I call 'the memory painting'. The successive stages of this carefully planned narrative contains valuable information for long-term episodic memory which can be assessed in a productive manner by neuroscientists.

In light of the immense scientific research on memory in recent times, it seems most appropriate to address the topic from the literary optic. Using literature as a laboratory for the workings of the mind, this book considers major authors of the past two centuries as 'subjects' of study that can shed light on the functioning of human memory. Correlations are made between the intuitive and experiential expression of memory by literary subjects and theories in neuroscience about the encoding, storage and retrieval of memory. This phenomenological study opens up links between the literary and the scientific in a time in which integrative approaches between the disciplines are at the cutting edge of knowledge.

This book is delimited by two golden ages of memory research. The late nineteenth century produced towering figures of memory research in an era of dynamic psychology who offered three pathways for the exploration of memory by fiction writers in the twentieth century. The pathbreaking psychologists were equalled a century later in the so-called Decade of the Brain of the 1990s by the many indefatigable neuroscientists who are having a powerful impact on the ever-evolving field of biochemical and physiological brain research. In fact, it is a field that is growing faster than the scientists can keep up with, as I have learned from immersing myself in it for over a decade and engaging in some dialogue with leading figures in brain research abroad. My chapter 'The Almond and the Seahorse' humbly selects some of the leading directions, with a metaphoric title that highlights two approaches to memory that are part of the current debate.

I am convinced, however, that in this fertile context of ongoing scientific exploration, the writings of selected literary authors become illuminating test cases of major trends in the understanding of the memory process. The scrutiny of literary texts by writers from Jean-Jacques Rousseau, the paradigm of early Romanticism, to Octavio Paz, the poet of modernist memory, provides valuable material for the classification of memory phenomena that can be fruitfully related to findings and directions in current neuroscience. These connections involve such topics as emotion and the brain, somatosensory trigger mechanism and localization of memory traces, long-term episodic memory, voluntary vs. involuntary memory, and confabulation. Such subjects have been discussed in science by articulate researchers such as Antonio Damasio, Edmund Rolls, Daniel Schacter and Jean-Pierre Changeux, to name a few.

The literary writers under consideration are herewith viewed as mediums for the unleashing of the memory process and its catalysis into artistic images. Human or 'subjective' time, what the French call 'le vécu', functions in personal, individual memory experiences. As the philosopher Paul Ricoeur has shown, narrative itself is an experience of time, and so, we may add, is memory. His plea to go from the cortical to the mental is momentous and challenging. Indeed, memory research can be expanded well beyond the brain scans and fruit flies of the neuroscientists. The literature of memory can provide a rich and complex array of data that is tantamount to field studies for capturing episodes of memory. At the same time, literary criticism can learn much from the scientific understanding of neurological phenomena that give rise to human behavior and image-making illustrated in these texts. Such scientific resources can provide more precise and objective criteria for evaluating mental phenomena in literary works than the vagaries and imprecision of standard psychological criticism.

My previous book *Aesthetic Autobiography* has been the background for the current one. There I scrutinized the transformation of raw materials of life into the art of the writers in question. Childhood memories are part of those ingredients and offer evidence of 'long-term memory'. In contrast to Freud's theories, I found that such writers lifted the screen of memory even if they sought to embellish their life secrets in artistic devices. Moving to complementary dimensions of autobiography and beyond, I am now analyzing the information about memory that can be gleaned from literature which has not been examined systematically in its specifically scientific context.[1] Moreover, in showing the linkage between art and its sources in actual life, I offer clinical proof of the saliency of real life experiences to the artistic work and, therefore, the inextricable link between author and text. Because so much of the literary material is overtly and emphatically autobiographical, it can profitably be explored as a series of case histories of a variety of operations of human memory. Given this kind of approach, the literary registering of memory phenomena of the authors under consideration is more directly tied to everyday experience than are the isolated and controlled conditions of a laboratory.

The tracking of memory in literature yields a dazzling panorama of orientations that are covered in separate chapters. I have categorized trends with descriptive titles to provide tangible classification in linking certain writers. The scrutiny begins with a grouping of Romantic writers who use emotion as a source of memory encoding. Rousseau is the most powerful example in this group, as he is self-reflexive and self-critical in attempting to judge the authenticity of the memory experiences he relates. Subsequently, Baudelaire and Huysmans demonstrate the bodily basis for the storage of the memory, pointing, innovatively for their period, to the physical brain as its container. Because of Proust's undeniable concentration on memory, he is the subject of an entire chapter, which demonstrates his exploration of the sensory trigger mechanism of memory throughout his eight-volume opus of *A la Recherche du temps perdu*. Moving beyond the legacy of Bergson, he proceeds to differentiate between voluntary and involuntary retrieval of memory by repeated examples dispersed throughout his work. Concurrently, on Anglo-Saxon shores, the work of Joyce, Woolf and Faulkner offer cumulative developments in associative memory, following particularly in the pathways marked by William James, who had a large impact on the era as a whole. Although each of these major writers is rich enough to merit an individual chapter, I group them together because of their common 'stream-of-consciousness' technique, which unifies their processural approach to memory both in terms of associative encoding and retrieval. A sixth chapter is devoted to Breton and the Surrealists, who explore the fields of aleatory memory, instigated as they were by the pioneering psychological work on the subconscious in the School of Dynamic Psychiatry in their native France. Ultimately, I have found that a group of multicultural writers such as Nin, Paz and Borges seize upon the linguistic context for their creative expression of memory in what they regard as its distinct connection to and dependency on the act of language.

In this purview of writers, individual works stand out as exceptionally revealing models of the memory process. First there are the large novels, Proust's *Swann's Way* and *Le Temps retrouvé*, Woolf's *To the Lighthouse*, Faulkner's *The Sound and the Fury*. But equally revelatory are certain poetic texts such as Lamartine's 'Le Lac', Baudelaire's 'Le Balcon', Apollinaire's 'Zone', Breton's 'Poison soluble II' and Paz's 'Pasado en claro'. In addition, there are the intriguing and compelling shorter narratives of Joyce's 'The Dead', Nin's *Seduction of the Minotaur* and Borges' 'Funes el memorioso'. Along with Rousseau's and Proust's narrators who are obsessed with the memory process, I have probed characters such as Woolf's Lily Briscoe, Nin's Lillian Beye and Borges' Funes as highly illustrative examples of memorizing subjects. Valuable findings are also drawn from the distinct focus on the memory process of the 'little boy' figure in Proust, Joyce, Faulkner, Rimbaud, Breton and Paz. This heightened memory process – visible in both literary characters and the impressionable writers themselves – can be as intriguing as, for example, the impaired case of brain damage in the real-life nineteenth-century landmark case of the construction foreman Phineas Gage that the neuroscientist Antonio Damasio features in his book *Descartes' Error*.

Specific memory objects and landscapes also are uncovered and assessed. These vivid findings range widely from the perfume flask of Baudelaire, the madeleine and the boot button of Proust, the bucket of water in Faulkner, the Gaelic folk song in Joyce, the puddle of water in Rimbaud, along with the memory painting and lighthouse of Woolf, the crystal burrow of Breton, the shadows and footsteps of Paz, the thresholds and labyrinths of Borges, the subterranean passageways and grooves of Anaïs Nin. Such concrete images highlight aspects of the memory process that poetic analogy succinctly communicates. As the most graphic evidence of this image-making expression of memory, I present in the 'Afterword' three twentieth-century paintings – by the artists Salvador Dalí, Oscar Dominguez and René Magritte – which are rich resource material to probe. These paintings along with the poetic works also feature elements of unconscious memory, which has become one of the biggest challenges for the scientific researchers. This begs an even larger question. Since artistic expression in whatever form is a supremely human mechanism for retaining memory, should not scientists be most interested in the memory process that it reveals?

As this book ventures forth on its odyssey of the literary routes of memory, I borrow Nabokov's expression of 'Speak, Memory', which as he demonstrated is ultimately registered in language. So, too, I 'listen' to selected writers as they give us their characters, images and artistic technique as clues to the workings of memory, that can interest scientists and more general readers in the continued probing of the inexhaustible properties of the human brain.

1
Memory in the Era of Dynamic Psychology: Nineteenth-Century Backgrounds

Historically speaking, late-nineteenth-century French psychology provides a backdrop to the literary exploitation of memory and, interestingly and not fully acknowledged, a point of departure for current debates in neuroscience. What has since been termed Descartes' 'error' of mind/body dualism was already being explored under the rubric of 'esprit/cerveau' discussions during a decade 1880–90 when the subject of memory was being unearthed, called by some as its 'golden age'. France, in particular, with its tradition of theoretical debate, was a hotbed for new theories, originating in clinical psychology in Paris in the laboratories of the Salpêtrière, the famous mental hospital, and leading to courses at the prestigious Collège de France. Bold pioneers of an exciting, dynamic psychology were emerging.

Specifically, Henri Bergson and Pierre Janet stand out as key figures in France in an ongoing discussion and polemic about memory. Both born in Paris in 1859, they presented their respective theses in 1889: Janet's *Automatisme psychologique* and Bergson's *Essai sur les données immédiates de la conscience*. Both also had contributed preliminary essays on their work to the prestigious journal *Revue philosophique de la France et de l'étranger* founded in 1876 directed by their contemporary Théodule Ribot, the founder of experimental psychology in France, who was ironically taking the study of memory in a physiological direction away from the metaphysical concerns of consciousness.

Bergson and Janet seemed to be directly responding in their writings to Ribot whose pathology of memory *Les Maladies de la mémoire* of 1881 had categorically stated that memory is essentially an organic biological event: 'la mémoire est, par essence, un fait biologique'.[1] Let's set aside the psychic element, Ribot had emphatically said.[2] Ribot was reducing memory to its simple and most primary state of automatic repetition in his work of comparative psychology. He referred to organic memory as involving the formation of dynamic associations in the neural system. Ribot had explained that in his time memory was studied with respect to its power of conservation, of reproduction and of localization in the past. The third of these, localization – what was being called 'reconnaissance' or conscious recognition – was the psychological element of memory which in his single-minded view was dispensable.

Concurrently, Ribot's colleague, the meridional Alfred Binet, an experimentalist in the field of physiological psychology, was tackling a wide range of issues pertinent to the more recognized spokesmen of his era. In his book *Introduction à la psychologie expérimentale* (1894), Binet devoted the entire fifth chapter to the topic of memory. He saw limitations in the study of memory as a simple biological function, alluding to the reductionism of the likes of Ribot. The truth, he said, is that memory consists of a set of complex operations: 'La vérité est qu'elle consiste toujours dans un ensemble d'opérations complexes.'[3] While hailing the advances of the new era of psychology dating from 1878, he distanced his own work from the pathological approach, what he called 'la psychologie morbide', that was gaining widespread attention. In contrast, Binet was drawn to the experimental study of memory in normal human subjects, which could be studied outside the hospital laboratories in real world conditions – on for example, schoolchildren and eventually on his own daughters. Binet's focus on the issue of the conservation of memory was more in line with Janet's and Bergson's ongoing discussions.

In the meantime, the German psychologist Hermann Ebbinghaus was actually conducting experiments on normal memory and its relation to learning as well. But his work gave the appearance of a mechanical approach, involving experiments in rote repetition and using himself solely as the subject. In his short, classic treatise, *Über das Gedächtnis*, published in Leipzig in 1885, he claimed that with respect to the field of memory, generally speaking, 'psychical processes offer no means for measurement or enumeration'.[4] He described his experiments of testing memory quantitatively through the learning and recall of lists of meaningless syllables in variable time spans. Using simple models, Ebbinghaus introduced distinctions between short- and long-term memory. Also distinguishing conscious and unconscious acts of recall, he might have suggested the inextricability of unconscious and conscious memory, what Bergson and his ilk were not ready to explore.

Beyond such isolated treatments of the subject, Bergson and Janet were to pursue notions of graded, hierarchical designations of memory in their later works *Matière et mémoire* (1896) and *L'Evolution de la mémoire* (1926), which went on to address the controversial topic of consciousness. Although in such subsequent works Bergson and Janet refer to each other, it is clear that their theories evolved independently of each other, with significant divergences. Both men taught at the Sorbonne and held chairs at the Collège de France, Bergson in philosophy from 1900–21, and Janet in experimental psychology from 1902–36. Janet had a less stable reputation than Bergson because of controversies with the likes of Jean-Martin Charcot, Sigmund Freud and Joseph Babinski who were bringing spectacular attention to the clinical findings of the school of Dynamic Psychiatry at the Salpêtrière Centre. In fact, it becomes a subject of its own as to who borrowed from whom as certain theories and terminology emerged.

To add to the web of interconnections, simultaneously, in 1890, William James's *Principles of Psychology* appeared, and Janet and James cited each other as well. It is a striking fact that William James was extremely cognizant of his French counterparts, referring to them frequently, and dealing with similar issues in his own terms. Unlike his brother Henry, who was deploring what he regarded as the seedy naturalism of contemporary French fiction writers, William was fully open to the exploration of contemporary French psychologists. He drew attention in 1901 to 'the wonderfully ingenious observations of Binet and especially of Janet in France'.[5] It was indeed a great moment of interchange between France and America and between metaphysical and pragmatic approaches! In addition, there is even a common and uncanny frame of reference for both James and Janet to works in parapsychology. Concurrently, as years passed, James and Bergson developed a common awareness of the subliminal, despite their different vantage points in the memory process. In 1905, in a letter to James, Bergson wrote that he thought the unconscious was 'interwoven' with the fabric of consciousness, and wondered whether he was closer to him on this subject than he might have thought.[6]

Beyond this fascinating web of interchange, it can be shown that the inquiry that was forged by these three pioneers of psychology Bergson, Janet and James, led to memory literature in several directions in the first three decades of the twentieth century. It is curious that each of the three writers posited two different forms of memory – ultimately tackling the issue of 'reconnaissance', or the mind's conscious recognition in the operation of memory, that some of the physiologists of their time had shunned. Despite this similarity, their different orientations led toward literary adaptations that will be seen in the course of this book.

The French vocabulary itself emphasizes the dichotomies present in Bergson's mind/body theory and his distinctions between operations of the 'cerveau' (the physical brain) and the 'esprit' (the metaphysical mind). It is true that Bergson pointed out that his discussion of memory necessarily brought out the age-old dichotomy and its metaphysical ramifications, since he was basically distinguishing between memory of the body and that of the mind. Bergson unabashedly stated in the preface to the seventh edition of *Matière et mémoire*:

> Ce livre affirme la réalité de l'esprit, la réalité de la matière, et essaie de déterminer le rapport de l'un à l'autre sur un exemple précis, celui de la mémoire. Il est donc nettement dualiste.[7]
> [This book affirms the reality of the mind, the reality of matter, and tries to determine the relation of one to the other based on a precise example, that of memory. It is therefore clearly dualist.]

Despite this explicit avowal, which elicits vociferous objections from current neurobiologists such as Antonio Damasio and Jean-Pierre Changeux, Bergson has gained a certain validity among a group of scientists and philosophers including B. Andrieu, Philippe Galois and R. Jaffard, who point to Bergson's rejection of his age's brain-trace theories, offering instead a model of memory which has ramifications on current globalist approaches. For example, Pete A.Y. Gunter has stated that it is unnecessary to 'bury neither Bergson, nor *Matter and Memory* nor memory'.[8] In Bergson's own time, in the literary context, it was the prestigious writer Proust who reoriented certain theories of Bergson and made him a common reference point, as shall be seen.

Bergson had started his probing of memory processes in *Matière et mémoire*, in his early distinctions between what he called the memory of habit or 'la mémoire-habitude' acquired by acts of repetition in the brain, and pure spontaneous memory or 'la mémoire pure' of the mind, which truly recalls and 'sees again' ('revoir'). The memory involved in learning the lesson by heart, 'le souvenir de la leçon', acquired voluntarily by efforts of repetition, is inscribed on the brain ('cerveau') and becomes part of the present. The memory of having read the lesson, 'le souvenir de la lecture', returns involuntarily and belongs uniquely to a specific date and place in the past. In opposing the mechanism of the habit-formed memory to the spontaneity of what he considered to be the higher form of memory, 'la mémoire par excellence', Bergson was locating his version of involuntary memory which was tied to his notion of duration and of the order of the mind ('esprit'):

> On the contrary, the recording, by memory, of facts and images unique in their kind takes place at every moment of duration.[9]

Furthermore, he stated that this spontaneous memory has a dream-like quality which 'is as capricious in reproducing as it is faithful in preserving'.[10] He therefore warned that the more weighty spontaneous memory which hides behind acquired memory can capriciously reveal itself in a flash but vanishes or escapes ('se dérober') at the least movement of acquired memory:

> Ce souvenir spontané, qui se cache derrière le souvenir acquis peut se révéler par des éclairs brusques; mais il se dérobe, au moindre mouvement de la mémoire volontaire.[11]

For Bergson, the phenomenon of 'reconnaissance' involves the transition of such pure memory to acts of conscious perception. The three stages of memory are amply discussed: 'le souvenir pur' 'le souvenir-image' and 'la perception' – a far cry from a single level of sensory-motor organization of 'souvenir-habitude'. Here, Bergson was concerned with hierarchies of memory and gradations, which involved shifts from the metaphysical realm to the material level of bodily activity. He even considered bodily memory ('la mémoire du corps') to be 'a quasi-instantaneous memory',[12] consisting of sensory-motor systems organized by habit, but having true memory at its base. The memory process in its avatar 'reconnaissance' fostered the interplay of mind with matter – what he had first presented in his article 'Mémoire et reconnaissance' in the *Revue philosophique* of 1896. Concurrently, in *Matière et mémoire* Bergson stated: 'Pure memory, on the other hand, interests no part of my body.'[13]

Bergson rhapsodized on the effects of pure memory which in his view originated in the nonmaterial realm of consciousness and its 'durée'. In Proust's work, this would become the realm of 'the deeper self' or 'le moi profond', as shall be seen. Bergson's metaphysical approach brought forward in his lesser known paper 'L'Ame et le corps' (1913) considered thought itself or 'pensée' to be independent of the brain. It followed that memory was stored not in the brain but in the mind:

> J'accepterai... l'idée d'un contenant où les souvenirs seraient logés, et je dirai alors tout bonnement qu'ils sont dans l'esprit.[14]

[I will accept…the idea of a container where memories would be lodged, and I will then say quite simply that they are in the mind.]

For Bergson was convinced that true memory was something other than a mechanical recording ('enregistrement'), a psychological association, or a biological fact of animal life, as Ribot had affirmed. Bergson was clearly hostile to localization theory, stemming from Paul Broca, the French neurologist who in the 1860s had mapped out a language-related area of the brain in probing cases of aphasia – what, in turn, led to a fashion of brain trace theories. Bergson also firmly rejected the tradition of associationism which was gaining ground in his era, that in his view was another avenue of reducing the mental to the physiological. Intuitively, Bergson was preparing the way for a global approach to the study of memory as a process involving various regions of the brain. He would rather envisage true memory as being stored in the intangible mind ('l'esprit') than in the tangible brain ('le cerveau'), which could not be a container for the conservation of memory:

> Faire du cerveau le dépositaire du passé, imaginer dans le cerveau une certaine région où le passé une fois passée demeurerait, c'est commettre une erreur psychologique.[15]
> [To make of the brain the repository of the past, to imagine in the brain a certain region where the past once past would remain, is to commit a psychological error.] *Memory defies logic of mem...*

To justify this point, Bergson argues that in the event of a cerebral lesion in which verbal memory is impaired, certain memories can be revived by the stimulus of even an emotion: 'Il arrive qu'une excitation plus ou moins forte, une émotion, par exemple, ramène tout à coup le souvenir qui paraissait à jamais perdu'; ['It can happen that an excitation more or less strong, an emotion, for example, brings back suddenly a memory which appeared lost forever'].[16] Here, the reference to emotion suggests the spiritual-mental source of memory that Bergson envisaged. Bergson was thus attacking brain trace theories arising from studies of aphasia in his time. Also, Bergson even acknowledged the existence of unconscious memory in certain dream states, which were for him additional signs of a spiritual form of memory. He argued that the development of intellect was accompanied by a corresponding decrease of pure memory as evidenced in the growth from

childhood. In the adult, sleep itself can prompt the revival of spontaneous memory:

> But, if almost the whole of our past is hidden from us because it is
> inhibited by the necessities of present action, it will find strength to
> cross the threshold of consciousness in all cases where we renounce
> the interest of effective action to replace ourselves, so to speak, in the
> life of dreams.[17]

Throughout his writings, for over a period of twenty-five years, Bergson
offered numerous images to convey the cerebral process of memory.
According to Bergson, as he expressed in *L'Evolution créatrice* of 1907,
instead of conserving memory in a drawer or inscribing it in a register,[18]
the brain is a functional processing center which first hides ('masquer')
the past or drives it back ('refouler') and then only allows that which
can be practically useful to show through ('transparaître'). Such is the
relationship that he envisages between the brain and the mind. He also
described memory as being hidden under the veil of the brain and then
revealed. For Bergson, the brain materializes the potentiality of such
dynamic memory which needs to be uncovered. Bergson's other famous
analogue is that of the clavier or keyboard:

> It is like an immense keyboard, on which the external object executes
> at once its harmony of a thousand notes, thus calling forth in a defin-
> ite order, and at a single moment, a great multitude of elementary
> sensations corresponding to all the points of the sensory center that
> are concerned.[19]

This analogy suggests that the bodily mechanism of the brain can be
set into motion by exterior stimuli, even by emotions, or by internal
'souvenirs-images'.

Bergson addressed the nagging question of memory again in 1922
prompted by a wish to respond to Einstein's Theory of Special Relativity
in a book entitled *Durée et simultanéité: à propos de la théorie d'Einstein*. In
attempting to reconcile his own sense of continuity with the more
modern concept of instantaneity, Bergson declared that his philosophical concept of 'real' duration could be compatible with Minkowski's
and Einstein's space–time notions. He asks how physicists can reject
inner experience if they operate from the point of view of perceptions
which in his view arose from consciousness. In Bergson's formulation,
instants could only be conceived within the concept of duration. In

a convoluted manner, analyzing his own notion of 'durée' further, Bergson sought to better identify the human character of memory as an elementary objective process linking separate moments in time. He also compared duration to a musical melody which is indivisible and heard as a whole. Bergson was trying to connect notions of multiple time in relativity physics with psychological time, giving the latter a new validity. In contrast, Einstein had made a firm distinction between 'psychological time' and real scientific time outside of the subjectivity of perception and 'mental' constructions such as memory.

But for Bergson, memory was 'real' duration, 'la durée réelle', which incorporated what he considered to be real time, 'perçu', 'vécu', 'éprouvé', or experienced but not measurable. 'Le temps qui dure n'est pas mesurable' ['Time which lasts is not measurable'], he wrote.[20] Thus, memory links two instants in consciousness in large blocks of time, which does not flow. In this discussion, Bergson came forward with his concept of 'elementary memory' as a functional connecting process of consciousness:

> Sans une mémoire élémentaire qui relie les deux instants l'un à l'autre, il n'y aura que l'un ou l'autre des deux, un instant unique par conséquent, pas d'avant et d'après, pas de succession, pas de temps.[21]
> [Without an elementary memory that connects the two moments to each other, there will be only one or another, consequently a single instant, no before and after, no succession, no time.]

Corresponds with notion that memory is referential

Bergson regarded the unlived, physical clock time of the referee-physicist in relative motion as fictional time, the latter dependent on the bodily reference system of the observer to imagined systems that are 'spatialized'. On the other hand, Bergson's own concept of memory fit into a duration that was relative to a specific frame of reference. Some would argue that Bergson had not understood the fourth dimension outside the Euclidean framework of space. Modern authors, writing at the time of Bergson's later work, were trying in their fiction to give 'lived evidence' of their own experience of both instants and of duration. In the works of Proust, Woolf and Faulkner, one can identify such elementary memory processes through the spans of time that link objects serving as poles of past and present. Such fiction revealed the tensions between the separateness and the simultaneity of moments in time. But it is in this context also that Bergson left room for contemporary notions of discontinuity vis à vis the continuity of his fabled 'durée'.

Another perspective of the memory process emerged in the work of Bergson's contemporary Pierre Janet, who was a founder of what could

Research this connection ↓

be called an actual school of Dynamic Psychiatry. Whereas Bergson identified memory in the enlightened consciousness which suggested the 'au-dessus' (the 'above'), Janet was drawn to primitive levels of a subconscious existence 'au-dessous' (the 'below'), locating memory patterns in the elocutions of hysterics in their dreams and fantasies. Janet had garnered documentation for his pioneering hypotheses of the dual or split personality from actual observations of hysteria in the neurological clinic at the Salpêtrière, established by Charcot in 1882. Charcot, who ultimately became director of the entire hospital, was the master of what came to known as the grand 'hysteria of the Salpêtrière'. The famous painting 'A Clinical Lecture at the Salpêtrière' (1887) by André Brouillet makes vivid such demonstrations.[22] From Charcot's spectacular sessions which attracted students from all over Europe came the book *Iconographie photographique de la Salpêtrière* (1878), a volume of which André Breton possessed and several photos of which were reproduced in *La Révolution surréaliste*.[23] It is a known fact that the Surrealists drew from the findings of Janet and his contemporaries for their own purposes, which in turn affected their view of memory. ←

In the midst of such publicized activity, this less sensational Pierre Janet offered his pathblazing thesis, *L'Automatisme psychologique*. Here he emphasized that pure automatism of any sort emerges in the most simple psychological states when there is a narrowing of the field of consciousness: 'le rétrécissement du champs de la conscience'.[24] He stated,

> Plus l'état psychologique était simple et le champs de la conscience restreint, plus l'activité automatique était manifeste.[25]
> [The simpler the psychological state and the more limited consciousness is, the more automatic activity was manifest.]

Conversely, as thought develops and adapts to new elements of consciousness, the automatism is reduced. Janet then observed, in particular among patients of hysteria, a favorable territory for the development and study of the phenomenon of automatism.

Janet, in fact, had realized from the start that variations of memory could be scrutinized in the study of somnambulism, a kind of hypnotic sleep emerging in hysterical states, which had access to the subconscious. His test cases of the 19-year-old Lucie and 13 other female hysterics at the Salpêtrière actually provoked acts of memory during hypnotic states. As Janet indicated in his article 'Les Actes inconscients et la mémoire pendant le somnambulisme' (1888),[26] under hypnosis, the 'subject' Léonie Leboulanger revived her childhood nicknames and persona. Findings on automatic memory were garnered from these fields of mental instability, what Janet considered to be the most favorable states for experimental studies of psychology. What he called elementary memory emerges in states of hysteria dependent largely on primitive conditions of sensitivity:

La mémoire et l'oubli des phenomènes complexes se rattachent donc à ce même fait, la persistence ou la variation de l'état de sensibilité.[27] [The memory and forgetting of complex phenomena are connected to this same fact, the persistence or the variation of the state of sensitivity.]

An entire discussion is devoted to the particular kind of memory relative to somnambulists who were provoked by acts of suggestion at the onset of these states, which in turn produced automatic writing. It was particularly striking to observe that although memories would exist between somnambulist states, there would be no memory of the waking state: 'aucune mémoire de l'état de veille'.[28]

In the context of this discussion Janet distinguishes between his two types of memory, 'deux espèces de mémoire', a distinction which he elaborates upon years later. He labels the first memory as elementary or sensitive ('sensible'), 'that which consists simply in the recollection of this or that specific sensation considered individually' ('celle qui consiste simplement dans le souvenir de telle ou telle sensation particulière considerée isolement') and the second as a complex or intellectual memory, 'which supplies us with complicated ideas' ('qui nous fournit des idées compliquées') and can only exist in us as a function of language.[29] The French language lends itself to the distinction between the more personal and particular 'souvenir' and the larger 'mémoire', whereas German distinguishes between 'Gedächtnis' (a storehouse of facts, an innate capability) and 'Erinnerung' (a conscious recollection of psychic content). The vaguer English language has the general word memory, personalized by reminiscences and remembrances. In his case, Janet makes it clear that in the early stages of his career he is only concerned with elementary memory (involving sensation and emotion) and the conditions conducive to it.

It is intriguing that Janet should also cite at this time the parapsychological writings of Frederic W.H. Myers and Edmund Gurney, in particular Myers' 'Automatic Writing' (1887) and Gurney's *The Stages of Hypnotic Memory* (1886). Both men at that time were exploring hypnotism and forms of spiritualism: popular nineteenth-century currents that were found all over the Western world in a 'Gothic' antidote to rationalism. Myers's subsequent work *Human Personality and its Survival of Bodily Death*, published posthumously in 1903, was to feature some of the ideas that Janet was exploring and to predate some of the automatic resources of dream memory and hypnotic memory that the surrealist poets in particular were drawing upon in their poetry. Myers was to define 'subliminal memory' as 'the preconscious unselective memory' of dreams and hypnosis from which the consciousness makes 'its appropriate selection' and develops 'into distinctness certain helpful lines of reminiscence'. Myers argued that 'It is the memory furthest from waking life whose span is the widest, whose grasp of the organism's upstored impressions is the most profound.'[30] Myers referred to clinical cases of Charcot and Janet at the Salpêtrière to corroborate his views.

Interestingly, Myers spoke of the purgation of memory, the removal of inhibitions, enacted, for example, through states of hypnosis. 'The treasure of memory is mixed with rubbish', he said.[31] The expansion of memory corresponds to the expansion of consciousness to what Myers called the 'subliminal' level of sensations, thoughts, emotions, lying underneath the ordinary threshold of consciousness. Types of subliminal memory can lead to forethoughts, what again certain surrealist writers were to explore both in poetry and painting. Along with hysteria, hypnotism, trances and genius, Myers had perceived automatism to be the general rubric under which he could envisage the intervention of the subliminal in ordinary life.

Similarly, in the early work of Janet, dating from 1882–88, there is a concentration on the subconscious as manifested particularly in the clinically observed state of hysteria, which comes close to the popular notions of the subliminal of the parapsychologists of the time. Janet coined the word 'subconscious' intentionally to distinguish it from the Romantic theory of the unconscious of Eduard von Hartmann or the psychoanalytical designation of Freud, who reduced memory to trauma. However, it is ironic that after spending the bulk of this work on the study of automatism, Janet arrived at a conclusion in which he states that automatic recall is an *inferior* process of the mind, devoid of creativity. It will be seen that the Surrealists were to understand this level of activity in a totally different manner, as they exploited the primitive workings of the mind for the propagation of images, the more arbitrary they were, the more surrealist! A certain type of memory emerged for their verbal experimentations in this primordial context.

Janet, on the other hand, was to emphatically distinguish automatic memory from higher mental activities of reconstruction, thereby indirectly shedding light on what he considered to be the other variety of memory belonging to the mind. That is to say, in good French manner, fully representative of nineteenth-century intellectual discourse, he makes an analogy with the mechanistic law of the conservation of force: he sets the activity of automatism, involving the senses and emotions, against that of conservation, which involves an association of ideas that constitutes memory of a higher order. He adds that a normal mind achieves an equilibrium by allocating to automatism certain inferior acts of memory. In raising memory to a new mental level of synthesis, Janet refers to his concept of 'reconnaissance' or conscious reflection upon the past. He notes that in a state of mental disequilibrium or hysteria, disorders result from a total reliance upon primitive automatism due to the inability of those disturbed minds to adapt to new environments. The test cases of Lucie and others had demonstrated such inadequacy.

It is not surprising, however, that Janet's studies should culminate in a lesser known later work entitled *L'Evolution de la mémoire* (1928) which posits language as the fundamental agent of memory: 'l'acte propre de la mémoire c'est le langage'. From the sensory-motor memory of automatic acts involving repetition, he moved to the verbal memory of locution, incarnate in narrative and its consciousness of time. In the gamut of his career he had proceeded from the subconscious to the conscious. In *De l'Angoisse à l'extase* (1926) he had fabricated a metaphor for memory in the story about the sentinel, describing a level of memory which is independent of stimulation, elicited solely by the act of communication. Hence, he defines memory as a social act. For Janet, the speech of the sentinel to his captain reunites the two memories actually established by Bergson, 'souvenir pur' et 'souvenir moteur'. Janet gave the following analogy for his version of human memory:

> Quand une tendance mémorielle est constituée, elle reste latente jusqu'au moment où la question joue le rôle de stimulation et provoque l'acte de la remémoration. Une sentinelle, comme je le disais autrefois, voit arriver l'ennemi, elle fait d'abord les actes qui sont les réactions ordinaires à cette stimulation, se cacher, se défendre, fuir, etc., mais en même temps elle construit un discours relatif à cette apparition de l'ennemi. Ce discours n'attend pas pour s'activer une nouvelle apparition de l'ennemi ... comme cela a lieu pour les actes précédents de se cacher, de se défendre. Il est prêt à s'activer en l'absence de l'ennemi, dans le camp, simplement devant le chef et à l'occasion des questions qui celui-ci posera. C'est cette conduite intellectuelle qui constitue la mémoire humaine.[32]

[When a tendency to memorize is constituted, it remains latent until the moment when the question plays the role of stimulation and provokes the act of remembering. A sentinel, as I said before, sees the enemy arrive; he first makes the acts which are ordinary reactions to this stimulus; to hide, to defend oneself, to flee, etc; but at the same time he constructs a speech relative to the appearance of this enemy. To activate itself, this speech does not require a new appearance of the enemy, as it does for the previous acts of hiding itself and defending itself. It [the speech] is ready to activate itself in the absence of the enemy, in the camp, simply in front of the chief and on the occasion of the questions that he will ask. It is this intellectual activity which constitutes human memory.]

This condition of *absence* is therefore essential for the emergence of memory, suggesting that in this view memory recedes into darkness, in latency, and must be awakened by questioning which provokes a process of intellectual reconstruction, 'la remémoration'. Clearly, this 'higher' intellectual memory, distinguished from the elementary reflex phenomena of animals, is not circumstantial or contextual and therefore does not depend on a reproduction of specific circumstances or associations. It can reconstruct a whole memory from partial ones.

Against this sophisticated act of language, Janet views the lowly engram in its limited physiological sense,[33] what he described as a physical trace left in an organism. Having edited a volume of Malebranche,[34] Janet gave the former philosopher credit for the concept of physical traces as well as for the sense of habit-memory. In a systematic fashion, Janet circumscribed his own work in light of others. Even as he countered Ribot, he also criticized what he regarded to be the spiritual nature of the 'souvenir pur' of Bergson,[35] presumably independent of the body, floating in ethereal spaces, tied to the 'esprit' and not the 'cerveau'. In advancing beyond such dualistic mind/body notions, Janet was suggesting instead a dualism of consciousness, in which two types of memory could coexist.

Audaciously as well, with his aversion to the developing psychoanalytical practices, Janet criticized Freud, who having spent four months at the Salpêtrière laboratory in the service of Charcot (October 1885–February 1886) went on to publish with the Viennese physician Josef Breuer *Studien über Hysterie* in 1895. Janet was substituting the notion of the subconscious for Freud's unconscious. He refused to discuss the traumatic memory, what has come to be known as 'screen memory'.

It is interesting that Freud, having been specifically exposed to the school of the Salpêtrière at the height of Charcot's school of hysteria, went on to minimize automatism and the memory events which it could trigger. In fact, leaving this environment of dynamic psychology which was probing different expressions of the memory process, Freud developed a theory of forgetting linked to his new term of psychoanalysis. It is true that he formulated his own theory of male hysteria from the French experience as he examined instances of amnesia in hysterics. But with respect to memory *per se*, instead of concentrating on the free-play of memory events, Freud fixated on their suppression or 'refoulement'. With his theory of childhood amnesia that claimed that there are few memories from the ages of eight and younger, Freud proceeded to expostulate his well-known notion of screen memory. In 1901 Freud gave its definition as childhood memories which hide an emotionally significant event behind a trivial one: 'The indifferent memories of childhood owe their existence to a process of displacement: they are substitutes in [mnemic] reproduction, for other impressions which are really significant.'[36] In fact, Freud made a strong statement against adult memory:

> I started from the striking fact that a person's earliest childhood memories seem frequently to have preserved what is indifferent and unimportant, whereas . . . no trace is found in an adult's memory of impressions dating from that time which are important.[37]

It is worth noting that in 1905 the psychologist Carl Jung, who had even been a pupil of Janet at the Sorbonne in 1902, credited his contemporary Freud with equating forgetting with repression.[38]

Years later in 1924, Freud developed his major theory of psychoanalysis in an article specifically on memory 'Notiz über den "Wunderblock"',[39] this time using a metaphor of a gadget called a 'wunderblock' to suggest two simultaneous layers of memory inscription constituting our psychical apparatus. The magic block conserves durable long-term memory on the wax tablet as short-term memory is inscribed on the transparent celluloid paper. By analogy, Freud distinguished between the durable unconscious and the fleeting conscious memories: the wax tablet retains unconscious memories even as the celluloid surface receives the conscious ones. However, the implication is that the unconscious memories are syphoned off to forgetting, and repressed, prevented from reaching the consciousness. In such discussions, Freud spoke of the personal unconscious rather than the forgotten.

Although some twentieth-century psychologists adopted Freud's screen theory approach and accepted his idea of childhood amnesia, Freud was not fully accepted by his peers. It is a fact that in many overt statements, Freud himself kept emphasizing that he was unable to appreciate the artistic experience. Separating himself from the artists, he was going against the growing trend in his time, stressed by the Surrealists, which linked science and art. Even more astonishing is the fact that Freud stated in 1920: 'Biology is really a domain with unlimited possibilities. . . . Maybe the replies will be such that they will cause the whole edifice of our (psychoanalytical) hypotheses to collapse.'[40]

In the meantime, it was William James who pointed the study of memory in a different direction, away from the amorphous realm of what was to become the Freudian unconscious and toward a concrete physiological, empirical understanding of the memory process. In Chapter 16 of his treatise *Principles of Psychology*, James opened up a new perspective on memory for his era. James focused distinctively on memory as a conscious phenomenon of association, even as it differed from the British associationist tradition of John Locke, David Hume, Alexander Bain and John Stuart Mill. On the one hand, James could not accept the premise that sensory impressions were at the basis of all mental activity and that memory was a mechanical operation of association of these impressions. He dismissed the so-called 'mind-stuff' theories of the British Empiricists who posited material, atomic components of the unifying consciousness. On the other hand, James made it clear that unlike Bergson, he was not concerned with the metaphysical aspects of memory. Instead, he was examining its psychological workings.

Taking a rather advanced physiological approach from the start, James described 'primary memory', as he called it, as a permanent substratum consisting of neural pathways which are the conditions of retention. Such 'habit-worn paths' are physical brain traces. Moreover, Ebbinghaus's experiments had suggested to him the intricacy of such pathways due to associative networks, visual ones, for example. James insisted that such memory retention is physical, not a mental phenomenon; it 'is not mysterious storing up of an "idea" in an unconscious state'.[41] In his view, so-called elementary memory is linked to the present and not to the 'genuine' past, as others like Binet would have it. He wrote: 'But what elementary memory makes us aware of is the *just* past.'[42] For James, primary memory was never lost. Paradoxically, perhaps, it belongs to the present state of time and tied to what current neuroscientists call 'working memory'. Indeed, James's rather fluid discussion demands unraveling.

In contrast, James turned to 'memory proper' or secondary memo

> An object which is recollected, in the proper sense of the term, is one
> which has been absent from consciousness altogether, and now revives
> anew. It is brought back, recalled, fished up, so to speak from a reservoir
> in which with countless other objects, it lay buried and lost from view.[43]

Recollection, he said, is a 'psychophysical phenomenon' with a bodily
and mental side. Whereas the bodily side involves 'functional excite-
ment' of the neural tracts, the mental side 'is the conscious vision of the
past occurrence'.[44] The power of association is highlighted in this
method of recall both with respect to the accidental cue and in the associates of the past experience. But James minimized the exterior sensual
stimuli and focused on an interior landscape of mental objects which
themselves act as these 'accidental cues' and can trigger multiple memory patterns. Memory is voluntarily retrieved as the mind can return to
the 'warmth and intimacy'[45] of the environment from which remembered objects are never separated.

Like his French counterparts, Bergson and Janet, James offered his
own extended descriptive metaphor to explain the memory process:

> In short, we make search in our memory for a forgotten idea, just
> as we rummage our house for a lost object. In both cases we visit what
> seems to us the probable *neighborhood* of that which we miss. We turn
> over the things under which, or within which, or alongside of which,
> it may possibly be; and if it lies near them, it soon comes to view. But
> these matters, in the case of a mental object sought, are nothing but
> its *associates*. The machinery of recall is thus the same as the machin-
> ery of association, and the machinery of association, as we know, is
> nothing but the elementary law of habit in the nerve-centers.[46]

But unlike Janet, James did not deal with the absence or darkness into
which secondary memory sinks and from which it need be revived. And
unlike Bergson, James did not posit a past distinctly separate from the
present. Instead, he provided the basis for a notion of the continuity of
the past and the present – which 'the-stream of-consciousness' writers,
notably Joyce, Faulkner and Woolf, adopted. After all, it was James who
first defined the continuity of the stream:

> Consciousness, then, does not appear to itself chopped up in bits . . .
> It is nothing jointed; it flows. A 'river' or a 'stream' are the metaphors

by which it is most naturally described. *In talking of it hereafter, let us call it the stream of thought, of consciousness, or of subjective life.*[47]

In the context of this description, James commented that remembrance 'is like direct feeling' enabling a present thought to consider itself continuous with a past state and integrating the self in this way.

It is an intriguing fact that James overtly recognized the psychical research of his own time when it coincided with his own interest in religious mysticism.[48] For him paranormal and psychical phenomena betokened vast reaches of unexplored mental terrain fascinating to James yet off-limits, in view of the pragmatic, hard-edged research he chose to engage in. He saw memory as part of the 'normal' consciousness distant from the hazy otherworld of subliminal consciousness. Having praised Janet's dynamic psychiatry for its discovery of a subconscious or 'secondary consciousness',[49] and taking serious note of the popularization of the subject, James positioned his own orientation:

> Set over against this subliminal life, and in strong contrast with it, we find the normal consciousness, dealing primarily through the senses and the material world and in possession of faculties of attention, and in particular of memory, which are pitifully small in comparison with those which the subliminal consciousness wields. The normal consciousness is thus only a portion of our nature, adapted primarily to 'terrene' conditions.[50]

As opposed to what he called the 'cosmic environment' of the spiritual world, James willfully limited his own focus to the narrower physical consiousness in which he situates the normal power of memory, and he focuses on its voluntary aspect.[51]

From such communication and cross-reference, it becomes apparent that these three major figures moved the study of memory forward as they established three different orientations for the exploration of memory at the advent of the twentieth century. In the final analysis there is more similarity amongst them than they might have imagined, since all three thinkers were grappling with vestiges of philosophical dualism which they could not shed: Bergson with his metaphysical domain, Janet with his intellectual sphere, and James with his spiritual and religious dimension. Also, having in different degrees located elements of automatic memory, they each acknowledged it and allocated it to an inferior level. Nonetheless, they tried to integrate elements of the unconscious in their versions of dynamic memory. The different pathways that these three thinkers forged help categorize certain writers of the twentieth century who channeled their mental experiences creatively into the memory process that was divulged in their literary writings.

2
Rousseau and the Romantics: Autobiographical Memory and Emotion

The Romantic writers gave special prominence to memory through their natural inclination for nostalgia, a reverence for childhood as the pristine, edenic state, and their tendency toward daydreaming, solitary walking, musing, reverie and meditation. Think of the spare time spent by Rousseau in his *Rêveries*, Lamartine in his *Méditations*, Hugo in his *Contemplations* or Wordsworth and Coleridge on their walking tours which would allow the mind to be cleared and room for memory events to surface. For such writers, Nature had been the setting for those memories to be instilled, and in such settings they are usually retrieved. The Romantics' characteristic 'pathetic fallacy', which egotistically ties their feelings to the outside world, applies to the phenomenon of memory, linked as it is to place. There was no specific recourse to the dream state to recover such memories, because life could be turned into a perpetual daydream in real places. Many of the writers had no other specific occupation than to muse, exercise what they considered to be their greater 'sensibility', wallow in their egocentrism, and then write about their personal past, unabashedly exploiting the use of the first-person-singular pronoun.

Rousseau is a prime example of a writer with such Romantic self-indulgence, and it is a fact that memory is a process which he constantly resorts to in writing his *Confessions*. For Rousseau, memory was an act of the imagination both created and retrieved by the important ingredient of emotion. Claiming to be a Man of Feeling, he stated, 'I felt before I thought.'[1] He admits that 'objects generally make less impression on [him] than does the memory of them' (169) – which accounts for his subjective vision. Rousseau extensively uses the words 'mémoire' and 'souvenir' throughout the painstaking narration of apparently virtually everything he can remember. In fact, in the endings to many of the 12 chapters of his autobiography, he evaluates his own process of memory, pointing out its strengths and weaknesses.

It becomes clear that there is no particular stimulus needed for Rousseau's evocation or the provocation of memory, because he obviously rehearsed the events of his life constantly and colored them subjectively. Nothing is too insignificant for him to remember; hence there is an amazing range of minor and major memories that he invokes. His memory is vivid and visual, as he describes it:

> Not only do I recall times and places and persons, but all objects surrounding them, the temperature of the air, the smells and the colors, and a certain local impression only to be felt there, the sharp recollection of which carries me back there again (121).

In dwelling on himself exclusively, allowing very few exterior events to fill his brain, he allowed the imprints of memory to remain clear of interference and therefore to become stronger over the years. He also makes the point that the distinctive feature of his memory is that as soon as he relegates that memory to paper, it leaves him:

> Quand elle me sert ce n'est autant que je me suis reposé sur elle, sitôt que j'en confie le dépôt au papier, elle m'abandonne (Pléiade, 351).
> [When it serves me, it is only so long as I rely on it, as soon as I consign the deposit to paper, it deserts me.]

Thus, Rousseau seems able to hold the memory in his mind until the point of recording it on paper, at which time it disappears. It shall be seen how different this notion of memory is from that of certain modern writers like Octavio Paz who conversely depend on the physical act of writing to elicit the memory, which is viscerally bound to writing and in fact surfaces on paper.

Rousseau first claims to have written his autobiography without the aid of notes: 'I am writing entirely from memory, without notes or material to recall things' (128). Later, in describing his flight from Paris in 1762 at the time of the warrant for his arrest and the condemnation of *Emile*, he admitted that since he had intended to write his memoirs, he had 'accumulated a lot of letters and other papers' (537). As he indicates, the letters would have been for the most part from the 1750s and would help especially in 'the order of facts and dates' (560). But

Rousseau also claimed to have lost many of those papers: 'The papers that I had collected to make good the defects in my memory and to guide me in this undertaking have all passed into other hands and will never return into mine' (262). Whatever disjointed notes he might have actually had with him, there could not have been much to rely on, since Rousseau wrote his autobiography as a frantic fugitive. Briefly starting his autobiography on the island of Saint-Pierre on the Lake of Bienne in Switzerland, he subsequently wrote the first part in exile in England and the second part as a wanderer through France. Rousseau admits that his narrative necessarily contains some invention to fill in the gaps – what he considers to be unimportant lapses. However, despite Rousseau's admission to some fabulation on his part, many critics, including biographers and editors, believe in the rather amazing veracity of the account of his life, even if they question the accuracy of his dates.[2]

The *Confessions* is Rousseau's retrospective narrative of his life from his birth in Geneva in 1712 to his fugitive state at the Lake of Bienne in 1765, spanning 53 years. In literary history, it is considered to be the first 'modern' autobiography, composed between 1766 and 1770, and published posthumously in two parts, in 1782 and 1789. From the start, Rousseau overtly pleads with the reader to forgive him if there is any lapse in his meticulous, if not compulsive and comprehensive record of the emotional events of his life. As a fact, Rousseau claims that 'memories of middle age are always less sharp than early youth' (170). At the age of 53, in starting to write the *Confessions*, he finds his earliest memories the most vivid. These autobiographical memories include the famous incident of the combs and the more trivial incidents of his pre-teen years, such as the destruction of a walnut tree, the stealing of asparagus from a neighborhood garden, and an unsuccessful hunt for apples from a kitchen larder. Such activities were childish pranks that took place in the peaceful Alpine countryside of Bossey, France, where Jean-Jacques was sent away to board under the direction of a certain pastor, M. Lambercier. The French village of Bossey, a few kilometers outside of Geneva, was distinctly associated with his childhood years from the age of ten to twelve. Rousseau declares that he remembers the most trivial events of that time; his memory is highly visual, as he describes, for example, the decor of M. Lambercier's study. Rousseau recalls 'places and people and moments in all their detail' (31), which vividly revive in his older years:

> Je sens que ces mêmes souvenirs renaissent tandis que les autres s'effacent, et se gravent dans ma mémoire avec des traits dont le charme et la force augmentent de jour en jour (Pléiade, 21).

[I feel that these same recollections revive while others are erased, and that they print themselves on my memory with features whose charm and strength increase from day to day.]

Perhaps the reason Rousseau remembered so much of his early life was due to its peculiar nature. After all, he was virtually an orphan, his mother having died at his birth, and his father Isaac abandoning him when he was ten years of age. There is also the rather climactic memory when, at the age of 16, he became an outcast, being locked out of the gates of Geneva for not observing a curfew, and thereafter literally leading a peripatetic existence marked by bouts of human relationships which were breached abruptly. This unusual, often traumatic quality of his early years and his constant wanderings in the French countryside of Savoie, made this past memorable – more so than what a so-called normal and stable but uneventful youth would yield. Moreover, one can say that Rousseau had an extended childhood, which runs through the course of Part I of the *Confessions* to the age of 29 since his behavior and his locale more or less remained the same. The fact that Rousseau even admitted to remaining a child with a youthful sensibility can account for the immense amount of detail and particulars, or 'trifles' (87), that he remembers. His child-mind seems to have retained a plasticity, scientifically speaking, which created memory circuits well beyond the standard years of childhood.

As a true Romantic, Rousseau was overly concerned with the expression of sincerity and true frankness ('la franchise') in the writing of his autobiography. Addressed to the reader, his work is intended to live up to his own criteria of truth-telling and aversion to lying. Somewhat paradoxically, therefore, he constantly holds up his memories to the standards of the 'truth claim' despite the fact that he admits to some kind of 'insignificant' embellishment:

> ...and if by chance I have used some immaterial embellishment ('quelque ornement indifférent') it has been only to fill a void due to a defect of memory. (17)

But since it was Rousseau's natural inclination to exaggerate, he might well have filled his memories with an elaboration that might be the unintended fictions of his imagination. Given this proclivity, he would feel that he should not be charged with falsity, since his own subjective perceptions helped mold the memories. Certainly, there would be no intentional effort to 'lie' on his part. Such a rationale persists throughout the *Confessions* and is reiterated subsequently in the fourth promenade of *Les Rêveries du promeneur solitaire*. There he pointedly comments on the kind of memory which made up his earlier *Confessions:*

> I wrote them from memory; this memory often failed me or only furnished me imperfect recollections, and I filled in the gaps with details which I dreamed up, details which supplemented these recollections, but which were never contrary to them.[3]

Rousseau goes on to say that a certain nostalgia ('de tendres regrets') for that past might have prompted him to add certain embellishments to the recollection of it. He uses semantics to justify any fabrication in the rendition of memory: if he had forgotten something about that past, he would have recollected it in the way that it seemed to him that it must have been 'comme il me semblait qu'elles avaient dû être'.[4]

In Book 7 of the *Confessions*, Rousseau makes it quite clear that his is an emotional memory which accurately recalls a succession of feelings, rather than dates or facts:

> I easily forget my misfortunes, but I cannot forget my faults, and still less my genuine feelings. The memory of them is too dear ever to be effaced from my heart. I may omit or transpose facts, or make mistakes in dates; but I cannot go wrong about what I felt, or about what my feelings have led me to do; and these are the chief subjects of my story (262).

The use of the word heart ('coeur') in this passage underscores the emotional quality of such memory. In fact, it is interesting that Rousseau comments that a loss of recollection can only coincide with a dearth of emotion in a period of his life. Such is the case when, for example, his beloved benefactor and lover Madame de Warens temporarily leaves Savoie for Paris in 1732. Rousseau comments that he has a confused memory of this particular period of his life because 'rien presque ne s'y est passé d'assez intéressant à mon coeur pour m'en retracer vivement le souvenir (Pléiade, 130); hardly anything happened that was interesting enough for my heart to recount from it a lively recollection'. Here again the French word 'coeur' is used, focusing on the heart as the retainer of memory. Hence, if the heart is untouched, there is little memory.

In general, Rousseau distinguishes between the first part of his narrative as relating those memories which are happy impressions in idyllic settings of nature from the second part which relate ones of bitterness in his dealings in society and the alleged conspiracy of the French intelligentsia against him. He may be here admitting that his long-term memory is greater than his short-term one. He claims that he has the power to dismiss voluntarily the 'bad memories' and retain the good ones as he relives those better moments through his emotions as he recalls them. He also claims that he naturally forgets past ills: 'the memory of them comes back only dimly' (540) – which justifies some of the confusion he has in relating the circumstances of some of the controversies with his 'enemies' that he describes in reference to the second part of his life. Also, since the later part of his life deals with facts and dates in relation to others, he is less prone to remember such objective data. On the other hand, to demonstrate the strength of his memory, he turns in Book 6 of the *Confessions* to the period of his life which gave him most felicity – when he was in his 20s in the company of that maternal figure and sometime lover, Madame de Warens in Savoie, France. He states: 'Nothing that happened to me during that delightful time, nothing that I did, said, or thought all the while it lasted, has slipped from my memory' (215–16).

As an example of one such trifle of a recollection which was revived with 'force' (strength) and 'vérité' (truth) (Pléiade, 226), Rousseau recounts the memory event of the periwinkle, a modest blue Alpine flower that Madame de Warens had noticed on a walk with him. It was a detail which Rousseau himself claims not to have given much attention to at the time. On the other hand, it belonged to a very happy period of his life, when he stayed with Madame de Warens in the estate at Les Charmettes, right outside of Chambéry. During that time in 1738, Rousseau was at the pinnacle of his relationship with her, right before his final rift and journey to Paris. But Rousseau makes the point that twenty-five or so years later, when he came across the same flower in a different locale in Cressier, France, in different company, he claims to have experienced a delight in suddenly recollecting an entire stage of his past life through the sight of this insignificant flower. The association of the flower with the earlier ambience of happiness that was connected to Madame de Warens had remained and resurfaced at a later date. The flower itself resurrected the entire environment which apparently for Rousseau was one of bliss and which was remembered precisely because of its positive emotional content and the sheer nostalgia it might have evoked as Rousseau looked back. He wrote: 'The reader can judge by the effect on me of something so small, the degree to which I have been moved by everything which relates to that stage in my life' (216). For the likes of Rousseau, to be 'moved' by the slightest provocation is to remember. The state conducive to the registering of memory can be an interior one of sheer, innocent contentment.

Rousseau analyzes his own memory process with great scrutiny and in Book 4 the vocabulary he uses to describe it is especially revealing:

> Comme en général les objets font moins d'impression sur moi que leurs souvenirs et que toutes mes idées sont en images, les premiers traits qui se sont gravés dans ma tête y sont demeurés, et ceux qui s'y sont empreints dans la suite, se sont plutôt combinés avec eux qu'ils ne les ont effacés. Il y a une certaine succession d'affections et d'idées qui modifient celles qui les suivent et qu'il faut connaître pour en bien juger (Pléiade, 174–5).

> [As in general objects make less impression on me than the memory of them, and as all my ideas are in the form of images, the first features to engrave themselves in my head have remained there, and those which have subsequently become imprinted have combined with them rather than erased them. There is a certain succession of impressions and ideas which modify those that follow them, and it is necessary to know the original set before judging them.]

Having been apprenticed to an engraver in his early youth, Rousseau uses an engraver's metaphor and the French words 'gravé' (engraved) and 'empreint' (imprinted) to designate the first impressions of memory, which leave their marks indelibly on the head ('tête'). Earlier in Book 1, Rousseau had written more pointedly that his recollections 'se gravent dans ma mémoire' (Pléiade, 21); ['are indelibly imprinted in my memory']. According to his descriptions, such original memories are expanded through time and blended with others to produce a composite memory, strengthened through combination but not obliterated by later ones. In terms of autobiographical memory, for Rousseau, there is the stress on the source memory which he claims remains intact and which he is able to retrieve and identify in terms of time and place. Subsequent related memories which follow in the same vein fortify the original memory. Such could be the case of the periwinkle.

Uncontestably, the most striking and dramatic memory of the *Confessions* is that of Mlle Pontal's ribbon which remains distinct and unique because it is this emotional memory which Rousseau claims to be the source of his writing his autobiography. The incident refers back to the time when Rousseau was 16 years old in Turin, Italy, serving as a lackey in the household of Mme de Vercelli. Impulsively but unjustly accusing an innocent country girl, Marion, of a paltry theft, he carries the burden of such injustice for more than thirty years to the point of writing a work in which he confesses this transgression. As a 53-year-old writer, Rousseau claims that the memory of the event has become even starker over the years: 'in fact the bitter memory of it, far from fading grows more painful with the years' (86). He finds it necessary to confess this past incident on paper so that he might be able to eliminate this guilt from his conscience. In line with Rousseau's later statement that 'once I have written a thing down, I entirely cease to remember it' (328) the transfer of the memory onto paper apparently helps him to lessen its haunting effect. Nonetheless, the emotion of remorse not only had imprinted the memory but had continued to activate it over time as guilt. Rousseau writes about this 'cruel memory':

> This cruel memory troubles me at times and so disturbs me that in my sleepless hours I see this poor girl coming to reproach me for my crime, as if I had committed it only yesterday (88).

It is worth noting that in some way this memory event is a variation of an earlier memory recounted in Book 1 of the *Confessions*, which had left its mark on Rousseau, disrupting the serenity of his childhood. Rousseau claims that as a young boy under the tutelage of the pastor Lambercier in the village of Bossey, he had been unjustly accused of breaking the combs of Mlle Lambercier, the pastor's sister. This first memory of an act of injustice proved to be painful, having lasted 'nearly fifty years', Rousseau says (29). Rousseau describes the lasting impression on himself:

> Imagine the revolution in his ideas, the violent change of his feelings, the confusion in his heart and brain, in his small intellectual and moral being (29).

At this early stage of life in this incident of the comb, Rousseau had been the victim of an act of injustice, whereas six years later in the incident of the ribbon, he himself in turn had become the perpetrator of a comparable act. Obviously, both are long-term memories. In the juxtaposition of these two events, a certain pattern of repetition can be discerned, which strengthens both memories that relate to a period from childhood to adolescence. However, narrated as separate events, they retain their identity and are not connected in any psychological way which might be discerned later in the Bergsonian writing of Proust. Rousseau's memory patterns do *not* connect moments in time but rather isolate them as prevailing incidents or what might be termed as Wordsworthian 'spots of time', which are building blocks in the formation of that identity considered to be the soul.

Even with respect to the memory of an intellectual development, Rousseau recollects it by way of emotion. Rousseau recounts a crowning memory which uncovers a climactic turning point in his life. In Book 8 of the *Confessions*, Rousseau dramatically describes the episode at the age of 37 when he discovered his vocation as a political writer. He recalls the scene when he was on his way by foot to Vincennes from Paris and stopped to take a break under an oak tree. Pulling out a copy of the *Mercure de France* to read, he came upon a notice for a prize offered by the Dijon Academy. It would be offered for a winner of an essay regarding the question of the moral impact on society of the sciences and the arts. The time of this memory event is clear since this prize question actually appeared in an October 1749 issue of the periodical. But again it is the element of emotion that makes Rousseau's ruminations memorable because, as he says, 'my feelings rose with the most inconceivable rapidity to the level of my ideas' (328). What he remembers is experiencing a kind of delirium, 'une agitation qui tenait du délire' (Pléiade, 351), as he went on to write the essay 'Discourse on the Sciences and the Arts' that indeed gave him the prize in 1750 which launched his career of political writing. He even states that the rest of his life and even his misfortunes were the result of that moment of passionate insight. It was an excitation which even his fellow philosopher Diderot, whom Rousseau was visiting in Vincennes, witnessed.

It is interesting to note that in the case of Rousseau, particular memory events, often construed as trifles or momentary occurrences become exaggerated and then remembered because this political writer links them to grand ideas on justice, equality, virtue, liberty, nature, truth. A striking example is found in Book 7 when Rousseau is briefly employed as a secretary to the French ambassador in Venice. Having described his feisty confrontation with this incompetent ambassador, Rousseau briefly swerves from his narration in a rather startling digression. He describes an encounter with a beautiful courtesan that proves disappointing because of the shock of suddenly discovering her malformed nipple. Having first contemplated the woman as a masterpiece of nature, he is subsequently distraught, almost fainting, he says, and weeping as he witnesses first hand this 'vice naturel' (Pléiade 321) or flaw of nature. This flaw in turn becomes an obstacle which thwarts a romantic moment of fulfillment; this disappointment itself is memorable. In this incident, Rousseau's reaction is emotional, and it is registered as such in his memory, because it challenges his Romantic idealism. The small individual experience of the past becomes aggrandized and retained because of its connection to social ideas.

A reading of the *Confessions* in fact can show the very process by which Rousseau arrived at elements of his social philosophy from his own limited life experiences which he vividly remembers. The famous Savoyard vicar of the incendiary *Emile* finds its origin 34 years earlier in a certain Monsieur Gaime whom Rousseau recalls meeting in Italy when he was 16 years old. In Book 3 Rousseau writes in retrospect that Monsieur Gaime's lessons in natural religion had made an impression on his heart ('coeur'); in fact, it helped shape his own views of Deism. In this context, memory imprinted again through such emotional empathy is later strengthened by its intellectual attachments.

Through the many personal events Rousseau actively recalls in his *Confessions*, he gives the reader concrete instances of the workings of his emotional memory, both engraved and later recaptured through feeling. It is interesting to note that Rousseau does not use the word 'mind' or 'esprit' in connection with memory. Wordsworth and Hugo were to use the word 'soul', that Romantic seat of memory known to Descartes but dismissed in the course of the nineteenth century. For the Romantics, the soul represented neither the heart nor the mind, but was the seat of sensibility which combined the two. Hence, an innate spirituality defines their memory events. Such Romantics are also able voluntarily to revive their memories through the restoration of emotion often in states of tranquility. Emotion has instilled the long-term memories, which are recovered through self-imposed acts of voluntary concentration and musing.

Subsequently, the poet William Wordsworth was to specifically associate the soul with memory. His autobiographical poem *The Prelude* spans his development as a poet from childhood to his early 20s, from his boyhood in the native countryside of the English Lake District through the period of the French Revolution and its aftermath of the Reign of Terror, during which he spent a year in France. Like Rousseau, Wordsworth intentionally unearths certain isolated recollections, which for him fortified his identity. In Book II of his autobiographical poem *The Prelude*, completed when he was 35 years old, he had written:

> . . . but that the soul,
> Remembering how she felt, but what she felt
> Remembering not, retains an obscure sense
> Of possible sublimity (II, 315–18).[5]

For the Romantics, the soul did represent the identity and temperament of a person that would remain after death. That soul often identified the character of a person, the innate tendencies, the personality. It is not only the seat of consciousness, but the seat of conscience as well. Memory helps form that identity.

It was Wordsworth who coined the much used term 'spots of time' which can be associated with the encoding of such Romantic memory events. In Book XII of his long autobiographical poem *The Prelude*, Wordsworth described 'spots of time' as impressionable events in his life, most often gleaned from childhood, which nourish him in later years and which are never forgotten:

> There are in our existence spots of time
> That with distinct pre-eminence retain
> A renovating virtue...Such moments
> Are scattered everywhere, taking their date
> From our first childhood (XII, 208–9; 223–5).

Such isolated emotional moments become lasting memories, later to be recalled in tranquility. Two striking examples are featured, at the beginning and toward the end of *The Prelude*, that of the elfin pinnace in Book I and the gibbet in Book XII.

The elfin pinnace memory is one that stems from Wordsworth's childhood. Wordsworth describes a summer evening during which he secretly embarked on a little rowboat on the quiet Esthwaite Lake near Hawkshead where he lived and attended grammar school. It is not long before the young boy on his elfin pinnace encounters a huge dark mountain crag. He remembers the fact that he was trembling with fear as he steered back to the mooring-place, and in deference to the power of Nature returned to his home in 'serious mood', (I, 390) to be obsessed with his vision thereafter. This emotional contemplation of nature, which disturbs his carefree tranquility, is memorable to the growing poet. Likewise, another childhood memory, that of the gibbet stirs his emotions. His remembrance, as he calls it, is that of journey over hills and dale with a friend, when suddenly he finds himself separated from his comrade and face to face with a gibbet-mast 'where in former times/ a murderer had been hung in iron chains' (XII, 235–6). To add to the unexpected, disturbing sight, he remembers seeing the murderer's name inscribed on the turf beneath the gibbet. He remembers that this ominous sight left him 'faltering', 'faint', and disoriented.

In his well-known Preface to his *Lyrical Ballads* of 1798, Wordsworth made the following statement regarding memory:

> I have said that Poetry is the spontaneous overflow of powerful feelings: it takes its origin from emotion recollected in tranquility: the emotion is contemplated till by a species of reaction the tranquility gradually disappears, and an emotion, kindred to that which was before the subject of contemplation, is gradually produced, and does itself actually exist in the mind.[6]

According to Wordsworth, then, a state of tranquil meditation is necessary for emotions to be remembered, which thereupon summons scenes or events where earlier versions of the same emotions were felt.

It is significant to take note that Wordsworth articulates, what Rousseau had already demonstrated, that *no* particular external stimulus is needed in this process of retrieval:

> ...the Poet is chiefly distinguished from other men by a greater promptness to think and feel without immediate external excitement.

Wordsworth's poem 'Tintern Abbey', whose very subject is memory, is demonstrative of this claim. The situation of this blank verse poem is as follows: the poet Wordsworth, aged 28, returns to Tintern Abbey on the banks of the River Wye in Southwest England five years after an initial visit 'when first I came among these hills; when like a roe/ I bounded o'er the mountains' (ll. 66–8). Whereas in the earlier visit he had been alone, in 1798 he is accompanied on this walking trip by his beloved sister Dorothy who is only a year younger than he. The light in her eyes at the fresh contemplation of the 'beauteous' nature landscape of hills, streams and trees, seems to reflect the same mindset that he had five years before, contemplating the scene for the first time. Wordsworth is said to have composed the poem within three days to capture the gleam in her 'wild eyes' so much akin to his first experience, which he recollects in the tranquillity of the scene. However, he also admits that he has been capable of reviving those feelings even amidst his sojourn in the cities and towns away from the scene:

> These beauteous forms,
> Through a long absence, have not been to me
> As is a landscape to a blind man's eye:
> But, oft, in lonely rooms, and mid the din

> Of towns and cities, I have owed to them
> In hours of weariness, sensations sweet,
> Felt in the blood, and felt along the heart;
> And passing even into my purer mind,
> With tranquil restoration. (ll. 24–30)

The poet has been able to create his own inner state of tranquility which is necessary for the restoration of these feelings. We also witness his effort to instill a memory, similar to his own, in the mind of his sister, to fortify her in the future against the inevitable anguishes of mortality:

> . . . and, in after years,
> When these wild ecstasies shall be matured
> Into a sober pleasure; when the mind
> Shall be a mansion for all lovely forms,
> Thy memory be as a dwelling place
> For all sweet sounds and harmonies . . . (ll. 137–43)

In this scene, therefore, there is simultaneous encoding and retrieval.

Subsequent to the British 'Tintern Abbey' poem, memory poems abounded especially in the French language.[7] Most notably, there is a cluster of three French poems, Lamartine's 'Le Lac' (1817), Hugo's 'Tristesse d'Olympio' (1837) and Musset's 'Souvenir' (1841) which feature the typically Romantic access to memory in the common nature settings. Each of these three highly lyrical Romantic poems, fraught with nostalgia connected to a past lover, depicts the poet's conscious pursuit of the retrieval of a particular memory of a loved one. In all three cases, there is a clear distinction between the past and the present; the happiness of the past has been replaced by the desolation of the present. Revisiting the locale in which a previous communion had taken place, the poet addresses Nature, searching for his memory which he ultimately finds within himself. The poet is typically inspired by the backdrop of the countryside which provides environmental cues and frames for the emotional events of the past.

Lamartine's famous poem from his collection *Premières méditations* situates the poet at the lake of Bourget in Savoie, France, on 29 August 1817. Vainly awaiting the arrival of his lover Madame Julie Charles, he remembers with nostalgia their day together at the lake in September 1816. Obviously, this is a memory event that is tinged with pathos since the 27-year-old poet knows that his 20-year-old loved one is suffering from an ailment – which actually causes her death soon afterwards in

December 1817. In the poem, the poet addresses the lake: 'Un soir, t'en souvient-il?';[8] ['One evening, don't you remember?'] He begs the lake, which is personified, to keep the memory of his evening tryst:

> Hé quoi! n'en pourrons-nous fixer au moins la trace?...
> O lac!
> Gardez de cette nuit, gardez, belle nature
> Au moins le souvenir!
> [What! May we not at least fix the trace?...
> O lake!
> Keep of this night, keep, beautiful nature
> At least the memory!]

He asks for memory traces to be engraved in nature – in the reeds, in the wind, in the breeze, fearing all the while that such memory can be ravaged by the passage of time. A tension is thereby produced between the poet's demand to retain the memory and Nature's apparent indifference. In this instance, the natural landscape itself nonetheless helps the poet revive the memory despite the intense awareness of the fleeting quality of human existence.

Such personal drama will turn into a longer-term memory, since years later in 1849 Lamartine composes his love narrative *Raphaël*, the fiction being based on this important relationship of his youth. This is a sentimental narrative in the tradition of such classics as Chateaubriand's *Atala*, Rousseau's *La Nouvelle Héloïse* and Goethe's *Werther*. At the beginning of the narrative, the persona Raphaël specifically makes a statement which links the retrieval of memory to the place in which it was conceived: 'On ne peut bien comprendre un sentiment que dans les lieux où il fut conçu: One can only understand a feeling in the places where it was conceived.'[9] For this very reason, when the beloved Julie dies, Raphaël returns to roam the Alpine countryside, which he shares in common with Rousseau, in the vicinity of the lake of Aix in Savoie to evoke the memory of her. He follows the traces of her footsteps ('ces traces de ses pas') as he revisits the nature scenes which harbored their love, breathing the air and remaining in a state of contemplation and memory: 'Je restai là en contemplation et en souvenirs.'[10] Away from the sacrosanct place, Raphaël has difficulty retaining the memory; however, when he returns again to the vicinity ten years later, contemplating the lake, the mountains, hearing the leaves rustle and the waters lap the shore, the memory of his soul-mate is retrieved in all its immediacy and vividness.

Lamartine shows in two other memory poems 'Souvenir' of 1819 and 'Souvenir' of 1845 an evolution in his view of memory. In the 1819 poem of profound grief sustained over the loss of Julie Charles, he holds that his memory of her can counter the ravages of time which attempt to erase memory 'sans laisser de trace' ('without leaving any trace'). He insists that even though he will grow old and his loved one has died, he will not lose the inner sight of his beloved 'tu n'as pas quitté mes yeux: you have not left my eyes',[11] he says. His voluntary power of memory, provoked by his emotional sense of loss or 'regret' can make her image reappear. The poet even explains in a commentary to the poem that he sat on a stone bench on a summer evening in 1819 in the woods of his uncle's château at Urcy and reveled in the melancholy mood which helped him write about the memory of his lost loved one.[12] This is a typically Romantic version of the power of reconstructive memory derived from nostalgic emotion. In the later 'Souvenir' poem (1845), addressed to the Princess of Orange whom Lamartine had met a year before in Italy, he turns totally inward for memory storage. He even goes so far as to dismiss the external, natural world of smells and sights to encode memory:

> Et moi, ce qui gravait ces nuits dans ma mémoire,
> Ce n'était pas l'odeur du vent de ces climats,
> Les astres, les cyprès, les flots d'or et de moire...[13]
> [As for me, what engraves the nights in my memory
> Was not the smell of the wind of this atmosphere,
> The stars, the cypresses, the golden and iridescent waves...]

What retains memory is not the sensory receptivity of the brain, as it will be with the poet Charles Baudelaire a decade or so later, but continuous, self-propelled rumination permanently engraving the image within the soul. Lamartine's final focus is on his self-sufficient capacity to retain memory through contemplative states.

Musset's poem, also entitled 'Souvenir', shifts as well from the exterior source of memory to the interior one. At the beginning of the poem, the poet-speaker returns in solitude to a place which harbors a memory of his past happiness with none other than the notorious mistress of so many Romantics, George Sand. Musset's biographer, his brother Paul de Musset, has offered documentation for the poem in recounting 'an unforeseen circumstance'.[14] Out of the blue, apparently Alfred had encountered his lost lover George Sand in the corridors of the Théâtre Italien. Thereupon, he is said to have gone home immediately and composed the poem 'Souvenir'. His recollection of her had been immediately awakened and put in the appropriate setting of the Forest of Fontaine-bleau, the site of an afternoon spent seven-and-a-half years earlier with George Sand in 1833 when she was 28 and he was 23 years old. Within the forest, sleeps the sacred memory of this remembered love which is more real than his current state:

> En osant te revoir, place à jamais sacrée,
> O la plus chère tombe et la plus ignorée
> Ou dorme un souvenir![15]
> [In daring to see you again, forever sacred spot,
> O the dearest and most unknown grave,
> Where the memory sleeps!]

The poet first perceives the memory as being dormant in the place where he had encountered his beloved. However, as the poet gradually doubts the ability of the external natural world of objects, of hills, heather, pine trees, stones, and the like to permanently lodge the memory, he retreats into himself as the more reliable container of that memory:

> Jamais ce souvenir ne peut m'être arraché!
> Comme le matelot brisé par la tempête,
> Je m'y tiens attaché.
> [Never can this memory be torn away from me!
> As the sailor wrecked by the tempest
> I cling to it attached.]

Ultimately, it is the domicile of the soul that permanently retains it: 'J'enfouis ce trésor dans mon âme immortelle.' The French word 'enfouir' suggests the metaphorical act of burying the treasure in the soul which then rises to the celestial region of God. The memory is a treasure for eternity, taken to the afterlife. A typical Romantic dichotomy is created in this poem between the worldly, present life and the afterlife. The poet ultimately rejects the ephemeral sphere of passing time and changeability of nature for the eternity of the spiritual afterlife which is connected with the permanence of memory. In effect, the poet ends by transferring the memory from nature to the interior region of the soul. It shall be seen how this is an entirely different approach from the Modernists' attachment to and dependency upon the outside material world as an objective anchor for the memory process.

   A similar movement to the past is made by Victor Hugo in his great Romantic poem 'Tristesse d'Olympio' from the collection *Les Rayons et les Ombres*. The poet actually returns physically to the forest scene in Metz, France, without his lover, the actress Juliette Drouet, in October 1837 simply to indulge in his memories. Even so, he deplores the way external nature has forgotten his previous pleasure with his beloved, two years before; hence the 'tristesse' or sadness which emerges from the scene. Hugo has his own persona 'Olympio' contemplating the beautiful nature scene as he revisits it, wanting to see everything over again: 'Il voulut tout revoir;'[16] the pond, the garden, the woods, the lake, the valley and remembering his previous adventures there with his loved one. In typically Romantic fashion, he asks a rhetorical question – whether nature, as an urn, has conserved those precious memories. He answers himself, by noticing the change in scenery and accepting the passage of time. He goes on to blame nature – 'Rien ne nous restera de ces coteaux fleuris'; ['Nothing will remain for us of these flourishing hills'] – stating that his traces are effaced and his name forgotten:

> Dieu nous prête un moment les prés et les fontaines...
> Puis il nous les retire. Il souffle notre flamme.
> Il plonge dans la nuit l'antre où nous rayonnons;
> Et dit à la vallée, ou s'imprima notre âme,
> D'effacer notre trace et d'oublier nos noms.
> [God lends us for a moment the meadows and the springs...
> Then he takes them away. He blows our flame.
> He throws into the night the cave in which we shine
> And says to the valley, where our soul imprints itself,
> To erase our trace and forget our names.]

Nonetheless, at this point, the poet turns inward from exterior nature to the dark region of his own soul; like a miner with a lamp he locates 'the sacred memory' mysteriously under a veil and amidsts the shadows of the interior:

> Comme quelqu'un qui cherche en tenant une lampe,
> Loin des objets réels, loin du monde rieur,
> Elle arrive à pas lents par une obscure rampe
> Jusqu'au fond désolé du gouffre intérieur.
> Et là, dans cette nuit qu'aucun rayon n'étoile
> L'âme, en un repli sombre où tout semble finir,
> Sent quelque chose encor palpiter sous un voile...
> C'est toi qui dors dans l'ombre, ô sacré souvenir.

[Like someone who seeks in holding a lamp
Far from real objects, far from the laughing world,
She arrives with slow steps by an obscure ramp
To the deep bottom of the interior abyss.
And there, in this night where no star shines
The soul, in the dark recesses, where all seems to end,
Feels something still quivering under a veil ...
It is you that sleeps in the shadow, o sacred memory.]

The metaphoric imagery is revealing here. Hugo associates the interior with the Romantic 'gouffre', or abyss, which he illuminates in his search. The poet's soul finds therein, under a veil, something alive, something beating, sleeping in the shadows, nothing more than the divine memory! What is particularly striking here is the probing nature of the poet in search of the hidden memory within himself. Latent in the darkness, that memory can be traced and revived. Initiated by himself alone and his acts of introspection, the poet is able to enact the recovery of his own memory, having frequented the scene which created it in the first place. In this case, returning to the scene merely sets off the search for the memory in the interior of the poet's soul. The sense that the memory is beating suggests its live presence; the poet is fully capable of reviving it in himself.

Such Romantics, therefore, locate their emotional memory initially within an exterior site of Nature in which their past feelings were lodged. All are active, voluntary searchers for memory in the lap of nature. Often, such peaceful meditative settings or even the recollection of them was the context for the individual memories to be revived. At times, they turn totally inward for storage sites through sheer contemplation; there, memories are revived through typical Romantic nostalgia – self-induced emotional states of longing for the past. It is especially interesting that no specific trigger is necessary for the recall to occur. In these cases, the stimuli function in the process of encoding rather than in the retrieval of memory. Rousseau does not need a ribbon or a comb to make him remember. Lamartine does not need a scent or a sight to engrave the memory on his soul.

The writings of Rousseau and his contemporaries seem to contribute to the neuroscientific hypothesis that emotion has an effect on memory storage. That is to say, 'the emotional arousal induced by an experience is an important determinant of the strength of memory for the event',[17] – which will be further discussed in Chapter 8. With their long-term personal episodic memory, the Romantics customarily look backward, and with this habit of mind, their memories were strengthened to nourish their spiritual lives. At the same time, the subjective element gave a natural character of confabulation to the memory events, as illustrated especially by Rousseau, whose tendentious imagination was so strong a factor in the reconstruction of memory. For the Romantics, memory was a voluntary operation, fully engaging the human sensibility, nutritive and actively summoned as a constant support system for the human identity.

3
Baudelaire, Rimbaud and 'Le Cerveau': Sensory Pathways to Memory

Baudelaire made it very clear in his poetry that memory was a function of the body. This seminal mid-nineteenth-century French poet took the Romantic subject of memory and nostalgia for the past and expressed them in a markedly physical way. The memories conveyed in his collection of poetry *Les Fleurs du mal* (1857) are not acquired through spiritual yearnings, as with the Romantics, but are reached directly by the senses, particularly by the primitive ones of touch and smell. Therefore, although he is a Romantic, dreaming of past love affairs and idyllic states of earthly paradises, his pathway to the past was through the senses. Sensuality itself is the environment from which memories of his many torrid affairs emerge. Baudelaire even went so far as to manipulate his sensory acuity to recover the desired past. For him, then, memory was largely a voluntary operation, involving a conscious and overt indulgence in the senses and their intermingling – which has been called synaesthesia.

Moreover, in his willful provocation of memory, Baudelaire sang of another intermingling, that of 'les transports de l'esprit et des sens', ('the bliss of the mind and the senses') – which suggested the cerebral connections to the sensory stimuli. This Baudelairean approach, set up in the poem 'Correspondances', innovative as it was for its era, introduced the brain, specifically invoked as 'le cerveau', as the setting for memory events. The fact that Baudelaire even uses in his poetry the word 'cervelle', an old French word for the brain of animals, gives a 'scientific' flavor to his expressions of memory. Other writers, connected to Symbolism, such as Rimbaud and Huysmans, were to follow this lead. After all, Rimbaud gave the senses priority in his description of his own poetry which creatively involved 'le dérèglement de tous les sens' ['the disturbance of all the senses'].[1] For such writers, an array of concrete symbols began to be used to depict memory phenomena, such as containers like flasks, cemeteries, drawers, puddles and lakes. Moreover, memory, once provoked, was like a drug which could put one on a journey, away from the present scene into the realm of the imagination. If memory is viewed as a form of inebriation, it sets the subjects not on metaphysical heights but in a kind of stupor as they re-experience a past event. Such an orientation reached its most demonstrative form in a prose work like J.K. Huysmans' *A Rebours* (*Against the Grain*) (1884), in which outright experimentation of memory provocation occurs in what could be called an artist's laboratory for the study of memory.

Baudelaire clearly opened up the way for the poeticizing of the memory process as he linked his concrete imagination to it. In an essay on his favorite American poet, Edgar Allan Poe, Baudelaire gave examples of certain sensory impressions, such as 'the sound of a bell, a musical note, a forgotten perfume' ('un son de cloche, une note musicale, ou un parfum oublié'),[2] which can be used to elicit memory and in turn provoke his imagination. In Baudelaire's view, the poet, with his extra-keen senses, is dependent on such exterior input for the retrieval and reconstruction of cherished memories. His choice of individual words and images as metaphors for memory are dramatically revealing in his poetry, such as the coupling of memory with wine in 'La Chevelure' and with perfume in 'Le Flacon'. It is telling that taste and smell, highlighted by Baudelaire's two major tropes, have been called the chemical senses by neuroscientists who have considered them to be immediate and vital cues to memory.[3] Indeed, for Baudelaire, there is a certain chemical 'feel' to his portrayal of the memory process. Baudelaire also introduces the concrete means of image-making as ways of expressing memory phenomena. The storage site for his strong, passionate memories becomes his poetry. He thereby pointedly demonstrates the poet's grounding of the memory process in the physical world.

The most striking poem demonstrating Baudelaire's expression of the memory process is the incantatory 'Le Balcon', which is a paean to memory. Here the poet evokes the site of a typical Paris balcony which suggested the locale of a past love affair. It has been widely recognized that this particular poem concerned his mulatto lover Jeanne Duval, often called his Black Venus, with whom he had had a passionate relationship for 14 years from 1842 to 1856. At the time of writing this poem, right after his rupture with that mistress, he provokes memories of his past pleasures, by addressing her and envisaging typical scenes with her on a balcony in the evening and into the dark night. With this willfull and conscious evocation of her, the poet instantly recalls the aromatic and nubile body of his mistress, who is actually designated as the 'mother of memory', the 'mère des souvenirs'. The memory is one of physical contact with her body, 'blotti dans tes genoux', as the poet recalls being nestled against his mistress's knees. Baudelaire challenges the darkness of the abyss, oblivion, to prevent his probing into what resembles the dark floor of the sea. The movement of memory is downward, as it pierces through the temporary darkness and replaces it with the illumination of sunshine, a sign of the recovery of the past. The poet flaunts his capacity to revive the past as a studied art, resulting from the sheer sensuality of his poetry:

> Je sais l'art d'évoquer les minutes heureuses
> Et revis mon passé blotti dans tes genoux,
> Car à quoi bon chercher tes beautés langoureuses
> Ailleurs qu'en ton cher corps et qu'en ton coeur si doux?
> [I can evoke the moments of our happiness,
> To live my past again, spent snuggled in your thighs,
> Where must one seek the languor of your loveliness
> If not within the body where your warm heart lies.][4]

The balcony image also suggests the vista of the mind, as it dominates the scene with a vast purview which reaches the past. Baudelaire's memory has the power of intoxication, which like his poetic art enables him to recapture that past in all its sensual intensity.

A similar effect is reached in the famous poem 'La Chevelure', which evokes the same mistress of his past, for whom he longs years later. Memories, he says, sleep in her hair, which he is able to recall: 'Des souvenirs dormant dans cette chevelure.'[5] The poet voluntarily remembers his hand in her heavy mane, 'drunken' as he is with sensuality. It is that sensual state which brings back the memory. Her hair is likened to a flask from which he drinks memory: 'Où je hume à long traits le vin du souvenir.' The French word 'humer' means to inhale or to suck. It is interesting that the poet follows the same pathways toward memory in the prose version of the poem called 'Un Hémisphère dans une chevelure' ('A Hemisphere in the Hair') from the collection *Petits poèmes en prose*. That piece begins with the poet inhaling the smell ('l'odeur') of the hair that he then fondles and waves like a fragrant handkerchief ('un mouchoir odorant') which rouses the memories in the air ('pour secouer des souvenirs dans l'air'). Baudelaire elaborates on the provocative quality of his mistress's hair, which he likens to an ocean and the journey of his imagination that transports him to the amorous scenes of the past:

> Dans les caresses de ta chevelure, je retrouve les langueurs des longues heures passées sur un divan.
> [In the caresses of your hair I find again the languor of long hours on a divan.][6]

Through the tactile caresses of her hair, the poet recovers those languorous days of the past in her voluptuous presence. Eventually, the poet speaks metaphorically of eating the memories as he bites at the heavy dark tresses of his mistress's hair:

> Quand je mordille tes cheveux élastiques et rebelles, il me semble que je mange des souvenirs.
> [When I gnaw your springy and rebellious hair, it seems to me I'm eating memories.]

In this piece, it is startling to witness the intense mixture of the olfactory, tactile and gustatory senses which produces the memory. In Baudelaire's poetry, memory is connected to a strong sense of physical presence.

A similar retrieval of memory can be observed in the poem 'Le Parfum' from a group of four sonnets comprising 'Un Fantôme'. This set of poems refers back to Baudelaire's passionate relationship with Jeanne Duval, who, much to Baudelaire's chagrin, had become a sickly, destitute being – a phantom-lover. Here, without the physical contact, *per se*, the poet gives the reader a metaphor for memory which arises specifically from the body:

> Ainsi l'amant sur un corps adoré
> Du souvenir cueille la fleur exquise
> [A lover from the body of his love
> Can pluck a smell as though he'd found a flower].[7]

In this poem the loved one is compared to a sachet, a living container of smells, which maintains the memory despite the ravages of time which have destroyed her physical presence. As the title 'Le Parfum' suggests, the sheer sensuality of the smell of the lover's body is the odorant which had been the stimulus for the retrieval of such memory:

> Charme profond, magique, dont nous grise
> Dans le présent le passé restauré!
> [Intoxicating sense of smell! You move
> The memory, restore the bygone hour:]

Ultimately, the poet prefers the portrait of the woman, the art which will store the memory of her sensuality, to her actual deteriorating and sickly body. Baudelaire's final statement in 'Le Portrait', another poem from the group, is that the enemy that is time, which can even succeed in erasing the crayoned lines that make up the portrait, will never be able to destroy the poet's memory of his sensuous Jeanne. This point of view was articulated as well in 'Le Peintre de la vie moderne'[8] ('The Painter of Modern Life') where Baudelaire states that true draftsmen draw from the recollected image in their brain: 'En fait, tous les bons et vrais dessinateurs dessinent d'après l'image écrite dans leur cerveau.' Again, in this instance, the telling word 'cerveau' is used for the durable registering of memory impressions.

Memory arises out of strong fragrances or drink in other poems as well, such as 'Le Flacon', where Baudelaire also envisages memory in gourds or flask containers. This poem is one of the strongest to suggest the resurgence of memory as a kind of resurrection from the musty corner of an abandoned armoire. There a flask lies, just found, containing the leftover perfume which retrieves a love that cannot be forgotten. It is, literally speaking, the flask that first remembers: 'Parfois on trouve un vieux flacon qui se souvient.'[9] It has been said that this poem was written about his memory of his love for the more stately and cultivated Madame Apollonie Sabatier. He had idolized her as his Madonna in a love affair and a cycle of poems, dating from 1852, which had followed that of his dark, exotic Venus, Jeanne. Triggered characteristically by fragrance, the memories are said to emerge from this flask through the next metaphor of a chrysalis. The comparison suggests the metaphoric passage from a quiescent, dormant stage of mind in which a thousand thoughts were in slumber ('mille pensers dormaient'), to an awakening symbolized by the flight of the butterfly: 'Voilà le souvenir enivrant qui voltige'; ['Here is the intoxicated memory which flutters around']. It is especially interesting in this poem to pay attention to the vivid word choice that describes the retrieval of memory in the Baudelairean landscape of the mind. The very use of the more studied

French word 'penser' instead of 'pensée' puts the accent on the process of memory which is unleashed rather than on the content. Verbs such as 'quiver' ('frémir') suggest the excitation of remembered thoughts which are liberated from inactivity in the heavy darkness of the mind's oblivion ('les lourdes ténèbres') and take flight 'prennent leur essor'. It is suggested that this memory is in a temporary state of retrieval since it can be thrown back into the darkness and shut back up into the flask. By the end of the poem, the container becomes an objective correlative for the poet himself and his own power of memory. The poem is an example of what Baudelaire had described as 'resurrectionist memory': 'évocatrice, une mémoire qui dit à chaque chose: "Lazare, lève-toi!"';[10] ['evocative, a memory which says to everything: "Lazarus, get up!"'].

For Baudelaire, memory is like a drug, often a temporary pleasure, which can be unleashed by the mind, as he himself might have experienced in binges of alcohol or opium, with their power of provocation. In his *Les Paradis artificiels* he likens the artistic process to drug-induced states in their common capacity to arouse memory. Memory takes Baudelaire from one pole of sensitivity to another: from states of ecstasy of 'L'Idéal' to states of depression of 'Spleen'.

In fact, so inebriated is Baudelaire by memories that he ultimately envisages his brain as a dark vault overwhelmed by physical traces of the past. The famous Spleen poem 'J'ai plus de souvenirs que si j'avais mille ans' presents a series of images which culminate in the brain – 'mon triste cerveau' – as the ultimate container. Baudelaire actually uses here 'le cerveau', the French word for brain, to stress the physicality of the process. He is a speaker who is virtually overwhelmed with past memories and feeling the weight of time and age as a result of this condition:

> J'ai plus de souvenirs que si j'avais mille ans.
> Un gros meuble à tiroirs encombré de bilans,
> De vers, de billets doux, de procès, de romances . . .
> C'est une pyramide, un immense caveau
> Qui contient plus de morts que la fosse commune.
> Je suis un cimetière abhorré de la lune . . .
> Je suis un vieux boudoir plein de roses fanées . . .
> [I couldn't hold more memories in a thousand years
> A heavy chest of drawers containing scraps of verse
> Check stubs, love letters, writs, a summons, a ballade,
> I am a cemetery hated by the moon . . .
> I am an old boudoir filled with the faded rose . . .][11]

This parade of images, ranging from a chest of drawers to a pyramid to a common grave and cemetery to a stuffy boudoir, gives various versions of the mind as a container of apparently useless remnants. But Baudelaire identifies these leftover objects as triggers for the revival of cherished memories: love letters, balance sheets, locks of hair rolled up in bills – such everyday items fill the brain and conjure up the past. Memories are not presented as abstract feelings, as with the earlier Romantic writers, but as sentient objects, and thus are tied to the physical world. Such an accumulation of memories encumbers the mind, which makes the poet feel old and abandoned like a 'lost sphinx' in a forlorn desert. These memories, in turn, produce the Baudelairean mood of Spleen, a depressed state to which the poet intermittently succumbs after his flights of ecstasy.

Two other poems in this same Spleen mood, 'L'Horloge' and 'La Cloche fêlée', focus on the sensation of sound to bring back memories which drown the poet in his spleen state. In 'La Cloche fêlée' ('The Cracked Bell') the poet's bittersweet memories revive at the sound of the chimes which ring in the misty streets:

> Les souvenirs lointains lentement s'élever
> Au bruit des carillons qui chantent dans la brume.
> [For distant memories that slowly rise
> Among the sounds of chimes in misty air.][12]

In this poem, the poet is engulfed in a state of depressed spleen and identifies with the cracked bell as a reminder of his dead and haunting past. 'L'Horloge', the final poem of the Spleen cycle, ominously brings the poet to moments of recall through the perception of an imposing clock, which seems to communicate the locution 'Remember' in the form of a command: 'Souviens-toi.' Baudelaire uses the French word 'chuchoter', meaning 'whisper', to describe the clock which, through its sound, makes him remember the past:

> Trois mille six cents fois par heure, la Seconde
> Chuchote: 'Souviens-toi!' – Rapide, avec sa voix
> D'insecte, Maintenant dit: 'Je suis Autrefois.'
> [Three thousand six hundred times an hour the tick
> Whispers: 'Remember thou!' And – speaking soft and
> fast, An insect's whine – the Present says: 'I'm now
> the Past.'][13]

With his great admiration for Edgar Allan Poe, Baudelaire facilely mimics the incantatory, auditory character of Poe's well-known poem 'The Raven'. Therein the repeated utterances of the emblematic black bird bring back sad memories of a lost lover, Lenore. Baudelaire seizes upon what Poe highlighted as 'Mournful and Never-ending Remembrance',[14] captured in a resonant, reiterated refrain.

But Baudelaire brings his expression of memory to its most subtle point in his Symbolist poem 'Harmonie du soir'. The entire poem is a controlled, indirect evocation of memory through the intermediary of symbols or what T.S. Eliot would later call 'objective correlatives'. As in, especially, 'Le Flacon' Baudelaire first evokes the memory of a past love (for Madame Sabatier) through the scent of perfume in a physical manner. But here the intensity of that trigger is further elaborated by analogies with another vehicle, the religious censer, the container in which incense is burned: 'Chaque fleur s'évapore ainsi qu'un encensoir';[15] ['Each flower lets off its perfume like a censer']. Hence, the analogy is created whereby memory rises in the way incense is spread in a church. Ultimately, the bittersweet memory, suggested by the melancholy and distant sounds of violins, ends up as a host in a monstrance, and this religious imagery shapes the ending of the poem: 'Ton souvenir en moi luit comme un ostensoir'; ['Your memory shines in me like an ostensorium'].

In this poem Baudelaire has found yet another receptacle for memory, but this time it is an awesome and solemn one – the receptacle of the host in Roman Catholic religious services has become the symbol for the container of memory. In 'Harmonie du soir' Baudelaire uses the verb 'luire', or 'glow', to suggest the radiating effects of memory. What is at work especially in this poem is the artistic technique of synaesthesia, the mingling of the senses. The poem has proceeded in its expression of memory of some past love of the poet through smell, hearing and sight. Through an intense experience of the mingling of these senses, the poet recovers vestiges of the past in fragments:

> Un coeur tendre, qui hait le néant vaste et noir!
> Du passé lumineux recueille tout vestige!
> [A tender heart, which hates the vast and black void
> Gathers from the luminous past every trace!]

In the recovery of the past in this poem, again the word choice is very revealing: 'vestige' suggests remnants and traces of the past; 'recueille', meaning gathering, reminds the reader of the flower imagery at the start of the poem and the scents which first suggested memories; 'lumineux', meaning luminous or radiant, also has the added connection in the French language with the lucidity achieved by the mind's heightened awareness. As such, the sensual triggers replete in the poem lead to the physical mind. Paradoxically, despite the fact that the afflicted heart is mentioned in its analogy to the sad tones of the violin, it is ultimately the mind which is at work in the memory process replacing the dark void of oblivion with the radiating shine of memory provoked by an overload of the senses. As always with Baudelaire, if the heart yearns, it is the mind which recovers.

Although the poet Rimbaud followed in the footsteps of Baudelaire, in this younger contemporary, memory events are tied up more to the state of childhood which the boy-poet Rimbaud retained as the source of his poetic vision. Here was a poet who spoke of art as the 'dérèglement' of the senses – in other words, the disorderly workings of the senses – which in fact included memory events. In general, this poet used varieties of water imagery, such as puddles and rivers, to suggest the source of memory. In considering Rimbaud's poetry, his well-known 'Le Bateau ivre' and the lesser known poem 'Mémoire' are involved in the recollection of unique and sparse scenes of childhood. In these poems, memories are derived from primordial puddles of water or rivers, producing not a stream but a series of disassociated concrete images. As a rule, this poet seeks liberation from his stagnant past by way of his unruly imagination.

'Mémoire' (1872) is Rimbaud's most overt treatment of memory, distinct in that it does not even use the French word 'souvenir' in the course of the poem. In its five sections and the sequence of scenes, it dwells on the implied totality of the memory of an evolving childhood instead of individually recalled moments. The critic Wallace Fowlie has called it 'a poem of sensations'.[16] Some critics interpret it autobiographically as referring to a time when Rimbaud, as a rebellious young teenager, left his mother and siblings and fled by train from his provincial home town to Paris in August of 1870. The poem moves through a succession of images proceeding from clear water 'l'eau claire' to muddy water 'cet oeil d'eau sans bords – à quelle boue?'; ['this rimless eye of water – in what mud?'].[17] This prevalent image of water is sensual in character as it frames the memory event from beginning to end. Whereas the first section of the poem evokes the memories of childhood through the image of the purity of childhood tears ('larmes d'enfance'), the last section transforms the scene into a motionless boat in gloomy water ('d'eau morne'). Autobiographically speaking, the transformation into the dark water initially suggests the advent of sadness in the life of the child Rimbaud upon the definitive departure of his father Captain Frédéric Rimbaud who deserted the family unit.

The pristine memory of childhood gradually becomes altered by the poetic imagination cumulatively into a prevailing and haunting image of an immobile state suggestive of the poet's later condition. A haunting image of the remembering subject, which is the poet, is that of his unexpected transformation into an old dredger on a motionless barge. It is he who dredges, only to find sediments and impurities from the past. The suggestion here, through this elliptical image, is that memory vestiges can be found at the bottom of water pools, solidified and lost in mud. Muddy waters separate the past from the present. The poem resembles Baudelaire's 'Spleen' poem in its evocation of a spleen mood derived from concentrated efforts at recollection.

The particular image of dark pools of water is known to readers of 'Le Bateau ivre', a poem of the same vintage, whose second to last stanza returns the poet after a phantasmagoric sea voyage to a cold, puddle in his native Charleville, on the Meuse river in the Ardennes:

> Si je désire une eau d'Europe, c'est la flache
> Noire et froide où vers le crépuscule embaumé
> Un enfant accroupi plein de tristesses, lâche
> Un bateau frêle comme un papillon de mai.
> [If I want a water of Europe, it is the black
> Cold puddle where in the sweet-smelling twilight
> A squatting child full of sadness releases
> A boat as fragile as a May butterfly.][18]

In both instances, the sight and feel of water provoked the memories of the past. In the case of this poem as well, there is a memory of a static situation. Here, the recollection *per se* is that of the little child bent over a puddle, floating a little paper boat, in a constricted space, in contrast to the vastness of the poetic imagination which involved the creative confusion of the senses. This puddle of memory will be appropriated by later writers as an apt image representing the origin of the memory process.

The Symbolist poet Mallarmé carries the sensuality of the memory process to its limit by demonstrably rarefying it. Here was a poet who proclaimed that he had exhausted every source of sensual pleasure: 'La chair est triste, hélas!/ et j'ai lu tous les livres';[19] ['The body is sad, alas, and I have read all the books']. Consistent with this statement express-ing his surfeit, therefore, Mallarmé takes the wine and the perfume, the two significant memory triggers of Baudelaire, and experiences them in their rudimentary forms of the grape and the flower. For another form of excitation, Mallarmé, instead, returns to the sources for the provocation of the sensory mechanism. Wine is the product of the grape; perfume is the product of the flower. Mallarmé is communicating the fact that the retrieval of memory by the senses involves the participation of the poetic imagination, which fabricates the memory from the raw materials of the past. The poet converts the sensory objects into outright symbols for memory, which incarnate its potentiality.

As an illustration, Mallarmé intellectualizes the sensual process of memory in his celebrated poem 'L'Après-midi d'un faune'. Here is the unusual image of inflating a grape of memory, which has replaced Baudelaire's more accessible wine of memory:

> Ainsi, quand des raisins j'ai sucé la clarté
> Pour bannir un regret par ma feinte écarté,
> Rieur, j'élève au ciel d'été la grappe vide
> Et, soufflant dans ses peaux lumineuses, avide
> D'ivresse, jusqu'au soir je regarde au travers.
> O nymphes, regonflons des souvenirs divers.[20]
> [Thus, when from grapes I have sucked the clarity
> To banish a regret by my ruse set apart,
> Laughing, I raise to the summer sky the empty grape
> And, blowing in her luminous skins, avid
> From intoxication, until the evening I look through them.
> O nymphs, let us reinflate the various memories.]

In this passage the poet, having sucked out all the possible sensual experiences, seeks to 'reinflate' the grape, the age-old Dionysian symbol of sensuality, which as seen in the quotation, is synonymous with the procreative aspect of memory. For the Symbolists, then, memory is both a welcome evasion for dreaming and an opportunity for creativity when the memories are resituated in art: 'la réminiscence de l'objet nommé baigne dans une neuve atmosphère';[21] ['the recall of the named object bathes in a new atmosphere']. Mallarmé here suggests that the object is the focal point for the recollection, and that it is transformed into the aesthetic symbol by the poet.

But bouts of splenetic boredom or forgetfulness intermittently block the memory process. It is here that the mind is being scrutinized. Mallarmé focuses on the difficulties involved in the eradication of memory from states of oblivion. Memory can be hermetically contained in frozen water and has become hard to retrieve. This ivory-tower poet, known for his creation of dense multivalent symbols in his poetry, offers this aspect of memory in two well-known poems, 'Le Vierge, le vivace et le bel aujourd'hui' and the poetic sequence 'Hérodiade'. In the first short poem, memory seems to be hidden under glaciers of ice, in layers, which are difficult to crack. The Mallarméan whiteness suggests oblivion, as in this case of the white lake and the white swan, the poet.

It is useful to note that the critic Harald Weinrich, in *Lethe*, his book on the cultural history of forgetting, dwells on Mallarmé's sonnet 'Le Vierge, le vivace et le bel Aujourd'hui' as a prime example of the poetry of 'l'oubli' or forgetting. Historically speaking, Weinrich claims that thematically forgetting takes the place of remembering in the post-Romantic era.[22] Weinrich's focus gives an interesting twist to the phenomenon of memory in Mallarmé. The lake, a traditional locale for remembering for the Romantic poets, has become a site for oblivion. It freezes all memories for the 'swan-poet' who is singing his swan song, divested of the inspiration that memory had provided: 'Ce lac dur oublié que hante sous le givre';[23] ['This hard forgotten lake haunted under the frost']. Packed in ice, the memories are difficult to extract.

The ice imagery continues in Mallarmé's longer dramatic poem 'Hérodiade', where the Biblical legendary princess, who actually suggests Salomé rather than her mother, stops for a moment of introspection. She symbolically looks into a mirror searching for memories. The passage is dense in connotation:

> O miroir!
> Eau froide par l'ennui dans ton cadre gelée
> Que de fois et pendant des heures, désolée
> Des songes et cherchant mes souvenirs qui sont
> Comme des feuilles sous ta glace au trou profond,
> Je m'apparus en toi comme une ombre lointaine.[24]
> [Cold water by boredom frozen in your frame
> How many times and during many hours, distressed
> By dreams and seeking memories which are
> Like leaves under your mirror with a deep hole
> I see myself in you as a faraway shadow.]

Literally translated, the memories are likened to leaves under ice. The double meaning of the word 'glace' in French as ice and mirror suggests the fact that memory can be either revealed as the reflected self in the mirror or frozen and submerged under a block of ice. In breaking through the ice to gather the leaves – what can be regarded as the remnants of memory – the poet can reach his other shadowy past self in the mirror. Unlike the facile method of recall by Baudelaire, for Mallarmé, the recovery process is sparse and uncomfortable and remains mysterious and unpredictable. There are no traces or vestiges left to be captured, nor containers lying around. The Mallarméan approach distills the sensual elements in language, where a flower is no longer a real flower with potent scent but a virtual flower created by words. At the end of his poem, Mallarmé depicts Hérodiade as waiting for the crisis moment in which memory mysteriously might reappear. The Princess says that she is waiting for something unknown: 'J'attends une chose inconnue.'

It is interesting that in the lesser known prose poem 'Le Nénuphar blanc', a white flower appears, here as the 'magical' water lily, which has a distinct connection to memory:

> Comme on cueille, en mémoire d'un site, l'un de ces magiques nénuphars clos qui y surgissent tout à coup, enveloppant de leur creuse blancheur un rien, fait de songes intacts, du bonheur qui n'aura pas lieu . . . [25]
> [As one gathers, in the memory of a site, one of the magic water lilies, closed up, that appears suddenly, enclosing with its empty whiteness, a nothingness, made up of inviolate dreams, of happiness which will not materialize . . .]

Rather than a chrysalis undergoing visible metamorphosis, as in Baudelaire's poem 'Le Flacon', it is a water lily in bud. In keeping with Mallarmé's Symbolist notion of the 'ideal flower' that is absent from all bouquets, this water lily is a symbol for an inscrutable memory that remains latent in the poet's mind. In contrast to the fertile darkness of the Baudelairean mental sites, the whiteness here suggests the mind's occasional ability to solicit memories by the uncanny predisposition of waiting for its slow emergence. The narrative itself, which describes a male speaker's walk in the countryside toward an estate of an idealized lady, waiting for her to emerge into view, is an extended metaphor for a possible tryst with memory, the imaginary prize 'mon imaginaire trophée'. Yet the outcome remains provocatively uncertain. Periodic bouts of oblivion prevent the poet at times from acquiring such trophies. There is therefore a different orientation toward the metaphor of the 'flower' of memory, which Baudelaire had associated with perfume. Whereas memory is viewed in its latent form by Mallarmé, for Baudelaire, the perfumed memory is actively recalled, easily 'plucked' and retrieved because of its physical accessibility and the poet's sensual activity.

Within Mallarmé's era, a more direct disciple of Baudelaire's functional memory process is the esoteric writer J.-K. Huysmans, whose notorious *A Rebours* or *Against the Grain*, called a 'breviary of Decadence' offered outright artistic experimentations with memory. Huysmans not only uses the word 'esprit' (mind) but 'cerveau' and 'cervelle' (brain) as well in describing certain memory events. It is as if approaching the end of the century, the artist has turned 'scientist' under the influence of Naturalism and Positivism that crowns the era. In this strange novel, the remembering subject is the odd persona Des Esseintes, a decadent 30-year-old aristocratic aesthete, who appears to be a case study of the Decadent in need of constant stimulation by the senses. Suffering from numerous disorders which include neurasthenia, anemia and dyspepsia, and disdainful of the materialistic urban Western world of the late nineteenth century, he goes off to the outskirts of Paris to a secluded villa at Fontenay-aux-Roses. To conquer his jaded boredom with much needed diversion, he fabricates his own sensually charged artificial world, which includes artificial means of provoking memory. It is as if he creates a laboratory situation for inducing memory phenomena.

Des Esseintes succeeds in experiencing bouts of memory events through a variety of sensory stimuli, but he also uses certain techniques to turn them on and off, according to his passing fancies. In other words, he has mastered the 'art' of manipulating memory in a pseudo-scientific fashion. In an avant-garde manner, the eccentric Des Esseintes regards memory as appearing in phases and classified according to short-term and long-term ones as they assault his mind ('l'esprit'). As he describes the onset of memories with a certain momentum, it appears that he is documenting phenomena of the mind. For example, he claims that a self-imposed concentration on certain readings can first 'hold back the current of old memories'.[26] But when he loses his attention on such readings, he gives himself up to reveries of the past which lead to a short phase of certain 'insignificant' memories on the surface of his mind. Such memories are floating metaphorically on sea waters where 'there drifted, like ridiculous bits of flotsam, trivial episodes of his existence, absurdly insignificant incidents.' The French word 'épaves' meaning 'debris' describes these recollections as insignificant fragments. They are actually associated with the superficial, mundane life that he had in Parisian society and from which he had fled. After a short pause when 'his memory took a siesta', there is reference to a second phase of memory.

The second wave of memories to appear are of 'a more distant period, yet they were clearer than the others, engraved more deeply and enduringly in his mind'.[27] Such memories refer to the period of his youth, of the Jesuit Fathers of his school years, which in turn lead him to ruminate seriously on his artistic development away from the atmosphere of Catholicism and toward that of Aestheticism. In the course of such self-analysis which accompanies such memories, Huysmans uses the word 'cervelle', and then 'cerveau', to show the shift from the mind to the brain. The physicality of the process is thereby stressed.

A litany of assorted memory events ensue as the eccentric Des Esseintes figure seeks further stimulation of his mind in order to entertain himself. In many instances, he mechanically elicits a continuous stream of disconnected memories as he experiments with the induction of sensations from a variety of rather unusual sources. These stimuli include exotic hothouse flowers, a chirping cricket, fine candies or 'bonbons', esoteric musical instruments, an assortment of perfumes and liqueurs, and strange knickknacks. Stimulated by all five senses, his cerebral cortex is like a stage setting for a series of memory events.

At times, the character elicits negative memories of the past, in an attempt to actually purge himself of them. Memory is triggered by a familiar sound which takes him back to his childhood:

> Thus, in hateful and contemptuous memory of his childhood, he had suspended from the ceiling of this room a little silver cage containing a cricket which chirped as other crickets had once chirped among the embers in the fireplaces at the Château de Lourps. Whenever he heard this familiar sound, all the silent evenings of constraint he had spent in his mother's company and all the misery he had endured in the course of a lonely, unhappy childhood came back to haunt him.[28]

At other times, memories of the past surge involuntarily. For example, in creating an elaborate hothouse of expensive and rare flowers for sheer amusement, he comes across a provocative cattleya. The smell of this orchid flower with its unpleasant odor of 'varnished deal' ('de sapin vernis') produces unpleasant memories of his childhood again, this time a recollection of New Year's day scenes in his childhood:

> Then he noticed that there was still one name left on his list, the Cattleya of New Granada . . . it gave out a smell of varnished deal, a toy-box smell that brought back horrid memories of New Year's Day when he was a child.[29]

Next he opens a box of purple candies, which turn out to be aphrodisiacs reawakening in him memories of carnal pleasures with an assortment of women in his past life:

> These bonbons . . . consisted of a drop of schoenanthus scent or female essence crystallized in pieces of sugar; they stimulated the papillae of the mouth, evoking memories of water opalescent with rare vinegars and lingering kisses fragrant with perfume.[30]

In this instance, there is a double stimuli, combining the taste with the scent and resulting in a sensual memory of 'the savour of some woman'. The taste of the candy unleashes a set of lascivious memories, a 'procession of mistresses' of his past debauchery.

Compound triggers of tastes and smells elicit memories, pleasurable as well as painful. For example, at one point when he is drinking Irish whisky, he is reminded of the scent of his visits to dentists over the years. In particular, he recalls a horrific tooth extraction of three years before:

> Little by little, as he drank, his thoughts followed the renewed reactions of his palate, caught up with the savour of the whisky, and were reminded by a striking similarity of smell of memories which had lain dormant for years.[31]

Through the sense of taste he recovers the unpleasant memory of a painful experience involving a horrible toothache; the narration becomes comic in its description of a frantic trip to the dentist and a virtual struggle with a dentist brutally pulling out his molar.

At another point, memories emerge from the sight of an astrolabe on Des Esseintes' desk. This object had been used as a paperweight for his books:

> The paper-weight stirred up in him a whole swarm of memories. Set in motion by the sight of this little curio, his thoughts went from Fontenany to Paris, to the old curiosity shop where he had bought it, then back to the Thermes Museum.[32]

This visual stimulus of an object sets in motion the recollection of a whole tour he had taken through the streets of Paris from the museum ending up in the taverns of the Latin Quarter. The character then muses about that contemporary Parisian life which he had sought to reject in his retreat to his artificial world as a practicing aesthete.

Ultimately, memory is like a drug which takes the place of what Des Esseintes calls the 'crude stimulants' such as laudanum, opium and hashish, that he claims to have rejected. For this subject, 'solitude had acted on his brain like a narcotic',[33] inducing a languor that set the stage for a passivity conducive to the arousal of a variety of memories. Like the poets Baudelaire and Rimbaud, Huysmans' artist figure Des Esseintes admits that memory serves his purposes best in prompting artistic dreamlike mental excursions, even though in his particular case they seem to bring back unfortunate past experiences from which he desires to be liberated. For the writers, however, whether it be a flask of perfume, a dark puddle, or a taste of candy, such particulars set off the memory process. Mallarmé portrayed certain blockages of memory when such outside stimulation was absent or avoided. On the other hand, the exaggerated access to memory in the Huysmans novel suggests the fascination that was intensifying about the artist's capacity to mechanically manipulate the senses as a trigger for creativity. With his Decadent persona's overstimulated brain ('un cerveau surexcité'),[34] Huysmans was perhaps even satirizing what the poets had already sensed: that memory events could be potently incited by the outside world and its sensory input. In particular, the 'perfumed' language of Baudelaire and Huysmans should be of interest to researchers who contend that among the sensory systems, the olfactory one has the most direct route to the limbic system and its memory processing. For its own time, this cluster of interrelated writings in the second half of the nineteenth century gave a very concrete sense of the memory process as a physical phenomenon that merited further exploration and study. The next step would come with the twentieth-century novelist Proust, who having surely taken note of both Baudelaire's and Huysmans' experimentations, proceeded to fixate on the involuntary mechanism that connected the sensory triggers to the mind.

4
Proust and the Engram: The Trigger of the Senses

Most psychologists cite Karl Lashley's 1950 paper in connection with the engram,[1] the physical change or neuronal trace in the brain both ingrained, originally, and later triggered by sensory signals – visual, auditory, gustatory, olfactory and tactile. It has been commonplace to cite Proust's madeleine episode as a classic literary illustration of the process whereby such a trigger of the senses evokes a memory. Proust called such memory events 'réminiscences',[2] dispersed throughout his mighty 8-volume continuous novel, *A la Recherche du temps perdu*, composed over the period of 1908–22. Following the initial madeleine episode in volume 1 of *Du Côté de chez Swann* there is a cluster of such memory events in the last volume of the work, *Le Temps retrouvé*. These engrams specifically involve the senses: the initial madeleine one (gustatory), the musty smell in a public lavatory on the Champs-Elysées (olfactory), the uneven cobblestones in the courtyard of the Guermantes townhouse (tactile), the noise of a spoon against a plate in the Guermantes library (auditory), the feel of a starched napkin wiped against the mouth. For Proust, the senses of smell ('l'odeur') and taste ('la saveur') are the most stimulating, for they bear unremittingly 'l'édifice immense du souvenir'; ['the vast structure of memory'].[3] The sense that is least involved is the visual one.

The validity of Proust's engrams has had different interpretations, both by scientists and literary critics. Let us remember that it was the post-Cartesian French philosopher Nicolas de Malebranche who in 1674 had spoken of changes occurring in the fibers of the brain[4] and the German biologist Richard Semon who in 1904 had first actually introduced the term 'mneme' to designate a permanent material change created by a stimulus.[5] Interestingly, Pierre Janet, who had edited Malebranche's writings, had referred to his notion of sensory traces, dismissing it as an inferior form of memory retention because they belonged to the body: 'ils laissent des traces dans le corps';[6] ['they leave traces in the body']. Proust obviously thought the contrary, incorporating the engram into the notion of involuntary memory in his fiction, yet giving it a metaphysical dimension. The playwright Samuel Beckett, in his short but important book on Proust, saw the memory episodes as mystic experiences in Proust's work and dutifully went on to list 11 examples of them.[7] With another point of view, the semiotician Gilles Deleuze interprets Proustian reminiscences as being merely 'sensuous signs' and analogues of metaphor which are part of an artistic world of virtual reality.[8]

On the other hand, current-day neuroscientists such as Alain Berthoz and Larry Squire[9] substantiate the veridicality of the Proustian madeleine case, as they single it out and interpret it scientifically. I would point out that although the well-known madeleine incident is dramatic and demonstrative, it is illuminating to go beyond this single, often cited reference. In particular, there is additional information to be gained from an examination of two more telling memory events: the recollection of the grandmother's death in the sixth volume of the *Recherche* and the *François le Champi* episode of the last volume. These two sections elaborate upon the specific requirements for the successful workings of the Proustian reminiscence.

Given the overwhelming presence of the memory phenomena in Proust's work, it is intriguing to first consider some reasons for Proust's absorption with the memory process. There were two great impetuses behind the conception of his work: a challenge from his father and a suggestion from a particular statement in the work of Bergson. Proust was nurtured in the medical environment of his father, Adrien Proust, a doctor of hygiene, professor at the *Faculté de Médecine* in Paris and Inspecteur Général des Services Sanitaires. Adrien Proust was also the author of the 1897 treatise *L'Hygiène du neurasthénique*. Marcel avidly read with personal interest the medical texts in his father's library, especially those concerned with nervous disorders and even hysteria, much in vogue at the turn of the century. These include notably Edward Brissand's *L'Hygiène des asthmatiques* (1896) and Paul-Auguste Sollier's *L'Hystérie et son traitement* (1901) and, most interestingly, *Les Troubles de la mémoire* (1892). Both doctors had tried to cure Proust of his own nervous maladies, which nonetheless led him to a sanitorium in December 1906.[10] But it should be emphasized that neuraesthenia, an acute form of mental exhaustion, was a much-discussed ailment at the time, made popular in literary circles by Huysmans' scintillating novel *A Rebours*.

In writing his own treatise, Adrien Proust might well have been publicly describing the weaknesses of his own son and in the process challenging him. Adrien Proust declared that memory was necessarily diminished among neurasthenics because of their pathological deficit in attention:

> La mémoire est également amoindrie chez ces malades. L'évocation des souvenirs est défectueuse parce qu'ils sont impuissants à soutenir l'effort d'attention nécessité par la recherche du souvenir perdu.[11]
>
> [Memory is also diminished among these sick persons. The evocation of recollections is defective because they [the sick] lack the power to maintain the effort of attention necessary for the recovery of a lost recollection.]

Could Marcel Proust have taken this exact phrase 'la recherche du souvenir perdu' and sought to refute what he considered to be the arbitrary conclusion of his renowned father? Adrien Proust went on to note that neurasthenics live in a perpetual state of distraction and therefore perceive life events with vagueness and incertitude. Hence, the conclusion that their forgetfulness is frequent: 'leurs oublis sont donc fréquents'.[12] Even the experimental psychologist at the Sorbonne, Théodule Ribot, who had written about the 'maladies de la mémoire' had pointed out the simple fact that fatigue was fatal to memory.[13] It would seem that Proust was out to disprove such theories by dedicating his entire artistic work to the vagaries of memory in both himself and his characters. It is ironic that Proust's father never lived to see his son's opus which goes so far as to state: 'la réalité ne se forme que dans la mémoire'[14] ['reality only shapes itself in memory'].

Regarding Bergson, it is well known that Proust, like others of his time, read the philosopher closely. The critical literature on Bergson's influence on Proust is vast and contestatory. It is the type of subject common to Ph.D. dissertations. The critic Joyce N. Megay, for example, comes to the conclusion that only in his 'aesthetic memory' does Proust come close to Bergson.[15] Despite such cases of fine tuning, however, there are substantial Bergsonian influences even if Proust redirected them to an aesthetic context. After all, influence can be a question of adaptation as well as imitation.

In addition to the many overt links between Proust and Bergson,[16] there is the significant fact that Proust annotated and reacted to *Matière et mémoire* in his notebook of 1908 at the time of writing *Contre Sainte-Beuve*, which contained an early version of sections of *Du Côté de chez*

Swann. It is also worth recalling that Bergson's treatise of 1896 had distinguished between the two types of memory ('mémoire pure' and 'mémoire-habitude'). Analogously, in *Contre Sainte-Beuve* Proust went on to distinguish between two forms of self connected to those two forms of memory, respectively, 'le moi profond' and an everyday self manifested in daily habits.[17]

Proust seems to have constructed his own view of the memory process from adaptions of Bergson's work. Specifically, a certain statement, already quoted, from Bergson's *L'Ame et le corps* (1913) could well have provoked Proust's own exploration of memory in its recovery stage rather than in one of conservation:

> ...une émotion, par exemple, ramène tout à coup le souvenir qui paraissait à jamais perdu.[18]
> [...an emotion, for example, brings back suddenly a memory which appeared lost forever.]

It must be recognized that Proust actually substituted the specificity of sensation for the vagueness of emotion as a trigger for memory. In a laborious way for his readers, Proust was out to extrapolate from certain distinctions that Bergson had made in *Matière et mémoire*. He might have come across Bergson's rudimentary statement regarding the emergence of pure memory from certain sleeping states: 'Des souvenirs qu'on croyait abolis reparaissent alors avec une exactitude frappante; nous revivons dans tous leurs détails des scènes d'enfances entièrement oubliées';[19] ['Memories, which we believed were abolished, reappear with a striking exactitude; we relive, in all their detail, the scenes of childhood which were entirely forgotten.'] Proust seems also to have been intrigued by the mysterious, metaphysical and diaphanous nature of 'spontaneous' memory as described in an early hypothesis of Bergson; the philosopher had stated that recollections become conscious by 'un véritable miracle, et nous ramèneraient au passé par un processus mystérieux';[20] ['a true miracle, and which would lead us back to the past by a mysterious process'].

It is readily apparent that according to Bergson's terminology, Proust was drawn to 'pure' memory as opposed to the memory of habit. What is more significant, however, is that Proust, unlike Bergson, sought out the specific access routes to the retrieval of such long-term memories. He fixated on the fortuitous side of such recollection recovered through sensations. In his literary work, Proust proceeded to firmly ground spontaneous memory in the material world through a concentration on the trigger mechanism which evokes it. He also considered the stratification of various sorts of memory in a kind of layering process. Despite this different emphasis, the interconnections between the philosopher and the writer become all the more pronounced when we realize that both men used the musical metaphor to illustrate the notion of duration which accompanies the memory experience well after any trigger that might have incited it. This time it was Proust who introduced the trope with the musical phrase from the Vinteuil Sonata triggering memories in Swann's mind in *Du Côté de chez Swann*. In his later work *Durée et simultanéité* of 1922, Bergson was actually to refer to a musical metaphor to capture the notion of pure memory. For the philosopher, the musical phrase was a moment of 'durée reélle', duration captured in clock time. Proust's last volume, *Le Temps retrouvé*, seems to capture the notion of Bergsonian elementary memory in stating that reminiscences produce time in its pure state, 'un peu de temps à l'état pur', with man freed from the order of chronological time, 'l'homme affranchi de l'ordre du temps'.[21]

In the opus of *A la Recherche du temps perdu* as a whole, it is even more fascinating that involuntary memory can actually become in some cases the trigger mechanism for voluntary memory. The introductory section to *Du Côté de chez Swann* presents a middle-aged narrator trying to sort out three types of memory that pertain to the recollections of Combray, the village where he spent the holidays of his childhood at his paternal aunt Léonie's home. In an autobiographical reading of this section, these memories would correspond to Proust's own experiences from the age of seven to thirteen during his visits to his aunt Elisabeth Amiot's home in Illiers. In the text, the memories can be classified as voluntary, involuntary and hearsay. The narrator envisages three kinds of memory as coalescing in a kind of stratification of certain rock formations. Proust's geological image gives a layered approach to the concept of memory:

> All these memories, superimposed upon one another, now formed a single mass, but had not so far coalesced that I could not discern between them ... if not real fissures, real geological faults, at least that veining, that variegation of coloring, which in certain rocks, in certain blocks of marble, points to differences of origin, age and formation.[22]

The narrator speaks of deposits on his 'mental soil' ('sol mental'). He asserts that he can sort out those that are the oldest and most 'instinctive', those that are inspired more recently by a taste or 'perfume', and those which are appropriated from another person's recall.

Is this Proust's response to Bergson's two sorts of memory? First, Proust presents the memory of sleepless nights in Paris in states of half-sleep which take the narrator back to scenes of Combray. The narrator admits that one such recollection is selective, in that it unearths a particular portion of the past 'as though all Combray had consisted of but two floors joined by a slender staircase, and as though there had been no time there but seven o'clock at night'.[23] Nonetheless, this initial act of memory is triggered by a physical event connected to the body. Proust opens his work elaborating on Bergson's notion of the quasi-instantaneous bodily memory because a particular way of sleeping prepares his body physically for the whirling gusts of recall, 'ces évocations tournoyantes et confuses',[24] that ensue. In *Du Côté de chez Swann*, Proust is tentative about classifying this sort of memory, but at the end of the work in *Le Temps retrouvé* he writes 'But it seems to me that there exists too an involuntary memory of the limbs, a pale and sterile imitation of the other . . . Our legs and our arms are full of torpid memories.'[25] For the narrator, it is first the body which recalls: 'Its memory, the composite memory of its ribs, its knees, its shoulder-blades, offered it a whole series of rooms in which it had at one time or another slept.'[26] This first kind of memory has effects of involuntarism, since his memory is 'set off' by the physical trigger of the body and gives suggestions of being in a semi-dream state.

A scene of episodic autobiographical memory from the narrator's childhood is evoked. It is the particular traumatic incident of one night in his bedroom at Combray when he was deprived of his mother's habitual 'goodnight' kiss because of the presence of Monsieur Swann. This episode, labeled 'the drama of the kiss', has been classified by most readers as a Freudian 'screen memory' with deep repressed psychological implications. It was what Proust was referring to as being among the most instinctive, the oldest 'entre les plus anciens'.[27] Monsieur Swann, the stockbroker neighbor and friend of the family, had come for an evening visit. But because this visit prevented the narrator's mother from going upstairs to kiss him, Monsieur Swann was regarded in a hostile manner as an intruder by the young boy. Hours of unforgettable anguish ensued, as the young boy awaited the arrival of his beloved mother. This emotionally laden event obviously had left its mark because of its traumatic nature and is appropriately linked to semiconscious states of sleeping.

By the end of the opening section of *Du Côté de chez Swann*, the narrator denigrates acts of voluntary memory or memory of the intellect ('la mémoire de l'intelligence'), which could naturally follow for the narrator. Proust had already stated in his Preface to *Contre Sainte-Beuve*: 'Ce que l'intelligence nous rend sous le nom du passé n'est pas lui'; ['What the intellect returns to us under the name of the past is not it (the past)'].[28] In the opening section of the *Recherche*, the narrator comments that voluntary memory would produce for him only residues or remains of memories against a shadowy background:

> ... et comme les renseignements qu'elle donne sur le passé con-servent rien de lui, je n'aurais jamais eu envie de songer à ce reste de Combray.[29]
>
> [... and as the information which it gives about the past conserves nothing of the past itself, I would never want to reflect on the rest of Combray.]

In contrast, what follows is for him the much more significant invol-untary memory of the madeleine episode which returns the middle-aged narrator to a moment in the more recent past. Back in the presence of his mother in Paris as an adult he drank an infusion of tea with a madeleine and was reminded instantaneously and viscerally of a child-hood scene in the company of his aunt Léonie in Combray, where he had first tasted the madeleine dipped in tea. In other words, he volun-tarily remembered a moment of involuntary memory resurrecting a more distant past. It is a chain process which gives him back the unadulterated sensation of childhood with broad and inclusive vistas of the past:

> So in that moment all the flowers in our garden and in M. Swann's park, and the water-lilies on the Vivonne and the good folk of the village and their little dwellings and the parish church and whole of Combray and its surroundings, taking shape and solidity, sprang into being, town and gardens alike, from my cup of tea.[30]

The narrator is very intent here on describing the incremental process by which the original act of involuntary memory slowly moves, rises, becomes disanchored from the depths of the mind to its surface. He is even able to repeat the process, once experienced, by removing all extraneous material from his mind and concentrating on this one event. Dramatically, he hears the rumblings of distances traversed in time. The effect is a strong sensation of a sudden flash of recollection appearing to him: 'Et tout d'un coup le souvenir m'est apparu.'[31] It is with this impetus of the involuntary madeleine incident, inspired in more recent times, that the narrator proceeds to conjure up distant scenes of his childhood at Combray. What follows are great efforts of voluntary memory and 'hearsay', second-hand memory of stories told to him of Monsieur Swann. Clearly, Proust shows the need of intermittent triggers to provoke long bouts of voluntary memory. These triggers involve the physicality of the body and its sensory mechanism. Thereupon, the tedious voluntary process of declarative memory can follow. In his long novel Proust seems to be enacting the two processes. The neuroscientist Jean Delacour has raised an important distinction in the consideration of Proust's reminiscences. Rightly so, he claims that the Proustian 'réminiscences' are actually part of a conscious memory process.[32] The involuntary part is *not* to be equated with unconscious memory, as many literary critics have done. In the Proustian context, it is rather an involuntary stage of a conscious, explicit retrieval process which unfolds.

To the point of being redundant, Proust gave priority to what he repeatedly designated as involuntary memory. This preference is confirmed by the painstaking amendations that Proust made on his manuscript with respect to passages on involuntary memory which he wanted to feature for the publisher. In the earliest version of the *Recherche* or the first volume originally called 'Les Intermittences du coeur', submitted to Gallimard in 1912, Proust specifically entitled the submission as 'Le Souvenir involuntaire. Chambres.'[33] The arrangement of memory events in this early typed version enables us to distinguish between more standard instances of autobiographical episodic memory, which includes the 'drama of the kiss' or what Freud would call screen memory, and a type of autobiographical memory which is more instantaneous, involving a greater form of involuntarism, emerging from the sensory apparatus of the taste of the madeleine. The latter is more vivid, since it brings with it sensations of the past in exact detail of time and place and seems to correspond to Bergson's description of pure, spontaneous memory.

Moreover, when Proust presented the typed montage of fragments to the publisher Gallimard in 1912, he included an extensive marginal handwritten addition, which sheds further light on the distinctions of memory that he was demonstrating. He demeans the process of voluntary memory, which he argues cannot revive the past authentically because it colors it with the present and dilutes the real past. What a different approach from the stream-of-consciousness writers, who follow in the tradition of William James, as shall be seen! Proust adds that the past of Combray would be dead for him had it not been for the element of chance which revived the past in its past taste, unadulterated. What emerges is a 'formula' for involuntary memory, which includes the element of sensation and the material object. The famous Proust passage is therefore circumscribed for the publisher, set up front in the draft version:

> And so it is with our past. It is a labour in vain to attempt to recapture it: all the efforts of our intellect must prove futile. The past is hidden somewhere outside the realm, beyond the reach of the intellect, in some material object (in the sensation which that material object will give us) of which we have no inkling. And it depends on chance whether or not we come upon this object before we ourselves must die.[34]

Accordingly chance triggering is exemplified in the tasting of the madeleine and the fact that his whole childhood springs up from the cup of tea. In the text, Proust, in willfully trying to elicit the experience, points out that simply the view of the madeleine would not have produced the involuntary episode because since the earlier time he had seen madeleines in pâtisserie windows which since would have acquired new associations distinct from the original event:

> The sight of the little madeleine had recalled nothing to my mind before I tasted it; perhaps because I had so often seen such things in the meantime, without tasting them, on the trays in pastrycooks' windows, that their image had dissociated itself from those Combray days to take its place among others more recent.[35]

However, the particular combination of taste and sight is what elicited the pure memory. In other words, the primitive sense of taste is more of a trigger than the visual stimulus, which produces a case of voluntary memory, but which cannot revive the immediacy or sensation of the past.

More than this carefully delineated madeleine episode, however, I consider the lesser known *François le Champi* episode as the key to Proust's concept of memory. A draft section of it, which was crossed out in the manuscript version submitted to Gallimard in 1912, was transferred to the last volume of the novel, *Le Temps retrouvé*. There the narrator alludes to the ritual of his mother reading aloud George Sand's book to him as a child in the bedroom of Combray. In the first volume of the novel, he had described his discovery of the book through its reddish color, the magical sound of its title, and the sweetness of his mother's voice reading it. He states: 'Je sentais comme une intonation, une accentuation étrange';[36] ['I sensed a strange, individual intonation']. In the last volume in the famous scene of the library of the Prince of Guermantes, when the then adult narrator happens by chance to take a copy of the *François le Champi* book off the shelf, he is suddenly haunted by a spontaneous chain of old childhood memories: 'C'était une impression bien ancienne, où mes souvenirs d'enfance et de famille étaient tendrement mêlés';[37] ['It was a very old impression in which my childhood memories were tenderly mixed in']. As he contemplates this occurrence, he also realizes that simply owning in his own library the original copy of the book that his mother had read to him would not produce the same revival of memory. He knows that his familiarity with the book would render him incapable of voluntarily bringing back the child of the past. His initial relation to the book had been a subjective experience of the senses. The following passage describes what could be a remarkable failure of voluntary memory to bring back the past:

Et si j'avais encore le *François le Champi* que maman sortit un soir du paquet de livres ... je ne le regarderais jamais; j'aurais trop peur d'y insérer peu à peu mes impressions d'aujourd'hui jusqu'à en recouvrir complètement celles d'autrefois, j'aurais trop peur de le voir devenir à ce point une chose du présent que, quand je lui demanderais de susciter une fois encore l'enfant qui déchiffra son titre dans la petite chambre de Combray, l'enfant, ne reconnaissant pas son accent, ne répondît plus à son appel et restât pour toujours enterré dans l'oubli.[38]

[And If I still had the *François le Champi* which Mamma unpacked one evening from the parcel of books ... I would never look at it; I should be too afraid that I might fill it little by little with my impressions of today, covering up completely those of the past and seeing it become at this point a thing of the present, so that when I asked it to elicit once again the child who unraveled its title in the little bedroom at Combray, the child, not recognizing its locution, would no longer reply to its call and would stay forever buried in oblivion.][39]

The 'call' ('l'appel') and the locution ('l'accent') which had marked the intimate relation between the child and the book could not be retrieved

voluntary fashion. As Proust wove this example in the first and
...me of his work, he was claiming that the conditions which
existed at the moment of encoding the memory and the state of sensibility which encoded the memory could not exist at the moment of
willful recall. In Bergsonian terms, the spontaneous or pure memory,
the memory of reading the book, 'le souvenir de la lecture' was not
retrievable voluntarily. No real memory of the first experience of the
George Sand book could be recaptured by the intellect:

> A thing which we saw, a book which we read at a certain period does
> not merely remain for ever conjoined to what existed then around
> us; it remains also faithfully united to what we ourselves then were
> and thereafter it can be handled only by the sensibility, the personality
> that were then ours.[40]

The narrator cannot voluntarily resuscitate the childhood associated
with the book because the real significance of the book lies in the sensory relations that the child had experienced in his first contact with the
book. In this context, the book itself becomes Proust's ultimate symbol
for voluntary memory which he considers to be deficient.

Earlier, in the prefatory section of *Contre Sainte-Beuve*, Proust made it
clear that the intellect or brain, so to speak, has nothing to do with such
'resurrections' of the past, which is the material for his art. For Proust,
true memories are conserved in the framework of sensations; if those
sensations are felt again, the memories attached to them are retrieved.
The narrator exalted this form of spontaneous memory:

> Ce que l'intelligence nous rend sous le nom du passé n'est pas
> lui ... chaque heure de notre vie, aussitôt morte, s'incarne et se cache
> en quelque objet matériel.[41]
> [What the intellect gives us back under the name of the past is not
> it ... Each hour of our life, once dead, embodies and hides itself in
> some material object.]

He adds that since we know material objects through sensations, they
serve as the gateway to real memory. This material factor is involved in
both the encoding and the retrieval of memory.

Proust introduced the word 'intermittences' to designate a particular
type of memory that surges sporadically and captivates him. He initially
used the word in the title of the first volume of the *Recherche* as 'Les
Intermittences du coeur', submitted to the publishers in 1912 and 1913.

Later this title was transferred to an entirely different section in *Sodom and Gomorrah* and used to designate simply a memory episode which could be called 'le souvenir de la grand-mère'. Like the *François le Champi* episode, this particular memory event has been untapped by the critics. With its delicate subtleties and large ramifications, the 'memory of the grandmother' climactically focuses on Proust's distinction between the memory of emotion and that of sensation.

At this point, the narrator revisits the seaside resort of Balbec in Normandy for the second time, even staying in the same room of the elegant Grand Hotel. Through what he specifically labels 'un souvenir involontaire',[42] he has a complete memory of his grandmother who had died a year before. Although the narrator admits that his chagrin at the death of his grandmother had diminished in the interim, it returns to haunt him by way of his spontaneous recollection. The physical action of bending down to take off his boots and touching a button reminds him of a moment in his youth when upon his arrival at Balbec on the Normandy coast, his beloved grandmother had undressed him and stooped down to unfasten his boots. The narrator thereupon describes this arousal of recollection which in typical Proustian manner occurs through contact with an object in the material world:

> I bent down slowly and cautiously to take off my boots...But scarcely had I touched the topmost button than my chest swelled, filled with an unknown, a divine presence.[43]

What was apparently forgotten had suddenly reappeared because for Proust such memories are never lost, they are merely set back in a latent state and preempted by others of a different order. For Proust, such memory events exist in separated compartments of consciousness in storage:

> ...dans un domaine inconnu ... refoulées par des souvenirs d'ordre différent et qui excluent toute simultanéité avec elles dans la conscience.[44]
> [... in an unknown region ... forced back by recollections of a different kind which excludes any simultaneity with them in consciousness.]

Instantly, however, the narrator, prompted by the sensation of the boot, perceives the face of the grandmother as real and immediate rather than the virtual image he had fabricated of her in the passage of time since her death:

> I had just perceived, in my memory, stooping over my fatigue, the tender, preoccupied, disappointed face of my grandmother.[45]

The narrator belabors this memory event, as he gives a poetic designation of the whereabouts of such 'real' memories. Here the vocabulary is especially revealing. Such true memories are 'dug' in him ('creusée en moi') like a mysterious 'furrow' ('comme un double et mystérieux sillon').[46] Such true memories form deep and permanent grooves. Once again, however, very pointedly, sensations have been the gateway to sudden retrieval, as is the case of the memory of the grandmother:

> Mais si le cadre de sensations où elles sont conservées est ressaisi, elles ont à leur tour ce même pouvoir d'expulser tout ce qui leur est incompatible d'installer, seul en nous, le moi qui les vécut.[47]
> [But if the framework of the sensations where they are preserved is recaptured, they have in turn the same power to expel all that is incompatible with them, and to install within us, the self that experienced them.]

Modern-day scientists would call this cue retrieval by way of the senses. Proust observes that such true memories have the power to expel all interfering memories of another kind. But having arrived at what he calls 'la réalité vivante', or living reality of the memory of his grandmother, his mind passes through other phases brought on by emotion which actually diminishes the acuity of the spontaneous memory. Hence, the narrator writes that 'aux troubles de la mémoire sont liées les intermittences du coeur';[48] ['with the disorder of memory are linked the intermittences of the heart']. Throughout this episode, Proust seemed to have been probing the kind of memory that is connected most specifically to grief.

In this situation, Proust is setting up a distinction of what he regards as lesser, more general, virtual memory. It is most interesting that for Proust, emotional memory can fit into this category. As the intensity of the flash of involuntary memory fades, the lesser memory of emotion and feeling takes over. The narrator suddenly recalls a feeling of remorse which habitually brought back the memory of his grandmother. He recalls that in his previous visit to Balbec he had unfortunately acknowledged Saint-Loup's photograph of his grandmother, which presented her in a coquettish manner. He remembers how badly he felt afterwards to have seen her in this light and to have mocked her in this way. Since his grandmother's death, such regret on his part had been associated with remembering her. But he had wished that he had stronger links with this memory than could be forged by such feelings of guilt:

> Je sentais que je ne me la rappelais vraiment que par la douleur, et j'aurais voulu que s'enfonçassent plus solidement encore en moi ces clous qui y rivaient ma mémoire.[49]
> [I felt that I only remembered her by pain, and I would have wanted those nails to be riveted more solidly to me.]

The 'nailing' of memory to the deeper self through sensation proves stronger than any retention of memory through emotions such as remorse.

In fact, for Proust, it is especially striking to note that memory weakens once it is associated with emotion, which creates only partial and general recall. The common scene at Balbec was of no use to its revival. Hence, Proust subsequently describes the fading of the sharp and concentrated memory into oblivion. Memory undergoes the inevitable process of arousal and effacement, analogous also to the phases of Proustian love which buds and dies, as in the case of Swann's love for Odette de Crécy in *Du Côté de chez Swann*. Proust then gives a provocative description of the power of forgetting ('l'oubli') in sleep. He poetically invokes the image of the river Lethe flowing along his veins in the arteries of the subterranean city of his interior: 'I sought in vain for my grandmother's form . . . ; yet I knew that she did exist still, if with a diminished vitality, as pale as that of memory; the darkness was increasing'.[50] With the classical reference of Lethe and the solemn figures of Hades, this passage is evocative of Homer's presentation of the unconscious world of the dead in *The Odyssey*, in which memory had been obliterated. So, too, in a dreamlike state, the narrator's memory dissolves into a faded view of the grandmother – unlike the precision of the involuntary awakened memory.

This protracted and intricate memory episode involving the grandmother is followed in *Le Temps retrouvé* by four succinct instances of involuntary memory, which produce, in contrast, states of delight connected to aesthetic pleasure. These reminiscences (rather than intermittences) have been identified as the uneven cobblestones, the noise of the spoon against the plate, the feel of the stiff napkin and the noise of the water in the pipes. It is in the last volume of his work where Proust seems to multiply the memory events in a short span of time, making analogies between them. These involve the tactile and auditory senses. Each is obviously a detail standing out in time. All are insignificant mundane material objects: a spoon, a napkin, a cobblestone, even a pipe. In contrast, a book in a library, which could become a piece of intellectual material, might not be the best springboard for memory.

In this last volume the narrator succeeds in being invited to a high society matinée reception at the Princesse de Guermantes' after being isolated during the war years in a sanatorium. All four memory events provoked unexpectedly by sensations recuperate old autobiographic episodes from the narrator's past in the period of his teens and youth – in Balbec and Venice. For the most part, the recollected events do not have the high and sustained emotional content of writers such as Rousseau and Woolf. Instead, they elicit a passing feeling of delight, comparable to an aesthetic pleasure, as a past sensation is replicated in the present, invading the Guermantes library in sudden caressing gusts of recall. Since they rely heavily on a moment of provocation, they relate entirely to the exterior material world and the specificity of the sensory stimuli. Their ostensibly random, unexpected nature creates an element of surprise which constitutes this *arousal*-form of memory. Perhaps this is the reason that Proust speaks of such memory events as being 'resurrections of the past' ('résurrections du passé')[51]; he metaphorically views such recollections as wrestling with the present to gain priority: 'Always, when these resurrections took place, the distant scene engendered around the common sensation had for a moment grappled, like a wrestler, with the present scene.'[52]

The narrator specifically chronicles these four 'réminiscences', which can be read like data from human subjects. First, there is the tripping incident on two uneven cobblestones in the courtyard of the Guermantes' townhouse. The narrator writes: 'Je posai mon pied sur un pavé qui était un peu moins élevé que le précédent';[53] ['I put my foot on a stone which was slightly lower than the preceding one']. This instantly reminds him of the sensation of happiness ('félicité') of the madeleine episode: 'The happiness which I had just felt was unquestionably the same as that which I had felt when I tasted the madeleine soaked in tea.'[54] As the narrator repeats the movement of his foot, another recollection surges forth, this time of Venice when the narrator stood on two uneven stones in the baptistery of St Mark's Church. In this manner, the recollection of Venice and Combray are joined through the comparable sensations of pleasure that they give.

Next, waiting to be introduced in the library salon, the narrator hears the delightful sound of a spoon against a glass. Proust writes: 'Un domestique en effet venait...de cogner une cuiller contre une assiette';[55] ['A servant in fact...had just knocked a spoon against a plate']. This reminds him of a sound of a hammer on a train wheel that he had heard in Combray.

Then, the stiffness of the napkin that the Proustian narrator wipes against his mouth when given a glass of orangeade by a maître d'hôtel: 'Je m'essuyai la bouche avec la serviette qu'il m'avait donnée.'[56]

> I thought that the servant had just opened the window onto the beach...for the napkin which I had used to wipe my mouth had precisely the same degree of stiffness and starchiness as the towel with which I had found it so awkward to dry my face as I stood in front of the window on the first day of my arrival at Balbec.[57]

This sensation against his mouth, similar to one he felt with a stiff towel at Balbec, restores the memory of the particulars of a past scene on the Normandy coast. It actually revives what could have taken place in Proust's own life at the Grand Hotel of Cabourg with the phenomenological detail of autobiographical memory such as the view of the sea, the smell of the hotel room, the speed of the wind, the desire for lunch.[58]

The fourth reminiscence is that of hearing the harsh noise of water running through a pipe, 'le bruit strident d'une conduite d'eau',[59] which takes him back to the sound of the steamers on the Normandy coast, again to Balbec and the Grand Hotel's elegant marine dining room overlooking the sea, and the painful recollection of his dead lover Albertine who would frolic on the beach before him:

> And now again, at the very moment when I was making these reflections, the shrill noise of water running through a pipe, a noise exactly like those long-drawn-out whistles which sometimes on summer evenings one heard the pleasure-steamers emit as they approached Balbec from the sea.[60]

But the narrator makes an important qualification to the memory that he evokes. He insists that this is *not* a case of nostalgia for that past: 'the painful recollection of having loved Albertine was, however, absent from my present sensation'. Instead, in this reminiscence, as in the previous ones, 'the sensation common to past and present had sought to re-create the former scene around itself'. He insists that the sensations are not echoes of the past but the authentic ones of the past. Such memory experiences are a total immersion into the past, bringing back the entire associative context with it so that momentarily they give the impression of a blackout from the present.

Given such forthright handling of memory in Proust's opus, the question always remains as to how authentic all these experiences really were, for the narrator, or for the author behind the narrator. Why does Proust concentrate on so many in his last volume? Clearly, the artistic patterning of such episodes into the rhythmic structure of the Proustian novel makes Proust vulnerable to questions about their veridicality, although the events described seem valid as a type of involuntary memory that is easily verifiable in human subjects.

Proust was attempting to unite various strands in his view of the memory process. After all, Proust's formation was affected by a certain spiritual philosophy that marked the Sorbonne of his time. The professor Paul Janet, the uncle of Pierre Janet, and Marie-Alphonse Darlu, Proust's teacher at the Lyceé Condorcet, had both offered a metaphysical reaction to Positivistic trends, claiming the existence of a spiritual realm. It is also true that along with the constant recourse to the involuntary trigger mechanism of engrams, a large part of the memory process in Proust's work is voluntary and autobiographical, and as such, some memory events figure in the category of conscious and not unconscious recall. On the other hand, in resurrecting large blocks of time through the involuntary process, the Bergsonian 'durée' is simulated.

It is the specificity of Proust's engrams that brings this author's deepest insight into the memory process. The triggers of these engrams are not especially visual. Nor are the engrams marked by an emotional or affective aspect as in the case of Rousseau where emotion itself instills memory. However involuntary Proust's memory is, it is not necessarily unconscious. In comparison with the sensual stimuli of Baudelaire and its earthy contours, the sensory mechanism of Proust's memory process has vast repercussions beyond the initial trigger. Such engrams are deeply embedded and ingrained over years of retention, yet magically summoned at an instant. Given these qualifications, they are unique and distinguishable from Romantic 'spots of time', from the interrelated cues of stream-of-consciousness flow and from random retrievals of images in the surrealist memory process.

5
Woolf, Joyce and Faulkner: Associative Memory

The stream-of-consciousness technique which unites the modern fiction writers Virginia Woolf, James Joyce and William Faulkner situates their approach to memory within an associationist context. The expression that William James himself had coined in 1890 in *Principles of Psychology* – 'the stream of thought, of consciousness, or of subjective life'[1] – set the path for the literary experimentation with associationist memory in the early twentieth century. James had insisted on the notion of a fluid consciousness: 'Such words as "chain" or "train" do not describe it fitly... It is nothing jointed; it flows.' These novelists intuitively saw that their characters could express the workings of the mind in the flow of words, images and ideas. This succession of thoughts depended for the most part on acts of perception. The reader is drawn into the flow of the key characters' minds wherein memory occupies a dominant place. As all three writers were thoroughly obsessed with memory events in their lives, they transferred such obsessions to their novels. Moreover, their personal memories mingled with cultural ones as they depicted the change they witnessed in their respective societies in the years from 1890–1920: Woolf's late Victorian England, Faulkner's postbellum American South, and Joyce's premodern Ireland. In all three cases, a deep sense of collapsing moral and social orders provokes an obsession with an historical past, which is projected selectively in vivid memory episodes in their fiction.

Key novels of these authors feature principal characters who are immersed in the flow of memory events. Such characters can be examined as subjects. There is Lily Briscoe in Woolf's *To the Lighthouse*, Mrs Dalloway in the novel of that name; there is Joyce's Gabriel Conroy in 'The Dead' and Stephen Dedalus in *A Portrait of the Artist as a Young Man*; and there are the idiot Benjy Compson and his brother, the suicidal Harvard student Quentin, in *The Sound and the Fury* as well as Darl and Addie

Bundren in *As I Lay Dying*. For such characters, memory controls the workings of their minds in a variety of ways that create a continuous interchange with the past. That interchange is especially striking in the juxtaposition of clock time – a day in *Mrs Dalloway* and in each section of *The Sound and the Fury*; ten days in *As I Lay Dying* and ten years in *To the Lighthouse* – with subjective human time in the form of memory which intrudes upon the chronological time and distorts it.

The French existentialist writer Jean-Paul Sartre helps highlight a distinctive use of time among the stream-of-consciousness writers. In his 1947 article on time in the work of Faulkner, Sartre made a pertinent comment in differentiating the American writer's treatment of the past from Proust's: 'For Faulkner, on the contrary, the past is never lost, unfortunately; it is always there, it is an obsession.' Sartre accounts for the difference in the fact that as a Frenchman and 'classicist' – one might add rationalist – Proust inevitably realizes the barriers between the memories and the present. Sartre makes the following generalization: 'The French lose themselves only a little at a time and always manage to find themselves again.'[2] In contrast to Proust, that more permanent immersion in memory that Sartre detects in Faulkner can also be observed in Woolf and Joyce within their stream-of-consciousness approach to the memory process.

For Virginia Woolf as for William James, the past is always present; memory facts are latent and ready to be recovered. Woolf specifically commented that her sense of reality involved 'the present...backed by the past';[3] the intrusion of the past into the present occurs in peaceful moments of consciousness, when the present runs smoothly 'like the sliding surface of a deep river'. This depiction contrasts with the isolated, intermittent views of the past in Proust's work. Woolf analyzed her own memory process, specifying that her recollection of scenes of the past was 'not altogether a literary device'.[4] She vividly explained how the significant moments of the past survive 'undamaged' and enter her present consciousness:

> The sensation that we are sealed vessels afloat on what it is convenient to call reality; and at some moments, the sealing matter cracks; in floods reality; that is, these scenes – for why do they survive undamaged year after year unless they are made of something comparatively permanent?

Woolf's main personal obsession, as she admitted in 'A Sketch of the Past', her autobiographical piece written at the end of her life, had been the death of her mother, Julia Stephen, and the desire to eternalize the memory of what she had cherished the most. For this reason, memory became the shaping force behind her fiction. Her work involved a very conscious act of retrieving her personal past and coming to terms with the bygone Victorian era which was part of it. From the point of view of neurological taxonomy, she demonstrated the process of long-term autobiographical memory, produced voluntarily, and depending foremost on visual perception.

From the vantage point of a memoir written 44 years after her mother's death, Woolf gives evidence of having retained to the end of her own life a very visual recollection of her mother:

> Certainly there she was, in the very centre of that great Cathedral space which was childhood; there she was from the very first. My first memory is of her lap . . . Then I see her in her white dressing gown on the balcony. . . .[5]

Woolf uses the sense of sight to unearth particulars concerning her mother and that past: seeing her hands and her fingers, nails and rings. Woolf also evokes specific scenes relating to this early period of her life, stating: 'But, whatever the reason may be, I find that scene-making is my natural way of marking the past.'[6] Throughout this piece, Woolf is trying to analyze her own resources of memory, which are essential not only to her life but also to her art. She describes the type of memory she is endowed with. She considers her propensity to remember through the preservation of visual scenes as her particular endowment – what she then transfers to her fiction:

> Obviously I have developed the faculty because in all the writing I have done, I have almost always had to make a scene, either when I am writing about a person; I must find a representative scene in their lives. . . .[7]

Such had already been the case with respect to the recall of her mother and the transposition of that enduring memory into the creation of the Mrs Ramsay figure in *To the Lighthouse*.

Woolf explicitly discussed this transposition of memory in her commentary about the novel. In her mind and in the novel she re-presented the context and the places of her early childhood. It is this associationist method that had allowed for her childhood memories to be resurrected. At the early age of 13, Woolf's life had completely changed upon the death of her mother, Julia Stephen; in particular, the summer house at St Ives Cornwall was sold and the customary family summer vacations came to an end. In the hands of her severe and erudite Victorian father, Leslie Stephen, Virginia became isolated, having lost the deep bond she had with the central maternal figure of her life. In 'A Sketch of the Past', Woolf wrote about the genesis of the earlier novel from her cherished memories of her mother:

> It is perfectly true that she obsessed me, in spite of the fact that she died when I was thirteen, until I was forty-four. Then one day walking round Tavistock Square I made up, as I sometimes make up my books, *To the Lighthouse;* in a great, apparently involuntary, rush. One thing burst into another ... I wrote the book very quickly; and when it was written, I ceased to be obsessed by my mother.[8]

Late in her life, Woolf posed her most arresting question, which she seems to have already answered in her fiction: 'I feel that strong emotion must leave its trace; and it is only a question of discovering how we can get ourselves again attached to it'.[9] She had not realized perhaps that she had herself already discovered that emotion leaves its traces in memory. Current neuroscientists such as Antonio Damasio, Joseph Ledoux and Edmund Rolls have been discussing the notion of the emotional brain, suggesting that emotional traces contribute significantly to the genesis of memory. Woolf had answered her own query in part through the visual object of the lighthouse in her major novel of 1927. In real life she obviously tied the 'deep emotion' of the loss of her mother to the image of the Godrevy lighthouse in St Ives, Cornwall, which was the view from their summer house that they enjoyed over the years of her happy childhood. For Woolf, the lighthouse was associated with the central mother figure as a unifying presence for a family threatened by flux and changing values. Woolf makes this association powerfully throughout her novel; she recreates her mother both through the character of Mrs Ramsay (who also dies) and through the Godrevy lighthouse which becomes a fictional lighthouse on an island in the Scottish Hebrides.

To the Lighthouse (1927) is the quintessential memory novel. Notably, in it Woolf presents three aspects of the memory process, as it reflects her own personal experience of memory. This novel, divided into three parts, distinctly traces the encoding, the storage and the retrieval of memory. The encoding is *sealed* by the emotion which ties the central figure of the mother to the different characters, especially to the Lily Briscoe figure. It is this artist, who will retain the memory of the mother figure through the creation of an actual painting depicting her. The act of retrieval, therefore, becomes overtly made through the sense of perception which links the lighthouse to the mother figure in the artist's mind.

Since Woolf herself recognized that sight was so important in her own memory process, it seems understandable why she designates the artist Lily Brisoce as the principal remembering subject in the novel. Both the novelist and her character use a process of 'tunneling' which had been described by Woolf in her journal of 1923, as a way of retrieving the past incrementally by 'installments'. Common to both the writer Woolf and her character the painter Briscoe, there is the retrieval of memory through the means of their respective art. This is made clear by the statement about Briscoe's physical act of painting in the third part of the novel: 'And as she dipped into the blue paint, she dipped too into the past there',[10] and 'She went on tunnelling her way into her picture, into the past.' The memory is materialized in the painting, just as Woolf's memory of her mother is materialized in her novel. It can be called a memory-painting.

In the novel, significantly, the lighthouse itself is the visual focus which provokes the memory by way of conceptual association. For the artist, the lighthouse as an object *and* place incites the memory process. Lily Briscoe had always seen Mrs Ramsay in her summer house against the background of the lighthouse. Lily had begun a painting of Mrs Ramsay and returns to the same setting to complete that unfinished painting ten years after the death of Mrs Ramsay. A little detail highlights the artist's approach. Lily finds herself sitting at the same table and viewing the same tablecloth of ten years before when Mrs Ramsay presided over the 'last dinner'. By staring in particular at the design on the tablecloth, Lily remembers the flow of thoughts which were contributing to her painting in its early stages, when the model, Mrs Ramsay, was still alive. In contrast to an example from Proust, it is not a touch of the napkin which suddenly recalls a past, but the sight of designs on a tablecloth and the thoughts associated with it. Here the power of association is shown to be fully at work in the memory process:

> Suddenly she remembered. When she had sat there last ten years ago, there had been a little sprig or leaf pattern on the tablecloth, which she had looked at in a moment of revelation.[11]

Also, later, when Lily is on the verge of completing the painting at the end of the novel, she remembers, standing in the very place she had stood years before observing the live Mrs Ramsay, the emotions of the past:

> It was some such feeling of completeness perhaps, which, ten years ago, standing almost where she stood now, had made her say that she must be in love with the place.[12]

Here it is the physical place which is the source for the retrieval of memory. Certain emotions become part of the associative context of this concrete place, so that the artist is able to retrieve such original emotions which had inspired the painting. In neuroscientific terms, Woolf seems to have demonstrated the classic memory phenomenon of 'cued retrieval', as indicated by the psychologist Endel Tulving in his notion of the associated networks of retrieval. Tulving has noted the interaction between the encoding of memories and the very conditions of their retrieval:

> Engrams, too, must be specified in terms of both their antecedent conditions – particular events particularly encoded in particular cognitive environments – and their consequent conditions, including the circumstances surrounding their subsequent retrieval.[13]

Demonstrably in the novel, the encoding, which originally introduces the links of association, are the basis for the retrieval in a similar environment. That encoding is produced by striking scenes which the mother figure had unwittingly created for those around her. Woolf calls such lasting impressions 'moments of being', which stop the flow of time in its subjective experience of *kairos*. She gives an image of such encoding in the following metaphor:

> She rammed a little hole in the sand and covered it up, by way of burying in it the perfection of the moment. It was like a drop of silver in which one dipped and illumined the darkness of the past.[14]

Accordingly, the memory was created by Mrs Ramsay in the first place, dug like a hole in the sand; it is associated with a drop of silver that the painter dips her brush into to illuminate the past. The digging and the dipping suggest the encoding and the retrieval respectively.

In contrast to these permanent moments stored as they are in the brain, there is the long span of storage, in the paradoxical guise of forgetting, which is made highly vivid and striking in the central part of the novel called 'Time Passes'. There, Woolf allows ten years to pass, following the death of the Mrs Ramsay figure, in which the Great War takes place and the summer house is abandoned. It seems as if this period is a necessary one for the gestation of a long-term memory that appears ten years later. For when the family returns after the War to the same place, its associations have remained to provoke the memories of the dead mother. Physical objects such as the lighthouse are the anchor for such retrieval, made possible by acts of perception. When the family and the artist had been away from these landmarks, the memory had been put into parentheses. In the meantime, the passage of time itself, had provided for the strengthening rather than the weakening of such memories.

In another revealing novel, *Mrs Dalloway* (1925), Woolf also features the memory process, though less autobiographically. In the course of writing the novel, which she first called *The Hours*, Woolf represented memory in spatial terms. She noted in a diary entry of 1923: 'I dig out beautiful caves behind my characters; ... The idea is that the caves shall connect, and each comes to daylight at the present moment.'[15] Such 'caves' are like pockets of memory that emerge in increments. A few months later, Woolf went on to specify her means of actualizing memory. It is worth noting that she considers this process to be deliberate:

It took me a year's groping to discover what I call my tunnelling process, by which I tell the past by installments, as I have need of it.

The Mrs Dalloway figure is presented on one June day in London in 1923 after the Great War. Woolf has this 52-year-old wife of a Member of Parliament virtually open the windows onto her personal past, as she prepares for an official party at her home in Westminster at the end of the present day. At the start, the noise of the hinges, as the doors are dismantled in preparation for the evening party, and the fresh flavor of the June morning set off by association a visual memory of her youth. Her long-term memory is activated to recall a time in the Cotswold village of Bourton when she was 18 years old:

What a plunge! For so it had always seemed to her, when, with a little squeak of the hinges, which she could hear now, she had burst open the French windows and plunged at Bourton into the open air.[16]

She is so fully transported to the past that she remembers the sensation of the early morning air as she looked out of the window of the country home. The 'irrevocable' sound of Big Ben soon draws her back to the present, as she continues to walk in Westminster on her round of errands, fully absorbed in the noise and traffic of the current day in London. Repeatedly, however, the Cotswolds scene guides her day and underlies her quest of selfhood. She yields to bouts of memory which take her back to that early scene: 'She could remember scene after scene at Bourton.'[17] It is as if her memory is set into motion, as it alternates with the pending present. As if by coincidence, during the June day, Mrs Dalloway experiences a lifetime well of memory events, provoked further by the appearance of a past lover, who, having written her that he would arrive from India in June or July, suddenly appears at her house. Although such a plot could appear contrived, the memory process is plausible. A person associated with the past brings back the past with him. Mrs Dalloway then ruminates on a past which never became present because of the alternate marriage choice she made and her present status as the society lady married to a Member of Parliament. Nonetheless, the sudden and unexpected sight of her former lover, Peter Walsh, provokes real visual associated memories of the countryside place which circumscribed that past. For example, Mrs Dalloway reminisces from the trivial to the significant in a stream-like flow of thoughts. In his presence, she is drawn into the past: 'Now I remember how impossible it was ever to make up my mind – and why did I make up my mind – not to marry him?'[18] Addressing him, 'Do you remember,' she said, 'how the blinds used to flap at Bourton?' She goes on 'Do you remember the lake?'[19]

Woolf further experiments with such memory events in this novel, as she presents simultaneously two different characters having memories. For there is also the shell-shocked war veteran who roams the streets of London and is totally absorbed in an obsessive way with traumatic images of the past in his dreadful experience of the Great War. This other memory subject, Septimus Warren Smith, has visions of his friend Evans, who had died in that war. In this case, such memories are not provoked by any objects in the London streets but seem pathologically ingrained in the young man's mind. The disturbing visions of the past, along with voices, are juxtaposed with sights of the present as Septimus walks through Regent's Park on his way to an appointment with a psychiatrist. He is also, ironically, on his way to his death, as he will frantically plunge out of a window at the office in the ultimate dissolution of the self, which has been shattered by a haunting past.

In the novel, Woolf has gone from a normal process of memory to a pathological one, juxtaposing both subjects on the same London streets.

Could the Septimus figure be a symbol for a type of secondary memory, which lurks beneath the primary memory of Mrs Dalloway? Whereas Septimus is completely engulfed in his memory, Mrs Dalloway is able to discard her memories at the end of the day as she hosts a significant society party at her home in the presence of the Prime Minister. In both cases, memory is aroused into the present consciousness to be reconciled with the present. For the figures Lily Briscoe and Mrs Dalloway, it is completely linked to the perception of place – what can interest scientists like Alain Berthoz, who ties memory to the mechanism of perception in the brain. Moreover, in the modernist context of Woolf's fiction, emotional memories are attached to material objects and places by association; they are dependent upon the exterior world to be revived. This is quite different from the Romantics, for whom memory may be projected upon a locale yet remains independent of it, residing within the subject and aroused by the individual's autonomous sentience.

In the cases of the double characters Mrs Dalloway and Septimus Smith, however, it is not a question of sudden 'intermittences' or flashes of memory that return characters to blocks of time in the past, as in Proust. For Woolf, the memory event involves a full-fledged intrusion of the past into the present, giving a multidimensional quality to the characters. Both figures seem particularly alert, with a heightened attention which allows their consciousness to be permeable to memories. As mentioned, contrary to a Proustian return to the past, where the present seems to be temporarily effaced, the Woolfian memory process integrates the past and present in the search for a definition of selfhood.

Woolf's formidable contemporary Joyce fits into the same associationist context when he overtly fictionalizes his personal memories in *A Portrait of the Artist as a Young Man* and when he focuses on distinct memory episodes in his stories, 'The Dead', 'Eveline', and 'Araby'. In all his works, the Irish environment is especially important in the revival of memories. Notably, that environment harbors a wealth of very tangible memory cues which can be detected. The sense of place was of particular importance to Joyce, who wrote in self-imposed exile from his native land, the memories of which were stored as raw material for his fiction.

In the case of the novel which closely follows his life events to the age of 20 as documented by the biographer Richard Ellmann and by Joyce's devoted brother Stanislaus, Joyce's approach to memory can be carefully scrutinized for its factual authenticity. Joyce started writing *A Portrait of the Artist as a Young Man* in 1904 at the age of 22; the work was first published serially in *The Egoist* from 1914–15. In his fictional autobiography Joyce reproduces his own memories through a third-person narrator who penetrates the thoughts of the young boy growing into the adult writer-figure. As opposed to a standard autobiography which would have taken the vantage point of the writer writing it in later time, this autobiography reverts to the consciousness of the subject originally experiencing the prior events. In effect, a double memory process is going on. The entire fiction is a reworking of remembered events. Within these recalled events of the author, the fictional subject has memory episodes that vivify the retrieval process experienced by the author himself.

Joyce, therefore, presents two facets of memory in this work. In *A Portrait*, unlike Proust's narrator in the *Recherche*, Joyce easily retrieves the boy in the memory event. The little boy is not lost, as in the case of the Proust persona who realizes that it is only through sharp sensory stimuli that he can occasionally recapture the past. In those momentary shifts to the past through distinct engram experiences, the return is temporary and distinctly separated from the present to which the narrator inevitably returns. In contrast, at the very beginning of his auto-biographical novel, Joyce relives his early childhood sensations through the mind of his character. The work starts with the mundane content that makes up a child's first memories, and the book evolves through the consciousness of the growing boy who turns into the young adult-poet rebelling against his Irish society and its past – and writing about it. Joyce was intent on presenting the various ingredients which contributed to the formation of his consciousness as a writer. That consciousness consists of sensory memory events flowing from one scene to another of the first twenty years of the artist's life. The reader experiences the writer's life from the interior, witnessing the encoding and the retrieval of memories simultaneously.

In this work, the environmental memory cues of place and locale are highlighted in the stream-of-consciousness retrieval process of the past. Moreover, the actual naming of such places as Clane, Clongowes and Cork as well as the places themselves create a connotative associative context which revives the memories for the persona Stephen. Specifically, the sense of hearing is the prime sensory trigger for this writer who loved music and was particularly sensitive to the sound of words. In his formal definition of 'retrieval cues', the psychologist Endel Tulving included instances of cues expressed by language which readily apply to Joyce:

> A retrieval cue can be thought of as the especially salient or sig-
> nificant part of retrieval information, those aspects of the individual's

physical and cognitive environment that initiate and influence the process of retrieval ... This definition covers particularly well instances of retrieval where the cue assumes a symbolic form – a word, a phrase, a question, a spoken hint. ... [20]

In a narrative which appears to be outwardly disjointed, with sudden shifts from scene to scene, the connections are in the flow from one retrieval cue to another achieved by the power of association in the consciousness of the subject. As opposed to a generic, general remembrance of the past, Joyce returns to vividly remembered interconnected details that had obviously made the most striking impressions on him in their emotional and sensorial intensity. For example, a sequence can be traced in the first chapter. There is a very specific recreation of images of the playground of the Catholic preparatory school, Clongowes Wood College, which Joyce himself attended from the age of six and a half to nine. That very place, in turn, revives memories of some of Joyce's boisterous, rough schoolmates who ostracized him because of his younger age and weaker physique. Out of this scene come words and expressions used by the boys, which the character Stephen Dedalus remembers his mother having told him specifically not to use. As a potential writer, the young Dedalus had been sensitive to the sound of words and therefore retained them. Later, such forbidden words make him think of his mother and the emotional parting scene, when she left him at the school in the first place. In this instance, the sound of language triggers the next memory. A flow can be charted from the playground to the boys to his mother, and so forth.

As the narration continues, the author's recollection goes from the everyday to two momentous events in the period of his early childhood and confirmed as life facts by Joyce's biographer, Richard Ellmann. These memory events are the political dispute at a certain Christmas dinner in Bray, Joyce's family home, where he had returned for the holidays, and earlier the traumatic unjust punishment he received by the prefect of studies at Clongowes for having lost his glasses. The Christmas dinner scene is a kind of flashbulb memory, encoded when Joyce was a nine-year-old boy and retained because of its association with the striking news about the death of the infamous Irish nationalist, Charles Parnell in 1891. The vociferous sounds of serious disagreement between husband and wife over politics resonate in the mind of the impressionistic young boy.

The act of injured innocence, the unfair punishment that the boy receives at the boarding school, Clongowes Wood College, for losing his glasses, is connected to the remembered sensation, not to feeling, as it would be in Rousseau. Whereas Rousseau remembers an event over time and associates it with political theory or past emotion, Joyce remembers it by association with its sensory immediacy, the actual pain, the exact sensation of being pandied on the hands. This is just one of a series of remembered sensations, ranging from this momentous moral event to lesser, mundane recollections of the sounds of the drips of water or the sights of coarse materials in the bottom of a jar. The senses set the memories in motion for the stream to follow.

For Joyce, even a city such as Dublin is a remembered sensation: 'Dublin was a new and complex sensation',[21] writes the narrator in the second chapter. The very name of his native city is a cue which conjures up his roaming alone the grey, drab streets as a boy of twelve upwards, contemplating sordid details such as the 'thick yellow scum' of the docks and the 'corks that lay bobbing on the surface of the water' seen from the quays at the Dublin port. In the adolescent period which follows, reaching crisis proportions in the trip to Cork with his decadent father who sells off the family properties, the narrator suggests that the childhood memories are temporarily failing: 'The memory of his childhood suddenly grew dim.'[22] This avowed memory lapse can be documented in 1894 in Joyce's own life when he was 12 years of age. Joyce is demonstrating a process whereby certain activities of his adolescence, traumatic in their own right, temporarily dim the earlier childhood ones. At this moment of disheartening, the narrator states that he retains only the names of the past; 'He recalled only names: Dante, Parnell, Clane, Clongowes', which have temporarily lost their power of arousal because of the overpowering financial concerns of the present and the isolated locale of Cork which lack a connection with Stephen's past. Instead, Cork is a hotbed of memori

Jesuit school he attended at Clongowes. By the association of the two similar environments, Stephen unearths and reexperiences the particular
sensations of the past which include smell, hearing and sight:

> The shadow, then, of the life of the college passed gravely over his
> consciousness...The troubling odour of the long corridors of
> Clongowes came back to him and he heard the discreet murmur of
> the burning gasflames....His lungs dilated and sank as if he were
> inhaling a warm moist unsustaining air and he smelt again the warm
> moist air which hung in the bath in Clongowes above the sluggish
> turfcolored water.[23]

In fact, the bath at Clongowes with its 'turf-colored water' becomes
a focal point for a number of memory events. This dreary image is
brought back again in the period of Dedalus's university years described
in a memory episode in the fifth chapter. There, the protagonist contemplates his desolate home life at breakfast one morning before going
off to his university. The dregs of the watery tea that he drinks prompts
a stream of associations that lead him back to the bath at Clongowes,
which has become for him a depressing representation of his past:

> He drained his third cup of watery tea to the dregs and set to chewing
> the crusts of fried bread that were scattered near him, staring into the
> dark pool of the jar. The yellow dripping had been scooped out like
> a boghole and the pool under it brought back to his memory the dark
> turfcolored water of the bath in Clongowes.[24]

For such sudden spurts of memory to appear, however, the author
recollects the whole stream of which they were part. To use the words
of William James, he treads 'the habit-worn paths of association'[25] and
recaptures consciously the past experience in all its 'warmth and
intimacy'. In other words, in the fashion of William James, James Joyce
recreates in his narration the 'neighborhood' or vicinity of the events in
which the negative experiences were originally ingrained. For Joyce the
sudden flashes of memory emerge as common moods joining that
which was apparently dormant, but never hidden nor lost.

The sustaining impact of environment on memory is demonstrated
in Joyce's shorter work 'The Dead', a well-known story of the collection
Dubliners. This story presents the older persona Gabriel Conroy as a
fitting parallel to what Joyce would have become had he remained in
Ireland. Gabriel feels stultified by the regressive atmosphere of his

homeland. In this story Joyce fabricates an impressive memory event in which the protagonist shifts to the past with nostalgia and regret. How does Joyce makes this shift occur? By a power of association which has been building all evening long in the Christmas party of the elderly aunts of Gabriel Conroy who belong to that past world which the present Ireland is rejecting and by the special power of music to trigger those memories of the past.

To recount the story, Gabriel Conroy, a middle-aged newspaper journalist arrives at the annual Christmas party given by his two maiden aunts at their Dublin townhouse on the banks of the river Liffey. From the outer world, which is cold and snowy, he enters the old house filled with convivial warmth and holiday festivity. As he demonstrably scrapes off the snow from his galoshes, it is as if he is warding off that outside world and entering an airtight container of memories. Thereupon, as if he were performing a ritual, he allows himself to be instantly engulfed in the customary chatter of the guests who are the same ones from year to year. The evening follows a pattern of dancing, music, speeches, dinner – repeated annually. Most of the same guests are present, so that the atmosphere is a familiar one which doesn't seem to change much despite major changes in the Irish society at large. As the articulate member of the gathering and the only intellectual, Gabriel is the one called upon to make the annual speech at the dinner table. It is a speech intentionally designed for this old-fashioned audience which resists change. It is full of nostalgia and expresses the sentimental regret that the modern society is discarding some of those past values of 'humanity, hospitality, of kindly humour which belonged to an older day'.[26] Gabriel therewith attempts to revive common memories held by the audience, and the speech is applauded. If past days are gone, he says, 'let us hope, at least, that in gatherings such as this we shall still speak of them with pride and affection, still cherish the memory of those dead and gone'.

Whereas the first part of the story resurrects the memory of the dead collectively through the general atmosphere which elicits a common associative context, the second part deals with a very specific personal revival. A musical motif from a well-known Gaelic folk-song, 'The Lass of Aughrim', heard by Gabriel's wife in the course of the party becomes the retrieval cue for a memory event after the party when she is alone with her husband in a Dublin hotel room. When Gabriel attempts to embrace his wife, she retracts, admitting perversely to him that the song had evoked her long-lost lover, dead many years before: 'I am thinking about a person long ago who used to sing that song.'[27] In one sense, there is an experience of an engram. But it is part of a larger context. The Galway lover had been 'awakened' from the dead, triggered not only by the specific folk song but by the general atmosphere of retrospection and nostalgia produced at the party.

The physical place, the group of people, the conversations, had all prepared the ground and created the susceptibility for the revival of the past. At the end of the story, Gabriel painfully realizes that his own presence is less strong than the memory of the dead boy. Gabriel's own memories of a happier personal past with his wife are conveyed physically as if his arteries are flooded with warmth. But they are overshadowed by the memory of Michael Furey, who was from the Irish nationalistic region of Galway, and, symbolically speaking, might stand for Ireland's past. By way of this strong recollection and through the motif of the snow falling all over Dublin, Gabriel, too, connects to that past, the memories of which are made a part of the present. The isolated memory event seems to bring with it an entire element of the past as his own 'soul had approached that region where dwell the very hosts of the dead'. The story ultimately has autobiographical implications. If Joyce, himself, was deploring such memories, having escaped to the continent of Europe for most of his adult life, he nonetheless realized how easily they might be revived. For Joyce, music was a catalyst for memory. So that even though in his own lifestyle he was trying to dispel the past in becoming the modern 'European' writer, he was admitting indirectly through his subject matter that it was impossible to shed that past, which was so easily retrievable through the least suggestion.

The shorter Joycean stories contain capsules of the memory process. As a rule, the evocation of memory, frequently through the sense of sound, produces a paralyzing effect on the characters. So, too, in the story 'Eveline' the past is awakened by an Irish air which the title character, an abused and oppressed 19-year-old girl, hears played by a street organ down the avenue. She cannot leave Dublin in an escapade with a sailor, because she cannot get rid of the past which is awakened by a song. The melancholy song, which she had heard in the past as her mother was dying, reminds her of the promise to her mother, 'to keep the home together as long as she could'.[28] In the gemlike story 'Araby' the young boy protagonist associates a Dublin bazaar with a query which was uttered by a would-be-girlfriend. His inability to get the girl a present at the fair associates the very name of 'Araby' with the unfortunate memory of this missed experience.

Contemporaneously with Joyce and Woolf, Faulkner further cultivates the associative networks of the memory process as he produces the major American version of 'stream-of-consciousness' fiction of the time. Like Joyce, Faulkner was haunted by his cultural past, a preoccupation which also finds literary expression in distinct memory episodes in the fiction. A stylistic experimentation with memory is a notable component of Faulkner's major works. As a quintessential regional and insular writer, Faulkner situates such fiction in the countryside of his youth – the American South. It is well known that he changes the real locale of Oxford, Mississippi, into Jefferson of the fictional Yoknapatawpha County and links its fictive decaying Compson family to a previous historical era. However, what actually must have had a powerful impact on Faulkner's treatment of the memory process was his only foreign experience in a brief stay in France. His sojourn in Paris in the fall of 1925 was an opportune moment for him to absorb the various theories about time rampant 'in the air'. Notably, there had been an outburst of such theories following in particular the dissemination of Einstein's work since 1920 and the subsequent response of Bergson to Einstein in *Durée et simultanéité* of 1922. When asked about possible influences, Faulkner said 'sometimes I think there must be a sort of pollen of ideas floating in the air, which fertilizes similarly minds here and there which have not had direct contact'.[29] That pollen may have carried different ideas about memory. When asked pointblank about his conception of time, Faulkner stated:

> (There isn't any time...In fact I agree pretty much with Bergson's theory of the fluidity of time). There is only the present moment, in which I include both the past and the future, and that is eternity. In my opinion time can be shaped quite a bit by the artist.[30]

This rather vague statement indicates that as an artist, Faulkner was understandably not altogether clear as to how to categorize his own treatment of time and memory with respect to the theories that were circulating around him. As a result, he experimented with a variety of memory experiences in his work.

It is interesting that after his brief sojourn in France in 1925, Faulkner went back home to write his 'time novels' and related stories in which he visibly experimented with the memory process. Two major novels of this genre had already been conceived: Joyce's *Ulysses* and Woolf's *Mrs. Dalloway*, taking place on single June days. More than even Joyce and Woolf, Faulkner explored multiple dimensions of time *within* the stream of consciousness of his characters who have an associative range of memories. He juxtaposes those characters who can retreat to the past in Bergsonian experiences of 'durée' with those who remain more strongly connected to the present by a 'mathematical' consciousness of time. He also alternates between voluntary and involuntary memory sequences in his work. Faulkner was able to retrieve the consciousness of 'the boy' figure in all the immediacy of the past experience. For example, the boy and the adult are fused in stories like 'Barn Burning' and 'That Evening Sun'. It is also true that often those characters who are most fully engulfed in memory are sensitive or deranged, like Benjy in *The Sound and the Fury* or Darl in *As I Lay Dying*.

In *The Sound and the Fury* (1929), Faulkner instinctively juxtaposes different experiences of the memory process focused upon the tragic history of the young girl Candace (Caddy) Compson, two of whose brothers are particularly significant remembering subjects. The life of the Compson family in Jefferson is recovered in disparate past episodes involving the parents and their children. The common memories of Benjy and of Quentin are juxtaposed respectively in the first two successive sections of the novel. It is as if Faulkner were contrasting Bergsonian and Einsteinian contexts for the memory processes. It is commonly observed that whereas the character Benjy lives entirely in the continuous past, Quentin is not enabled by his memory to escape to that past, and therefore his only way of escaping 'present' time is his suicide on that June day. Whereas Benjy experiences instants of time within a 'durée' that fuses past and present, Quentin retains his vantage point in the present defined by the course of a particular day and the clocks which pursue him. Quentin is denied the prolongation of such past instants by any overt connecting factor. In the novel there is even the complicated use of italics, albeit not consistent, to designate the shift in time zones. At the beginning of each of these two sections, there are memory events; the arousal of memory in Benjy's consciousness in the midst of an action, the memory of father and grandfather that Quentin experiences one morning upon awakening.

It would seem that Faulkner creates the mentally retarded character Benjy in order to depict an uncontrolled intrusion of memory which completely breaks down rational barriers between the present and the past. With this character, Faulkner is refashioning the Bergsonian notion of time as duration while considering alternatives as well in the experiences of Quentin. First, the 33-year-old Benjy effortlessly shifts back to early childhood and is absorbed in that past which exists simultaneously with his present. The activity of his brain is virtually limited to memory, often stimulated by sensory objects or physical sensations. Faulkner later made the following observation about his 'idiot' character's experience of present time which incorporates the past:

> To that idiot, time was not a continuation, it was an instant, there was no yesterday and no tomorrow, it all is this moment, it all is [now] to him. He cannot distinguish between what was last year and what will be tomorrow.[31]

The major focal point in the shift to the past in the novel is the obsessive memory of Benjy's cherished sister Caddy, who eventually disappeared. This is not a case of a real-life loss on the part of the writer, as with Woolf and her mother, but of an invented one, which, according to Faulkner, pertained to the sister he never had. In the beginning of the Benjy section, at the opening of the novel, Benjy is caught by a nail in a fence as he is about to go out into the fields to search for a lost quarter with Luster, the grandson of the family servant, Dilsey. Instantly, the snag of the nail as a physical sensation triggers the 33-year-old Benjy's recollection of his distant childhood – some twenty-eight years in the past – when his sister Caddy had disentangled him from a fence. But this is not an isolated trigger, as it would be in Proust's work. The fence itself is an integral part of the past, as it is associated with the scenes of family life that are not frozen in the past, but flow from one to another through continuous dialogue. This type of memory enables the adult Benjy to *become* the boy and reemerge as a full participant in the talk and action as he relives certain smells and sights and discoveries of his childhood. As Benjy returns to the past and his dead sister Caddy, he is immersed in all the activity associated with the 'fence experience' on the day just before Christmas. Benjy even reverts earlier to that same day when Caddy came home from school; he brings back his past impressions of her through the repeated thought statements like 'Caddy smelled like trees.'[32] Such phrases are lasting cues attached to the different scenes that are remembered.

The power of Benjy's associative memory is similar to the impression given by Joyce in *A Portrait of the Artist as a Young Man* where the cold bath at Clongowes is a reference point for the past. For Benjy, the specificity of the remembered day of 23 December gives a semblance of authenticity to the autobiographical source memory which starts off the sequence of his recollections. He recalls sensory details connected to this scene, such as being warned about the coldness of the day. Benjy's subsequent shifts to the past, provoked initially by a simple sensation of the 'present' day in 1928, moves from the first recollected scene to a number of dated events in the past involving Benjy's mother, Caddy herself, and other family members over a 14-year period from 1898–1912. In these 15 scenes, Benjy is not a detached observer but an active participant.

The case of Quentin is different, as Faulkner moves from the mind of an idiot to that of the intelligent Harvard student, the scion of the Compson family. Faulkner had already prepared the Quentin character in his short story 'That Evening Sun'. In that story, the Quentin character reverts (after one paragraph in the 'present' time of 1914) to 15 years before when he was a 9-year-old boy. Here, the boy and the adult coexist as the adult shapes the boy's view of the past from the perspective of the present. Such relative simultaneity allows for a reconstruction of the past from the present vantage point. In specific terms, Quentin, in the dialogues he recalls and participates in, can critically remember, for example, the unfortunate social situation of his family's black laundress, Nancy. In developing this character Quentin for his novel, Faulkner shifted the focus to the memory of the sister Caddy and her loss of virginity. As a memory subject, Quentin selectively remembers this recent event because it symbolizes the loss of his moral idealism and his traumatic break with the past.

The Quentin character who emerges in *The Sound and the Fury* seems time-obsessed, not free from present time as is his brother Benjy. Most intriguingly, time pieces, like watches and the clocks' chimes as well as natural signs of time like shadows of light, haunt Quentin throughout his peregrinations in Boston on the ill-fated 1910 June day of his suicide. In particular, the multiplicity of time pieces resonates with Einsteinian relativity theory. This flavor of relativistic mathematical time is what Quentin will unconsciously seek to reject in the course of the day as he intermittently resorts to memories, fragments of human time, which fleetingly pass through his mind. Yet Quentin's memories do not occupy a Bergsonian 'durée' that could circumscribe them and make his past stable.

Faulkner sets up what will become a fatal conflict for Quentin, since memory for Quentin is a less satisfying alternative than it is for his brother Benjy. The opening scene sets up a memory episode. Quentin is awakened on the June morning with a consciousness of time, 'a shadow of a sash', a shadow coming through a window of his room which was a visual indication of time for him corroborated by a watch: 'it was between seven and eight o'clock and then I was in time again, hearing the watch'.[33] This watch was his grandfather's handed down to him by his father. Church bells continue to mark the invasion of time upon his consciousness that morning as Quentin walks in the Boston streets. In a 15-minute sequence, the sound of the church chimes prompts by way of contrast the resonance of the past: the reflections about his sister's premarital affair with a certain Dalton Ames. The name 'Dalton Ames', repeated five times, rings obsessively in Quentin's mind, leaving him with the image of his sister standing at the house door after her immoral escapade. Quentin, suddenly back in the present, proceeds to break the watch of 'chronological time' – an act that foreshadows his ultimate rejection of it in the course of a day which will lead to his suicide:

> I went to the dresser and took up the watch, with the face still down. I tapped the crystal on the corner of the dresser and caught the fragments of glass in my hand and put them into the ashtray and twisted the hands off and put them in the tray.[34]

Despite such willful and violent action, the watch ticks on, the quarter hour chimes sounds in the streets, the shadow reaches the stoop, the sun shines. Another memory event intrudes, which involves the next stage in his sister's life, her forced wedding to Herbert Head. Quentin, walking aimlessly in the Boston streets, passes a jeweler's shop and enters automatically, with the conditioned instinct to have the watch repaired. He notices in the window a display of a dozen watches all telling different times: 'There were about a dozen watches in the window, a dozen different hours . . . Contradicting one another.'[35]

With this sight, his struggle with time continues. Quentin asks the jeweler if any of the watches in the window 'are right'. The jeweler responds with a 'no' since he says they have not been regulated. As Quentin views the dozen watches contradicting one another, he hears again his own watch ticking in his pocket, and he continues his walk through the streets.

Therefore, throughout the fateful day, Quentin cannot relieve himself of the presence of time and of the time of the present. Shadows follow him all day long, clocks sound. Simultaneously, he is haunted by intermittent memories of the past which shape his present perceptions, such as Caddy's wedding, her lost virginity and death, Damuddy's earlier death, conversations with his father. In contrast to Benjy's memory of similar scenes, for Quentin there is less access to concrete visual details than to interconnected thoughts about them. His mind links the past and present thematically. Quentin's memories are of relatively short term, since the suicidal subject is situated in 1910, closer to the critical events which plagued his family. Unlike his brother's memory, Quentin's is compromised as the present moment intrusively invades his consciousness – which leads to his suicide. Such is an alternative to the coherent kind of memory which preserves the less intelligent sibling in a state of blissful inertia.

It is interesting that Faulkner's next novel, *As I Lay Dying* (1930), continues with an exploration of memory events in the provocative situation of the death of a mother figure who herself had questioned her own sense of motherhood. In this uncharacteristically short novel, which Faulkner nonetheless considered his 'tour de force', there is the morbid view of the coffin of Addie Bundren that mechanically sets the memories of her family in motion. The novel describes the burial journey of the family to the fictional town of Jefferson where Addie had requested to be buried. And during that seven-day journey, delayed by cataclysmic interferences of fire and flood, the consciousnesses of the various family figures, including Addie's five children and her husband are displayed. Faulkner explores different consciousness and different types of memory within the same reference point of Addie Bundren's death, the objective event and catalyst which merges the past and the present. But along with short bouts of memories, a strong sense of the present time prevails because of the designated mission in progress. In an uncanny way, even Addie's own memories are elicited. Faulkner multiplies the memory events by presenting a stream of consciousnesses, shifting from one to another, unified by the common situation and purpose of present time. The burial itself, and the threatening obstacles that have to be overcome to achieve it, unleash the common flow of disparate memories simultaneously. As in the case of Woolf, the simultaneity of memory flow suggests a notion of ubiquity as the past and present are interwoven in a ten-day period through which the lifetime of the family is revealed.

The characters who are most prone to memory events are Darl, Vardaman and even the 'dead' Addie herself. Most poignantly, Faulkner probes the memory of the deranged Darl, a sensitive and isolated character, who later becomes an arsonist during the journey and is eventually hauled off as an insane person to a state asylum. Even so, Darl has often been compared to an artist figure, with a high state of awareness, instinctively reacting as his memory is triggered by raw, sensory signals. Initially, his memory is aroused by the taste of water in a bucket which brings back other associative memories of feeling and touch experienced in his childhood:

> They look around as I cross the porch and dip the gourd into the water bucket and drink . . . And at night it is better still. I used to lie

on the pallet in the hall, waiting until I could hear them all asleep, so
I could get up and go back to the bucket.[36]

Two successive memory events are produced, which take him back to
two stages of that childhood when he would contemplate the dark
bucket in the wee hours of the night alone or in the early morning
when the household was asleep and he could relish the darkness and
the 'cool silence'. Such flashbacks suggest the solitary nature of Darl's
childhood. As Darl returns to the present, he focuses on his younger
brother Jewel riding his horse. Later, in the course of the journey Darl
again becomes engrossed in another memory event involving Jewel
and the horse. As Darl is obsessed by his mother's preference for her
illegitimate son, the sight of Jewel sitting on his horse triggers a memory of three years before which had demonstrated Addie's affections.
The remembered scene is when Jewel, 15 years of age, secretly bought
himself the horse. Having been reprimanded by his angry father for
squandering money on this purchase, Jewel had received the sympa-
thies of his mother. Darl recalls that on the night of the incident, his
mother was sitting and crying as she watched over the sleeping Jewel.
Hence, the horse is the cue for an understanding of the close relationship between Addie and Jewel, which Darl acquires in his recourse to
memory. Such retrieval cues are parts of associative networks.

In contrast to Darl's intermittent memory episodes, Addie's own
memory is confined to one long chapter. It spans her entire life from
her schoolteacher days to her marriage to Anse, to their series of
unwanted children, and her betrayal of a husband she never loved. It is
an extended monologue of voluntary memories strung together by the
subject in a dispassionate and negative review of her past. Faulkner
reconstructs the memories of the deceased Addie, who voluntarily
recalls the past chronologically. In contrast, the 'living' Darl weaves in
and out of past and present, inhabiting the past sporadically through
involuntary associations.

Such memory sequences in this novel, though separated and disparate, contribute to a collective stream of consciousness. Strikingly,
however, the corpse itself proves to be the morbid trigger reminding the
characters of their different views of their common past, even as they
attempt to bury it forever. Although the characters are together on the
same journey, it is as if they occupy different locales which in turn
create different memory perspectives. For Faulkner, therefore, memory
is the vehicle for the multiple perspectives that derive from relative
simultaneity.

In the case of these three writers, the stream of consciousness is the conveyer of memories, perpetually linking the past and the present. In the narratives, the past weighs heavily on the present, psychologically and culturally. A prime illustration of this fact is that with all their ramifications, 'the dead' – Mrs Ramsay, Michael Furey, Addie Bundren – become living presences in the minds of the characters. When it comes to the remembering subjects – Septimus Warren Smith, Gretta and Gabriel Conroy, Darl Bundren – some of them are psychologically disturbed or have a heightened sensitivity. For most of the characters, past and present are commingled in a continuum of give and take as they search for their identities, stimulated by environmental cues which set off the memory process. Noticeably, the writers expand the array of such cues that elicit and link memory sequences. The physical environment of specified places is an important source for such cued retrieval. In some cases, there is evidence of involuntary memory, which serves as another form of trigger for a voluntary chain of recollected events. Ever present, memory phenomena float on the surface of the mind, ready to be awakened. As these literary works furnish rich examples of factual, autobiographical memory, they demonstrate how the power of conscious association can govern the memory process.

6
Apollinaire, Breton and the Surrealists: Automatism and Aleatory Memory

For the surrealist poets, memory, which was disdained in its conventional meaning, was to become involved with the aleatory functions of walking, writing or sleeping. The pen or the foot retrieved in an unstructured manner memory traces from the realm of the unconscious. From Guillaume Apollinaire to André Breton, to Louis Aragon and Robert Desnos, there is an experimentation with the involuntary, unconscious aspect of the memory process. All such writers sought to cultivate the creative aspects of memory extracted from nocturnal peregrinations or from the uninhibited dictation from dream states. In fact, these could be labeled as 'dream-memories', in keeping with the early psychologists of the Salpêtrière. For the purposes of the Surrealists' art and even life, the overt coupling of memory and imagination shaped the present moments and engendered future ones. The fragments of memory were strung together *without* apparent connecting links or rational threads. The surrealist mode announced a discontinuity of memory events which removes memory from an associationist context.

Critics have all too readily dismissed the subject of memory for the Surrealists because it has been regarded in its conventional sense connected to the process of logical reasoning. It is important to understand the reason why the Surrealists on the whole detested memory, 'strictly speaking'. Breton claimed in the first *Manifesto of Surrealism* (1924) that memory intrusively assumed the right of 'cutting up' the dream: 'seule la mémoire s'arroge le droit d'y faire des coupures'.[1] The Surrealists were objecting to the mind's rational packaging of memory as it deleted the unconscious ingredients. Furthermore, although they borrowed from

Freud's studies of the unconscious, as shall be seen particularly in the case of Breton, they did not basically accept his notion of retroactive causality. That was the notion that the present could alter the past. Instead, as seen in their artful exploration of the memory process, the Surrealists turned the tables; they actively used the past to alter the future.

Breton's intentionally paradoxical phrase 'Il y aura une fois',[2] awkwardly translated into English as 'Once upon a time there will be', is revealing in this respect. It is a word play on a verb tense which takes a formulaic fairy-tale construction designating a distant past and abruptly moves it into future time. In the prose piece, Breton, who loved fairy tales, challenges mankind to uncover mysteries found in a new type of spontaneous memory. A common orientation can be found in the use of memory by the Surrealists who give it free play and dislodge and transplant it for artistic purposes. Three significant surrealist paintings will serve as graphic illustrations of this process in the epilogue of this book.

Before Breton, Apollinaire provided a concrete trajectory for memory, as he walked the Paris streets and reminisced about his past, his lost youth and lost loves. But with his peripatetic poems, Apollinaire was no mere Romantic dreamer, wallowing in the past and lost there. After all, like those Surrealists who followed him, his mind was on the future and what he specifically called 'l'esprit nouveau' or the new spirit in his famous lecture of 1917, 'L'Esprit nouveau et les poètes'. As an innovator of modernist aesthetics in the first decade of the twentieth century, he also coined the term 'Surrealism'. Apollinaire's literary use of memory events is connected to the aesthetics he was promoting for the avant-garde. Taking the poetic imagination into a new dimension could in turn uncover unknown properties of the human mind.

Through his poems Apollinaire seems to go through a series of approaches to the memory process. At first, he suggests that standard, sentimental memory is fragile and weak. On the one hand, he evokes the fleeting nature of the past in love poems which contain agonizing recollections, reverberating faintly in the hunting horn motif of such poems as 'Cors de Chasse' from the collection *Alcools*. He writes: 'Les souvenirs sont cors de chasse/ Dont meurt le bruit parmi le vent';[3] ['Memories are hunting horns/Whose sound dies amidst the wind']. The loss of his lover the artist Marie Laurencin, was an inspiration for many of these poems, as the popular one 'Le Pont Mirabeau' 'Ni temps passé/Ni les amours reviennent';[4] ['Neither time past/Nor past loves return']. In a short but striking poem 'La Boucle retrouvée',[5] the memory of a loved one is reduced to a curl of hair which is found/remembered, but that fleeting memory also seems to die with the expiring day. However, it is interesting that as the word 'boucle' becomes specifically linked to memory in the expression 'boucle de souvenir', with the second meaning of 'loop of memory', it turns into a poetic metaphor of circular meandering.

Apollinaire proceeds to perceive memory in a more innovative manner in his series of short stories in the volumes *L'Héresiarque et Cie* (1910) and *Le Poète Assassiné* (1916). In such prose, he creates characters who not only mentally return to the past but use such memories to distort the present moment through creative acts of disorientation. Apollinaire uses the resources of memory to destroy sequential time, to impose fantasy and dream onto the present, and to create what surrealist painters later would call 'the persistence of memory' or 'the memory of the future'.[6] In the little known strange *conte* 'La Fiancée Posthume', for example, a close couple, bereaved by the tragic loss of their five-year-old daughter, annul reality and over the years delude themselves into thinking that this daughter is growing in their midst. When, in their minds, she would have arrived at the age of marriage, they enlist a lodger in their home in Cannes whom they deem appropriate for their absent daughter. The use of the conditional verb tense in the statement distorts the memory of her in a hypothetical situation: 'Elle aurait seize ans. Qui sait? Notre pensionnaire lui plairait peut-être?';[7] ['She would be 16 years old. Who knows? Our lodger would please her perhaps?']. Although things work out perversely, the young man falling for the mother of the dead daughter, the couple has created an imaginary situation from their memories which have evolved into the future by way of displacement. In this and other stories, the act of memory provokes the imagination, allowing the dream to invade reality, and disorienting the characters from sequential time.

But above and beyond such quaint pieces, Apollinaire's most profound contribution to the literary expression of memory is his monumental poem 'Zone' of 1912 from his collection *Alcools*. Therein the poet-subject Apollinaire is able to recapture his past through a nocturnal journey in the 'present' time. This significant poem makes a powerful impression of unleashing simultaneous memory images in the experience of the 'present' moment. It is what I have labelled 'zig-zag memory'.

This lead poem is often characterized as Cubist in style because of its juxtaposition of fragments of experience from a range of time periods. It first sets the old Western world steeped in the tradition of Greco-Roman antiquity and the Christian religion against the new world advancing in the technological age, symbolized by the jarring and relatively new image for its time, the Eiffel Tower looming over Paris. The poem actually treats memory through the lonely poet's nocturnal walk, which, rather than producing a chronological succession of past events, passes through simultaneous time zones. Night-time is the appropriate environment for memory to emerge. In a gratuitous and desultory serialization of events and objects, there is a compression of space and time which produces instead a poetic expression of simultaneity. The poet juxtaposes his past and present through alternating the pronouns between the first person singular present 'I' and the second person singular past 'tu'. When the peripatetic poet emerges from a night escapade at the end of the poem, alone and alienated in a seedy Parisian urban scene, hearing the sound of milkmen making their rounds in the early morning hours, he trades his memories for the vacancy of the present moment. He returns to his diurnal self, which ultimately rejects the memory of the past as the physical movement of walking ceases.

What distinguishes this expression of memory from others of its time, in, for example, Proust's *Du Côté de chez Swann* and Joyce's *A Portrait of the Artist as a Young Man* is the simultaneous experience of the distinctly separate past and present through the process of memory. The 'you' follows a circuitous route coexistent with the present 'I'. While the 'I' voice continues along an industrial street of Paris, there emerges the 'tu' – which can be connected to early stages of Apollinaire's life, such as the pious child dressed in blue and white uniform being led by his mother to his Catholic school, the Collège Saint-Charles:

> J'ai vu ce matin une jolie rue dont j'ai oublié le nom ...
> Voilà la jeune rue et tu n'es encore qu'un petit enfant ... [8]
> [This morning I saw a pretty street whose name I forgot ...
> Here is the young street and you are still only a little child.]

Another 'tu' follows, under the lemon trees on the coast of the Mediterranean in the South of France:

> Maintenant tu marches dans Paris tout seul parmi la foule ...
> Maintenant tu es au bord de la Méditerranée
> Sous les citronniers .... [9]
> [Now you walk in Paris all alone amidst the crowd
> Now you are on the Mediterranean coast
> Under the lemon trees.]

Thereupon, the past 'you' travels in rapid succession from one city to another: Prague, Marseilles, Coblenz, Rome, Amsterdam, and back to Paris and its darker emotional moments which include a sad love affair at the age of 23. At this point the 'I' and 'you' merge in the present nocturnal time zone through the admission that 'J'ai vécu comme un fou et j'ai perdu mon temps'; 'I have lived like a fool and wasted my time.' Such is the condition of the present self standing at the counter of a dirty bar with the debauchees or mingling with a lowly crowd at night in a big restaurant. The 'you' is finally on the streets of Paris at dawn, walking to its destination of the outer district of Auteuil. As the poem wanes into the realm of daylight, it is as if the memory is covered up again by the territory of the night in which it is enclosed. The present self is once again severed from its past and the old, dead world. This rupture is indicated by the sparse play of words at the end of the poem which signal a definitive break: 'Adieu, adieu/Soleil cou coupé'; ['Farewell, farewell/Sun, a neck cut off'].

Such is a poetic nocturnal memory 'trip' provoked simply by the physical bodily movement of walking to a stream of disconnected images which relate to the poet's past through block shifts in time zones. Throughout this succession of disconnected states, without links or connecting threads between them, the past tense is mostly avoided as the present tense is used. As an avant-garde writer, Apollinaire was himself demonstrating the shift from chronology to simultaneity in the experience of time. Memory naturally was incorporated in this new perspective.

Early on in 1914, in his article 'Simultanéisme-Librettisme',[10] Apollinaire had argued for being among the true discoverers of simultaneity along with contemporary Cubist painters such as Braque, Picasso and Delaunay. Apollinaire therefore attacked the boasts of a contemporary writer, Barzun, who claimed he initiated poetic simultaneity in his theatrical works. The poem 'Zone' had already been Apollinaire's artistic statement regarding a budding version of simultaneity as actually being synonymous with a form of memory. Historically speaking, 'Zone' can be regarded as *the* twentieth-century poem on memory which subtly influenced other poets and artists who experimented with the manipulation of time dimensions in their works.

If Apollinaire had opened up the exploration of memory to the region of nocturnal dreams, Breton exploited the memory process further, imposing those dreams on diurnal reality. Breton was attracted to the primitive automatism that he gleaned from the writings of Pierre Janet, which he found a fertile territory for reaping poetic images to transpose into his writings. As an earthbound dreamer, Breton exploited the automatism of the mind in part for the uninhibited unleashing of unconscious memory. Such resort to memory-land created an atmosphere of incertitude, a wasteland territory in which words and images could form new unions. A striking statement in the first *Manifesto of Surrealism* sets the stage for Breton's particular way of cultivating memory. Breton feels able to retrieve the rich ground of the childhood state which for the Surrealists was the terrain conducive for the exercise of the unculti-vated eye (or 'I'):

> Des souvenirs d'enfance et de quelques autres se dégage un sentiment d'inaccaperé et par la suite de dévoyé, que je tiens pour le plus fécond qui existe.[11]
> [From childhood memories and some others emerge a feeling of free-dom and then of going astray that I consider the most fertile that exists.]

Here Breton was saying that a sense of freedom, of going off the beaten track from normal reality, emerges from childhood memories and creates a fertile environment for artistic production. There are no traces of traumatic experience or euphoric nostalgia as in Proust. The uncanny feeling of what the Surrealists call the 'insolite' elicits an atmosphere which is ripe for creativity. This seems to be an example of the 'terrain vague', off the beaten track, which was the ground for surrealist experimentation.

For a poet who detested the memoir form and who was not Romantic in his dreaming, there is for Breton less interest in the contents of mem-ories themselves than in the potentiality of the free functioning of memory that in turn elicits the art. For Proust, who cherished the past, memory was an end in itself, to which he could escape in his cork-lined apartment. For Breton, who exalted the present as he walked the streets of Paris, the free play of memory was a means for gratuitous mental alliances of images which offered passages to the future. After all, Breton was searching everywhere for new territories for artistic creation. The surroundings of the memory event, hence, are explicitly vague but provocative.

Accordingly, the concept of involuntarism that arises in Breton's sparse but acute recourse to memory is radically different from the strat-egy of Proust which retains a logical structure. No exterior trigger is called upon by the poet. It could be argued that Breton's use of involun-tary memory seems more authentic since it enters the realm of the unconscious and probes the implicit memories therein. This distinction becomes clear in an examination of Breton's evocation of his childhood scene, a rare act for him, which occurs in his early attempts of automatic writing.

In evaluations of Breton's automatic writing, there have been arguments by the critics as to how much Breton actually drew from the psychologists at the Salpêtrière. Breton had been a student at the Faculté de Médecine in Paris from 1913 to 1914, taking the introductory courses of Physics, Chemistry and Natural Sciences – known as P.C.N. During those years he had fully read Janet's treatise of *L'Automatisme psychologique* and no doubt was struck by the expression 'le rétrécisse-ment du champs de la conscience'[12] ['the narrowing of the fields of consciousness'], appropriating those so-called narrowed fields for a wider range of surrealist activity. Most specifically, he was an externe from January to September 1917 in the Hôpital de la Pitié, under Charcot's disciple Joseph Babinski. In fact, Babinski dedicated a copy of his book *Hystérie-pithiatisme* (1917) to Breton.

Certain documents do substantiate Breton's recourse to the investi-gations at the Salpêtrière. In his famous piece 'Le Cinquantenaire de l'hystérie (1878–1928)', Breton proclaimed the indebtedness of the Surrealists to the studies at the Salpêtrière and singled out Babinski as the most intelligent man to have tackled the subject: 'l'homme le plus intelligent qui se soit attaqué à cette question'.[13] In his 'hands on' observations of traumatisms of the Great War 'neurologie de guerre', Babinski was concerned with cures for hysteria by way of processes of persuasion and suggestion. Breton was to extract from these patho-logical studies an opportunity for poetic activity, as he reaped fragments or phrases as remembered from dream or hallucinatory states. 'L'Hystérie n'est pas un phénomène pathologique et peut, à tous égards, être con-siderée comme un moyen suprême d'expression.'[14] Breton's co-author of *Les Champs magnétiques*, Philippe Soupault, even confirmed that the reading of Pierre Janet had had an impact on their poetic creation.[15] Actually, Breton was reappropriating the term 'automatique' of Janet to give it an artistic application. Eventually, in order to explain his experi-ments in automatic writing, Breton expressed a preference for the word 'unconscious' ('inconscient').[16]

However, Breton's use of the word 'inconscient' is not the same as Freud might have had it. The critic Jean Starobinski has pointed out that Breton was closer to the more developed notion of the subliminal self that had been popularized by F.W.H. Myers, to whom the poet made numerous references. Starobinski writes: 'Car le moi subliminal est un inconscient valorisé'; ['Because the subliminal "I" is the unconscious of enhanced value'].[17] Breton had even directly acknowledged his indebtedness to the parapsychologist who, having written an essay 'Automatic Writing' in 1887, opened up for Breton another avenue into the unconscious:

> Chronologiquement, avant Freud...nous sommes bien plus largement tributaires que nous le croyons généralement de ce que William James, à très juste titre, a appelé la *psychologie gothique* de F.W.H. Myers.[18]
> [Chronologically, before Freud...we are much more greatly indebted than we believe to what William James has very rightly called the Gothic psychology of F.W.H. Myers.]

Breton's version of unconscious memory can be viewed in this particular context. It is well known that Breton himself focused on pure automatic writing early in his poetic career, up to the time of the first *Manifesto of Surrealism* in 1924. Breton explicitly made the point that this writing was a free uninhibited transcription of thought from the depths of the unconscious: 'Automatisme psychique....Dictée de la pensée, en l'absence de tout contrôle exercé par la raison'.[19] 'Psychic automatism...Dictation of thought in the absence of all control exercised by reason'.

Two specific pieces of Breton's automatic writing convey this free play of memory, derived as it is in part from psychic automatism. The first, a section of *Les Champs magnétiques* entitled 'Saisons', actually recreates remembrances of his childhood in Brittany followed by certain experiences in Paris as a schoolboy. The second part of *Poisson soluble* gives extended metaphors of memory, rather than any particular personal recollection. But what is most important is that the original manuscript demonstrates that the text is uncorrected and therefore fully automatic. Only later in his career, at the second stage of his surrealist adventure would he manipulate the automatic events for artistic purposes.

Les Champs magnétiques was an early experimental piece of writing. According to Breton it was composed within six days.[20] In the spring of 1919 two young poets Breton and Soupault, aged 23 and 24 respectively, collaborated in furnishing 'le minerai brut...l'or, dit Mme de Noailles, à son état primitif';[21] ['The crude ore...gold, says Mme de Noailles, in its primitive state']. In his notebooks of 1920, Breton applauded the practitioners of the Salpêtrière, who with full spontaneity, without constraints of modesty or anticipation, had allowed 'everything that passes through your head' ('tout ce qui vous passe par la tête').[22] In particular, he gave credit to Freud for liberating and refurbishing memory which was often censured and weakened by a sense of morality: 'Il redressa notre mémoire qui avait pris l'habitude de défaillir chaque fois que nous aurions eu l'occasion d'un remords';[23] ['He straightened up our memory which had taken the habit of weakening each time that we will have had an opportunity for remorse'].[24] Such an uninhibited free-flow of memory would be part of the experiment of *Les Champs magnétiques*.

It was in the article 'Entrée des Médiums' ('The Mediums Enter') that Breton, prior to the Surrealist Manifesto of 1924, was attempting to explain this type of automatic memory as crucial to the activity of surrealist writing. Breton elaborates on the keyword 'Surrealism' that he had borrowed from Apollinaire: 'Par lui nous avons convenu de désigner un certain automatisme psychique qui correspond assez bien à l'état de rêve';[25] ['By it [this word] we have agreed to indicate a certain psychic automatism which pretty well corresponds to a dream state']. Breton then proceeded to allude to *Les Champs magnétiques* as the application of such a perspective:

> En 1919, mon attention s'était fixée sur les phrases plus ou moins partielles qui, en pleine solitude, à l'approche du sommeil, deviennent perceptibles pour l'esprit sans qu'il soit possible de leur découvrir une détermination préalable. Ces phrases, remarquablement imagées et d'une syntaxe parfaitement correcte, m'étaient apparues comme des éléments poétiques du premier ordre.[26]
> [In 1919 I was focused on more or less partial sentences which in full solitude at the approach of sleep become perceptible to the mind without it being possible to uncover a preliminary designation. These sentences remarkably full of imagery and with a perfect syntax appeared to me as first-rate poetic elements.]

At first, Breton had himself produced such spontaneous poetic phrases at the approach of sleep. Later, in the automatic writing of *Les Champs magnétiques*, he apparently simulated the sleep environment to provoke similar verbal results. Breton called the whole project a magic dictation ('dictée magique') or a dream narrative ('récit des rêves') for which he himself was the medium or a passive receptor. He thus emphasized the lack of any artistic intervention. The critic Anna Balakian has described Breton's approach in this early work: 'There seems to be no labor involved, as though the author in fact acted as a sort of medium between his subconscious memories and their transformation into spontaneous images.'[27]

Breton also made very overt statements with respect to memory, which shed further light on *Les Champs magnétiques*. The first *Manifesto of Surrealism* (1924) makes it very clear that Breton was attempting to reshape the functioning of the memory process. First, he deplores the negative aspect of memory, which has been conditioned to function in the daily context of rational progression:

> C'est que l'homme quand il cesse de dormir, est avant tout le jouet de sa mémoire, et qu'à l'état normal celle-ci se plaît à lui retracer faiblement les circonstances du rêve . . . le rêve se trouve ainsi ramené à une parenthèse , comme la nuit.[28]
> [That is that man when he ceases to sleep is before all the toy of his memory and that at the normal state that [memory] pleases itself to weakly recount the circumstances of the dream . . . the dream is thereby brought back to a parenthesis, as the night.]

As a function of voluntary, rational thought, memory amends and edits reality by putting the dream state in parenthesis. For this reason Breton declares a real disdain for ordinary rational memory as a confessional operation. However, what is less recognized is that he was reorienting the memory process to reap a larger recuperation from its unconscious state. These findings would in turn help create a voyeurism of the future as memory became endowed with a prophetic character:

> Le grand voile qui tombe sur mon enfance ne me dérobe qu'à demi les étranges années qui précéderont ma mort.[29]
> [This big veil which falls over my childhood hides only half of the strange years which will precede my death.]

Once again, a strange combination of tenses brings the future tense in relation to the past. Breton is saying that his childhood was only half-way hidden by a veil. His future is inscribed in this childhood, however. It is suggested that if he can fully unveil his childhood, he might be able to predict the future.

The 'Saisons' of *Les Champs magnétiques* is written in the present tense, suggesting an immediate experience of the past in its raw primal state. If the title was inspired by Rimbaud's famous little poem 'Ô Saisons, ô Châteaux', the word 'season' could have a similar connotation suggesting the passage of time and the past. Breton himself specified that in this section he evoked his happy childhood memories of Brittany from the age of two to four. It contains involuntary configurations of memory events, marked by ellipses or spaces between occurrences which, according to Breton, only true memory could permit. There is no 'stream' here, but a succession of brute images, lacking narrative continuity and linkages. In his purview of the past, Breton gathers perceptions *without* connecting threads. In his esoteric essay of 1924 'Introduction au discours sur le peu de réalité', Breton specifically spoke of new mental processes such as the imagination or memory which proceeded 'sans fil' ('without thread'). The strange frontispiece to the 1927 edition of the article is a page of elliptical notes listing themes such as space and time, linking memory and imagination, and underlining a phrase 'le souvenir du futur'.[30] In one parenthetical statement Breton qualifies remembering or 'Je me souviens' by what he calls invention: 'ce que l'on m'accordera que j' invente *dans* ce dont je me souviens' ('what one will grant that I invent in that which I remember'). Memory meant invention.

The unleashing of earliest memories seem to be Breton's first product of such automatic writing. The actual text of 'Saisons' written by Breton includes a section of reminiscences which unravel the distant past for him. The freedom with which the images are evoked suggests a spontaneity of recall without recourse to association. The first recollection takes him back to the setting of Saint-Brieuc, when Breton was under his grandfather's care, 'cela vient du temps où l'on m'asseyait sur les genoux'.[31] We are struck by the particularity and specificity of the images he recalls that concern his life before the age of four. He evokes the images which surrounded his early childhood in this maritime, country village of Brittany. He sees an inn which seems big and bountiful with the garden around it. A whole universe of dreamlike images is evoked: the blue fountain which makes stones shine like gold and startles the frogs. He hears the women in the village washing at the public basins. Nature is alive with a forest, white agate stones, cactuses and honeysuckle. He remembers the swelling of the grass at night. He has a hard time going to sleep and engages in child lies to explain his sleeplessness. The section ends with his child games, in which he is the head of an army that imaginatively fights the hedges.

In the next section of the text, 'Eclipses', Soupault makes the following statement: 'Un homme ressuscite pour la deuxième fois. Sa mémoire est plantée de souvenirs arborescents et il y coule des fleuves aurifères.'[32] Here memory is resurrected in a twilight zone giving new life out of uncanny darkness. It creates tributaries that are arborescent and 'gold bearing', since this brute matter of recall is what the poet will alchemize in the gold of his art.

Whereas *Les Champs magnétiques* unearths some of the particulars of Breton's personal memories, *Poisson soluble* characterizes memory in striking metaphors. First of all, the expression 'poisson soluble' refers to Breton himself: born under the sign of Pisces, his mind was solvent, suggesting a dissolving of all time barriers. In Part I, an enigmatic piece 'Entre la source' refers to the source of memory as a well of the subconscious from which memory images involuntarily spring. The abundant images are a resource for his poetry. They are recovered individually in their pristine form without being adulterated by associative contexts.

In Part II of *Poisson soluble* Breton offers a series of probably the most cryptic metaphors for memory ever expressed, including a personification of it as both a seigneur who flatters his servants and a lady's companion ('dame de companie') who pours coffee into thimbles. Both analogies create a typical Breton medieval environment of mystery and distance from which memory may emerge through a slow process. Here is the dense passage about memory, marked by enigmatic juxtapositions which are jarringly provocative even in English, as suggested in the translation which I myself have rendered:

> A Memory, the first undoubtedly and the one that makes stars flourish, that opens hands. Those who summon it are grand. But the garden of persecutions closes its doors on them and they remain hounded by the tunas of the sea, by the strong workers of Les Halles, by the religious hosts with spiders' legs. This memory strokes its servants as a lecherous master does. The bedroom is divided according to perfumes, perfume of the South, jewelled star of Nubia, collars of a child who has disappeared . . . This memory, calmed, harmed, wrought like an iron gate, gives up its place sometimes to a ball of poison. The trolley which advances in the woods.[33]

As this passage may suggest, the obstacles to memory are like the crude workers of Les Halles or the clumsy tuna fish that would be insensitive to the poetic imagination. Also, memory arising from delirium or confusion would not be taken seriously. On the other hand, when memory is slowly and subtly at work, it creates its own enchanted dwelling, similar to a medieval castle of fairy-tale land which for Breton and other poets suggests a kind of dream environment of the mind that harbors the precious essence of memory. The strange reference to 'ball of poison' might even suggest a dose of opium which memory might be likened to. The erotic references to the seigneur and his bedroom suggest the fusion which memory needs.

The speaker describes a specific way of willfully extracting the magic of his memory:

> J'ouvre ma tête avec une serpe d'or pour en détacher ce gui merveilleux qui fait pencher les soleils.[34]
> [I open my head with a golden billhook to cut off the magic mistletoe which makes suns tilt.]

The billhook, a tool shaped like a sickle moon, is the legendary means from Celtic times of extracting the sacred mistletoe, as if the poet were digging out the 'ore' from precious dreams. Subsequently, with mysterious vigilance, the speaker also awaits memory in a kind of wasteland setting. The memory seems to emerge from the dream onto the surface of the earth, in an erotic tryst with reality:

> C'est dans ce terrain vague que j'attends la mémoire, folle de tous les rendez-vous qui se donne à la surface de la terre. Un rayon danse sur la taupinière de cristal et de cette taupinière sort la mémoire comme une gerbe d'iris pour la plus grande satisfaction des sens chiffonnés avant de s'ouvrir comme les tombeaux.[35]
> [It's in this wasteland that I await memory, crazy about all the rendez-vous which are made on the surface of the earth. A ray dances on the burrows of crystal and from this burrow memory arises like a bunch of iridescent irises creating a rainbow from the largest satisfaction of crumpled senses before it opens up like tombs.]

The language of this passage suggests that memory comes out from a burrow of the subconscious. However, rather than dark, the burrow is paradoxically crystalline; as a ray of light shines on it, it emanates off it like a wreath of irises, multicolored and iridescent like a rainbow. As the critic Jean-Pierre Cauvin has noted, 'crystal, a particularly frequent image in Breton, is defined by him as the perfect expression of spontaneous action and creation'.[36] Through the visual metaphors of mixed images, Breton communicates how the dream has opened up to reality through the emergence of memories.

In dramatizing the vagaries of memory with sudden and unexpected shifts in orientation, Breton anticipates the findings of certain current scientific experiments that identify incongruity, discontinuity and uncertainty as three main characteristics of the dream states. From a neurocognitive standpoint, J. Allan Hobson and Robert Stickgold conclude:

> The data indicate that while subjects frequently and rapidly reorient their visual attention while dreaming, they simultaneously experience a relaxation of the rules of associative memory.[37]

The writings of Breton's fellow Surrealists further corroborate this approach to the memory process. Having experimented with the recall of provocative phrases from what resemble self-induced artistic states, Breton also had vicarious recourse to the experience of hypnotic memory as he encouraged his notorious fellow poet Robert Desnos to go through bouts of somnambulism and hypnosis. Recognized as a hypnotizable subject, Desnos was provoked into retrieving memory fragments as vivid imagery. In a prose piece of his own 'Confession d'un enfant du siècle' (1926), Desnos directly admits that he mixes the dream and reality, the future and the past. In fact, he asks whether he even has standard memories: 'Ai-je des souvenirs au fait?'[38] The very word 'souvenir' or recollection is confining for him, because it is suggestive of everyday things or facts which can be catalogued in a limited temporal framework and arranged in narrative sequence. In his view, fluid dream events themselves are as memorable as discrete past actions. Desnos thereby undoes Baudelaire's statement that 'J'ai plus de souvenirs que si j'avais mille ans' – which suggests a static storage of memory in limited, designated time-frames of human activity. Desnos conveyed his approach to memory years later in a collection *Les Portes battantes* (1942) which included two highly revelatory poems on the subject, 'Erotisme de la mémoire' and 'Le Verre brisé'.

'Erotisme de la mémoire' presents a graphic illustration of memory in its fragmented perspective. The word 'erotic' in surrealist usage suggests unanticipated coupling of retrieved images and objects and can be applied to the memory process. The poem starts off with a fragmentation of the body of the mythical goddess of the moon and hunt, Diana. This mythic reference for a memory poem divorces it from a personal backdrop of a past love affair which is a typical trope for Romantic love poems. Poetics have shown that such moon imagery can suggest the passage of time. In this poem, the timeless nature of Diana is implied in her dissolution at daybreak as with a dream. Having established this setting of fragmented parts or metonymy, Desnos goes on in the poem to concentrate on debris left in the forest setting. These remnants of a dream include a bottle, an old book, a bird's feather, a piece of flint-stone, and a footprint deeply set on the earth. But such traces are not triggers to a specific scene in the past; they are disconnected and dislodged from any framework of past associations and integrated into the present perceptions.

In this light, Desnos's 'Le Verre brisé' seems to be a companion poem demonstrating the catalytic power of the mind to piece together the broken memory fragments in new ways. Desnos again undoes the Baudelairean trope of the 'wine of memory' which typically brings back a personal scene of the past. Instead, a broken glass on a table under-goes metamorphosis through the passage of time as in the succession Desnos presents of 'un verre à pied', or stemmed glass, a wine glass, and other kinds of glasses. At one stage, the glass is lost in the terrain and then found again by chance. A series of spontaneous and new associations are created. If the vagabond suggests the wandering poet, these meager mementoes might be memory fragments which he will gather and recycle into his art.

Another contemporary surrealist poet, Aragon, famous for *Le Paysan de Paris*, in which he exploited the vagrancy of the poet, offers yet another dream memory poem in his collection *Le Mouvement perpétuel* (1920–24). In his lead poem 'Sommeil de plomb' or 'Leaden Sleep', the poet recovers his childhood past through the intermediary of the heavy dream. It presents a sleeper who is awake, 'le dormeur éveillé', an active dreamer who sees life with the eyes of a little child. The implication is that the sleeping dream state is transposed onto ordinary reality. In the course of the poem, the speaker poet invokes 'the lady of memory', 'la dame du souvenir'. Like Desnos, Aragon seems to offer yet another outright response to Baudelaire's drinking of the wine of memory. Aragon sees memory as a reservoir not from which he drinks but into which he can willfully become submerged or literally drowned:

> Un grand trou s'est fait dans ma mémoire
> Un lac où l'on peut se noyer mais non pas boire[39]
> [A big hole was made in my memory
> A lake in which one can drown but not drink]

It is not a case of syphoning out individual memories but being immersed in the state of remembering. A concrete allusion to a bed continues the sleep motif. Literally, under the bed lies the territory of the dream from which the state of childhood emerges:

> Au pays souterrain du songe
> Alors je retombe en enfance
> [In the underground country of the dream
> I fall back into childhood]

And the young man is enthralled in the beatific forest of sleepers, as he retrieves his childhood condition of translucency.

In such a poetic evocation of the dream state, Aragon situates memory. In typical surrealist fashion, the primitive condition of childhood and the natural setting of a forest scene are the environment conducive to the free flow of memory. As with Breton, Aragon seizes upon the metaphor of a lady of memory who gracefully solicits the poet into this soft paradoxical atmosphere of sleepful awakening. Inevitably, this memory process requires a particular state of vigilance and a passivity which renders the subject receptive to the internally generated memory experience.

In unleashing the irrational and the automatic, the Surrealists brought therewith distinct innovations to the treatment of memory. Unlike the Romantics, they did not construe memory events as the emotional recall of specific incidents in specific places. Unlike Proust, they did not court memory or wallow in the introverted experience of stretches of past time. In fact, they disdained any overt reverence for memory or any directed search of it. Nor did they consider memory to be dependent upon external triggers of bodily sensation. They also showed little interest in exterior stimuli from vivid cues of perception that were highlighted in the associative treatments of memory of Woolf, Joyce or Faulkner.

Overall, the surrealist concern was with the complete liberation of memory from what Breton called the 'strings' or 'threads', that is to say, any causal links that would in any way hold memory within the confines of rationality or temporal chronology. As a result, the surrealist representation of memory had the arbitrariness and discontinuity of the dream states. These poets did not dramatize memory with a setting, character or chain of events, but rather presented memory in the context of bizarre montages and confused patchwork that totally obliterated the unifying logic of any pattern or sequence. For them, the past was not a previous time to be revisited, a time with a definite 'story' that informed the present. Instead, the past was mingled in an ongoing dynamic jumble with the present and the future. As a result, the Surrealists arrived at a new and revelatory perception of memory. They perceived what later dream studies would validate: that the human thought process is at least in part naturally discontinuous and fluid, instead of being completely ordered or sequential. In the same years as writers were demonstrating the carefully charted stream of consciousness in connective narrative, the Surrealists were offering another perspective as they reaped poetic harvest from a new territory that they had discovered of oneiric memory.

7
Nin, Borges and Paz: Labyrinthine Passageways of Mind and Language

For the writers Anaïs Nin, Jorge Borges and Octavio Paz, all of whom were modernist writers sharing Hispanic backgrounds – Cuban, Argentinian and Mexican, respectively – memory is not reimagined as experience, even disconnected experience, but rather is enacted in figurative or mythic language. Just as psychoanalysis moved from Freud and the signified to Lacan and the signifier, so with these modernist writers there is a shift from memory perceived as the substantial lived and even hidden experience of the signified to memory as a kind of 'jouissance', or pleasure of linguistic signifiers presenting polyphonic voices of the subconscious in a grammar of its own making. Language stores material traces of human memory in the brain, which appear, as Lacan would have it, as 'a succession of little signs'[1] in circular motion. Accordingly, the memory process is enacted on this sensorial level of the 'signifiant' or signifier.

These three multicultural writers, who show a long-standing interest in the nature of memory and its connection to writing use physical images to portray the memory process in spatial perspectives, which suggest versions of 'the fourth dimension'. Geographical inscapes convey the passageway of memory, along subterranean routes of earth and waterways. Long-term autobiographical memory is their concern, as all three writers unearth fragments of their childhood past in their attempts at self-exploration and probing through their language. Most revealing in this context is Nin's novelette *Seduction of the Minotaur*, Borges' poems 'Adrogué' and his story 'Funes el memorioso' and Paz's key poem 'Pasado en claro', which is comparable in impact to Apollinaire's 'Zone'.

All three writers follow the memory process through the labyrinth, which becomes a common and compelling metaphor for the spatialization of time. Language is like Ariadne's thread which retraces the footsteps or imprints, physically designated within the intricacies of the labyrinth. Nin envisages memory as a pattern which keeps repeating itself throughout a lifetime in analogous incidents and relationships. Borges crosses thresholds to darkness as the artificer whose craft of poetry is the catalyst for the retrieval of the remnants of the past. Paz sees a trail of footsteps that follow into the distant past, as words are bridges in the poetic journey backwards. It is also worth noting that all three writers resort to the common image of the mirror to suggest the self-reflective aspect of memory: Nin in the reflecting windowpane, Borges in mirrors of art, Paz in a mirror of words. As a psycholinguistic image, featured by Lacan, the mirror image of the self fills the gap toward 'otherness' by language, which becomes ingrained in the earliest memories.

Nin made her lifetime preoccupation with her past a priority in her continuous search for the father. Most Nin critics concentrate on the trauma that the missing parent had on her life. This impetus for her diary writing is visible as it is woven and rewoven in the recurring patterns of her fiction. On the one hand, her daily diaries, which she began to write at the age of 11 when her debonair musician father abandoned her family in Europe, present short-term memories of immediate events and experiences. On the other hand, her novels revisit those memories in long-term form, as she recasts the search for the father in fiction. The transmutation of short-term to long-term memory, in the passage from diary to fiction, occurs through the intermediary of aesthetic images. Nin writes that distance in time and her fiction writing yield the larger and truer representations of long-term memory:

> Every day of record counts against this bigger thing or can it be made so big and beautiful that it can become the whole thing – the infinite? Is the flowering possible only with forgetting, with time, with the rotting and the dust and the falsities?[2]

She is eventually able to fully recapture the memory of her father in the fiction.

Graphically, Nin constructs an archaeology of memory. For Nin, the image of the labyrinth represents the brain in its intricate layers of memory circuits, comparable to what the British neurologist Tim Shallice has called 'nested structures'. Her locales are often transformed into an inner space which she inhabits through the power of memory. Passageways such as tunnels, grooves, corridors, mazes in underground cities are the networks through which memories pass through the strata of consciousness. Nin explained why the configuration of the labyrinth intuitively attracted her from the time she had visually contemplated the labyrinthine structure of the city of Fez in 1936, which became for her a real-life model for the 'city of the interior':

> The concept of the labyrinth attracted me. It represented, first of all, mystery. One was lost in a maze. The unconscious is a maze. One does not know with the conscious mind, clearly, where one is going. There are many detours. When I saw the city of Fez, I saw in its design a huge, life-sized labyrinth. The whole city was a labyrinth. Later on, this fascination found not only confirmation in myths and legends, but in scientific images of the brain.[3]

In characterizing Nin's iconology, the critic Catherine Broderick refers to what she calls Nin's 'memory cities'.[4] Nin's collection of five novelettes under the title of *Cities of the Interior* (1959) does present the poetic inscape which harbors her strong and prevailing, often repressed, memories. *Seduction of the Minotaur* is the most significant in this series as it climactically produces a modern myth of memory in the figure of the minotaur which is associated with the labyrinth in the age-old Greek legend.

This 'memory novel' deals specifically with the persona's temporary return to an imaginary place called Golconda which evokes her childhood past in Mexico. The narrative pits the character's short-term memories against her long-term memories. The key figure, Lillian Beye, a housewife from White Plains, New York, who also happens to be a jazz musician, takes a three-month trip to Mexico to escape her mundane life and temporarily erase it from her consciousness. As she arrives in her interior city of Golconda, it soon becomes clear that despite her efforts at forgetting, the short-term memories of her immediate past are replaced by long-term memories of her childhood, connected with the Mexican scene and surging from it. It soon becomes clear that this is 'that underground city of her childhood'[5] in which her oldest memories, the painful memories of the past, are lodged.

Lillian's initial conversation with Dr Hernandez, a physician living in the Mexican city, reveals Nin's view of the memory process. Whereas Lillian admits that she is there to forget, the experienced doctor, who speaks like a psychoanalyst, claims that nothing can ever be totally forgotten, especially the traumatic memories which are embedded in the psyche. He advises her, therefore, to confront her memories rather than try to escape them. Highly revealing is the 'splinter' image of the following quotation. It conveys the sense of a deep, long-term memory that the doctor senses that Lillian will face during the trip to Golconda. He warns her: 'Some memories are imbedded in the flesh like splinters and you have to operate to get them out.'[6]

A chain reaction in the memory process occurs over the course of the three-month stay. First of all, the physical environment of the exotic, sunny land allows Lillian to forget the recent past and luxuriate in the present. As short-term memories are erased, there is room for long-term memories to emerge along with the pain associated with them. Such memories surface involuntarily by the power of association but most of all by particular visual stimuli of chance encounters. Since these prove to be painful memories which are extracted, as the doctor foresaw, there will subsequently follow a supreme effort to forget them. Lillian attempts to eradicate these involuntary memories through acts of voluntary forgetting. Such efforts occur in the latter part of the novel, as Lillian faces the minotaur of her remembered selfhood and recoils from the sight of it on her return to White Plains, New York, and her ordinary existence.

Lillian is shown to take a journey into the unconscious that is likened to a subterranean journey into the depths of the earth. In fact, one extended metaphor suggests a mining expedition. It is right after Dr Hernandez's death, and Lillian, now without his help, which she had previously rejected, must continue on her own:

> . . . if only they had gone down together, down the caverns of the soul with picks, lanterns, cords, oxygen, X-rays, food, following the blueprints of all the messages from the geological depths where lay hidden the imprisoned self.[7]

Nin speaks of the 'eyes of memory' which see through the darkness. All through this journey, such memories spontaneously spring up prompted by certain sensory signals which translate internally:

> It was a night journey into the past, and the thread that had pulled her was one of accidental resemblance, familiarity, the past.[8]

With the minotaur myth as the substructure of this novelette, it is intimated that the Ariadnean thread is the thread of memory which pulls her back along the labyrinthine passageways of the past. One particular 'cue' along the way is her meeting with a certain character, an engineer Hatcher, who happens to resemble her father and his hairy fingers: 'Hatcher had hair on his fingers, like her father.'[9] This Hatcher becomes an 'echo' from the past, as Lillian journeys with him through a tunnel on a side excursion in a place called San Luis. For Lillian, Hatcher lights up what she calls 'these intersections of memory which were like double exposures',[10] evoking a superimposition of past events – journeys divided into 'two, four, six, eight skeins' – another indication of the labyrinthine structure. In this context a simultaneity of past events is experienced:

> She was speeding at the same rhythm along several dusty roads, as a child with parents, as a wife driving her husband, as a mother taking her children to school, as a pianist touring the world, and all these roads intersected. . . . [11]

Nin introduces another visual cue for Lillian's memory on her plane trip home. It is the view of a 6-year-old girl running up and down the aisle, which 'carried [Lillian] by a detour into the past, to a certain day in her childhood in Mexico'[12] when at the age of six she would receive spankings from her father. The recollection of the father, and the past, is heightened by a recall of a strange mixture of pain and pleasure – hence, a sensory trace is part of this memory. As such accidental cues multiply, it appears as if there are layers of memory which become uncovered along the journey. Eventually, however, they are ostensibly covered up again upon her return home. For in the ultimate vision that the character has on the airplane, the dreaded minotaur image incarnates the repressed memory. It is seen as a reflection of herself upon the windowpane of the plane – connecting memory to the mirror of a past which she wishes to forget. As this memory appears involuntarily on the windowpane, it triggers a stream of associative memory which links together selected images of her past – of relationships with Jay and Sabina during escapades of infidelity in Paris, of selected childhood impressions of her father – all of which the character eventually purges herself as she returns to her present and to the relationship with her husband, Larry.

In this highly figurative novelette, Nin puts a linguistic spin on what in recent years scientists such as Joseph Ledoux or Edmund Rolls have called the emotional brain. For her character, Nin actually envisages emotional traces in terms of grooves developed from molds and physically marked on the brain. The French use the word 'ornière' in translating these grooves. Metaphorically, Nin conveys the memory process in terms of her own footsteps which trace these grooves. Her poetic language reaches these imprints – what she eventually wants to forget as she extricates herself from the 'labyrinth of remembrance' because of its painful import:

> Erasing the grooves. It was not that Lillian had remained attached to the father, and incapable of other attachments. It was that the form of the relationship, the mold, had become a groove, the groove itself was familiar, her footsteps followed it habitually, unquestioningly, the familiar groove of pain and pleasure, of closeness at the cost of pain.[13]

Throughout the novelette, there exists the dialogue of remembering and forgetting, what Nin herself disputed with several psychoanalysts with whom she associated in the 1930s. Most commentators hold that the Dr Hernandez of *Seduction of the Minotaur* represents Nin's real-life psychiatrist and transient lover, Dr Otto Rank; both Rank and Hernandez insisted on the salutary effect of uncovering memory to deal with past traumas. Hence, the statement of Dr Hernandez, the physician, who boasts of being able to manipulate memory through drugs:

> There are so many kinds of drugs. One for remembering and one for forgetting. Golconda is for forgetting. But it is not a permanent forgetting. We may seem to forget a person, a place, a state of being, a past life, but meanwhile what we are doing is selecting a new cast for the reproduction of the same drama, seeking the closest reproduction to the friend, the lover, or the husband we are striving to forget. And one day we open our eyes, and there we are caught in the same pattern, repeating the same story. How could it be otherwise? The design comes from within us. It is internal.[14]

Instead of affirming, like Proust, that the present erases the past, Nin finds that the present constantly affirms the past. This design is what Nin perceives as memory traces which are indelible because they are emotionally engraved and repeated continuously over a lifetime in analogous patterns. For Nin, memory is a substrate upon which layers are imposed. The forgetting of such states is temporary. In the story, the protagonist Lillian sheds tears at hearing Hernandez insist that she probe her long-term past – what she has been striving all along to cover up. 'She plunged into the deep water again as if to wash her body of all memories, to wash herself of the past'[15] – a futile effort in this context. Ultimately, his death triggers her epiphany of the long-suppressed traumatic memory of her father. She involuntarily acquires that memory in the epiphanic moment of revelation of the minotaur, and then she voluntarily rejects it to proceed with her present life. In other instances in Nin's fiction, the failure to probe memory produces situations of stagnation. For Nin herself, such stalemate is surmounted through recourse to verbal art which transposes memory onto fiction.

The drama of the memory process traced in this novelette is found in much of Nin's other fiction. For example, there is the striking example of the story 'The Labyrinth' in the collection of *Under a Glass Bell*. This short piece first portrays the Diary itself as a physical labyrinth and repository for memory, as it was in the real life of Nin: 'I was eleven years old when I walked into the labyrinth of my diary.'[16] This diary is then made analogous to the winding serpentine city of Fez with the metaphor of language appearing: 'I was lost in the labyrinth of my confessions' and 'I was walking on a carpet of pages without number.' The walk through the labyrinth conveys the way language uncovers memory traces in the circuits of the brain. When Nin speaks of 'silence' and dreams, she is suggesting that some of those memory traces are left and trapped in deep recesses of interior cavities. Again, only through the intermediary of her literary art can they be fully excavated and dealt with.

In *Winter of Artifice*, an early novelette written in 1936, the persona Djuna, transparently representing Nin, revives her long-term memories of her father. As a 31-year-old woman she is reunited with him 20 years after he had abandoned her. As she recalls the crucial scene of his abandonment of her that she had construed repeatedly over the intervening years, she remembers the strong emotions linked to this permanent memory. Here, the description of an emotional memory is once again revealing through the intense imagery:

> There seemed to be a memory deeper than the usual one, a memory in the tissues and cells of the body on which we tattoo certain scenes which give a shape to one's soul and life habits. It was in this way she remembered most vividly that as a child a man had tortured her.[17]

The imprint, metaphorically represented by a physical tattoo, is like the splinter image or grooves of *Seduction of the Minotaur*. Nin construes long-term memory traces in a concrete manner. Personally, in her case, they remain deep and permanent scars left by her remembrance of a father who had abandoned her.

Ultimately, Nin intimates that if the Diary 'hides' the deeper older memories, her art, as the novel *Seduction of the Minotaur* and other

fiction show, successfully uncovers them. In exposing her deeper memories, her fiction liberates her from the constrictions of the labyrinth
which her life and its transcription in the diary had created. Specifically, it is Nin's artistic language of myth and metaphor that enacts this
process of memory recovery and transformation.

As in the case of Nin, Borges, the cosmopolitan Argentinian writer,
gives topographical imagery to the passageways of memory, also often
perceived in terms of the Daedalean labyrinth. As the artificer of the
labyrinth of art, he presents himself as endowed with the godlike power
of memory which elevates him to the position of 'El hacedor' or the
maker of handiwork. In giving this title to a collection of poetry and
prose as well as to a specific prose piece (1960), Borges considers his art
to be a selective kind of cultivation of memory, connected with crafts-
manship, which is to be distinguished from more 'ordinary' instances
of everyday memories. Borges' particular circumstance of problems with
eyesight, which eventually led to his blindness in 1955, heightens his
resort to memory. The subject of the short prose piece 'The Maker', also
going blind, descends into his memories 'descendió a su memoria'[18]
and is filled with certain memories, one of which includes a search for
a woman in subterranean galleries that were like labyrinths of stone.
The journeys to the past occur downward into darkness along circular
pathways.

As a poet, Borges introduces the notion of a threshold ['umbral'] of
time to recover his own past. His poem 'Adrogué', the title of which
refers to his family's summer place on the outskirts of Buenos Aires,
recovers his childhood past once again through the imagery of footsteps
as designating the mental process of retrieval. The poem starts off with
the depiction of night in which the poet gropes for symbols. In such
shadowy territory, suggestive of a dreamscape, he finds a landmark of a
coach-house and its associated smells of eucalyptus trees which initially
bring back the vanished past. Such is the atmosphere necessary to cross
the threshold:

> My step feels out and finds the anticipated
> Threshold. Its darkened limit is defined
> by the roof, and in the chessboard patio
> the watertap drips intermittently.
> On the farside of the doorways they are sleeping.[19]

This itinerary suggests a journey to the paganlike land of the 'sleeping'
or unconscious dead which the poet undertakes. It is not surprising,

therefore, that Borges should associate himself with the blind poet Homer who fashioned a visit to the underworld in *The Odyssey*, where memories of the dead were uncovered. As Borges, the modern day poet, crosses the crucial threshold, he reaches another dimension through the memory process: 'but all this happens in the strangeness of that fourth dimension which is memory'.

Borges substitutes for a mythic underworld a fourth dimension of space–time in which memory is awakened. That Borges should actually use this highly charged scientific expression of his era suggests that he has devised his own understanding of spatial time which helps him create his poetic imagery of the memory process. Throughout his poetry he invents such spaces as a kind of no-man's land. Such areas lodge the memory events transposed from actual, personal scenes of his past. For even as his poetic imagination allows for such leaps across thresholds into bouts of recollection, there is the dialectical movement of constant passing time and forgetting which can equally erase that recall and bring him back instantly to the present.

The poems 'Curso de los recuerdos' ('The Flow of Memories'), 'Everness', and 'La lluvia' ('Rain') also present variegated instances of retrieval through the imaginative power of memory. 'Curso de los recuerdos' focuses on the garden of a house, whose gate opens to 'narrow spaces'. 'Everness', with its English title, presents a universe which mirrors memory within the framework of eternity. The sonnet 'La lluvia' connects to a personal past, as the rain evokes the voice of Borges' father. The mirror image is a dominant one in the representation of the myriad reflections of memory, which accompany Borges' own quest for understanding infinity.

Such are some of the images associated with memory. But Borges also explicitly tackles the notion of memory and time in several interrelated prose pieces, which include the essays 'The Nothingness of Personality' (1922), 'A New Refutation of Time' (1944–47), and the fictions 'The Garden of Forking Paths' (1941) and 'Funes el memorioso' (1944). Cognizant of philosophical theories of time from the pre-Socratic Heraclitus to more modern discussions by Berkeley and Hume and the renowned Bergson, Borges wrestles with the notion of continuity in connection with memory.

In 'A New Refutation of Time', he dramatically recounts a 'déjà-vu' experience he had on the street corner in Barracas – which gives him a sense of eternity in the feeling of an identical moment of thirty years before. As he strolls in an unfamiliar zone, led by the familiarity of names of places, beyond the trodden paths of Barracas that were part of his past and childhood, he arrives at unknown borders of the city. He writes:

> I am not speaking of the specific surroundings of my childhood, my own neighborhood, but of its still mysterious borders, which I have possessed in words but little in reality.[20]

When he arrives at one particular corner, he revives a similar scene of thirty years before. He points out, however, that the feeling of 'sameness' with respect to the past derives not from the recovery of the scene itself but from its surviving trace in the word 'eternity' ('eternidad'). He writes:

> This is the same as it was thirty years ago. . . . I guessed at the date . . . No, I did not believe I had traversed the presumed waters of Time; rather I suspected that I possessed the reticent or absent meaning of the inconceivable word *eternity*. . . . The impartiality and inseparability of one moment of time's apparent yesterday and another of time's apparent today are enough to make it disintegrate.[21]

This memory state does not provide a Proustian experience of the past but a heightened experience of the present. Memory resides not in a metaphysical mind but in the very language that describes it: 'let the real moment of ecstasy and the possible insinuation of eternity which that night lavished on me, remain confined to this sheet of paper'.[22]

Borges had directly confronted the meaning of memory in an important early article 'The Nothingness of Personality' to dispel any idealized notion of a synthetic process of consolidation. He writes: 'memory is no more than the noun by which we imply that among the innumerable possible states of consciousness, many occur again in an imprecise way'.[23] In other words, for Borges, memory is only an approximation, a mediating designation or circumlocution of a temporary state of consciousness. With the repeated statement that 'the whole self does not exist', Borges considers memory within the context of the disintegrated personality, lacking a unifying superstructure which would organize the random incoming material as a 'past plenitude' ('plenitud de pasado'). He emphatically attacks the idea that memory is a storage place, like a granary ('troj') or a warehouse ('almacén'). Instead, it consists of lapsed instants that can be lost because they might not have left lasting marks. Therefore, here and in other works, Borges envisages a 'babble' of language, confused memories, always incomplete, which flow existentially along circular paths unsequentially. On the other hand, through the intermediary of his poetry, he is able as a writer to seize intermittently epiphanic moments of recollection in their transient nature.

To further dispel the notion that memory involves simple content, Borges gives examples of the chaos of memory that he treats ultimately in the Funes story, years later. In the disturbing narrative 'Funes el memorosio' ('Funes, His Memory') (1944), Borges satirically presents a type of idiot-savant who, having fallen from a horse and been knocked unconscious at the age of 19, acquires a prodigious memory. For example, Funes is capable of recalling minute details in the past such as the forms of the clouds on a particular day in 1882 and compare them to the veins in the marbled binding of a book that he once saw. He is able to perceive every grape that had been pressed into glasses of wine. He is able to learn instantly many languages like Latin, for example, reciting passages from Pliny's *Natural History* and a short section in which actual cases of prodigious memory are listed.[24] It is especially interesting that Funes remembers every detail of every dream he has ever had. As with the surrealist perspective, this suggests that rational logic blocks out aspects of memory and prevents normal people from reconstructing the totality of the dream. In contrast, Funes admits: 'My dreams are like other people's waking hours.'[25] Funes has a kind of unconscious memory, automatic in nature, but not controlled or retained in artistic language.

Jarringly, therefore, this character becomes immersed in a babble of language. If, as he admits, his memory is 'like a garbage heap', this prodigious memory, which collects every particular detail, interferes with his ability to reason or synthesize the incoming material. Borges may be unwittingly confronting an empirical model of memory which involves storage without the organization that the imagination gives. In this ironic display of a character, memory reaches its ultimate postmodern stage of chaotic disintegration.

Borges, himself, as a writer, did not go so far, admitting for one, that his own memory was fortunately faulty, that forgetting was necessary for the reconstructive faculty of the imagination to come into play. His story 'The Zahir' suggests that true memory requires a fixation or concentration rather than a proliferation of thought. Often that fixation is on a discrete object. In one of its meanings as a coin, the Zahir is a distinct object which reminds the narrator-persona of a beautiful dead woman, Teodolina. The concept of the 'hypostat' in Borges' stories – to borrow a term used by the critic Carter Wheelock – clarifies this aspect of memory which reifies and enlarges. In his book *The Mythmaker*,

Wheelock defines the term as: 'one aspect of reality that is momentarily elevated above all others'.[26] When applied to the memory process, this focus suggests selectivity and concentration. When interviewed at the age of 80 by Willis Barnstone, Borges made the following comment regarding his own memory:

> But of course, I live in memory. And I suppose a poet should live in memory because, after all, what is imagination? Imagination, I should say, is made of memory and of oblivion.[27]

Borges goes on to refer to his character Funes who 'goes mad because his memory is endless'.[28] Through the distorted manifestation of Funes's memory, Borges had examined the insignificant scope of human memory, in contrast to his own more selective and artistic memory.

Whereas Borges was demonstrative and analytical in dealing with memory, as the Funic situation showed, his younger contemporary Paz subsumed memory to the larger process of poetic creation. Many of his poems from the 1950s to the 1970s graphically depict the emergence of memory through the act of poetic writing itself. One of the most poetic monuments to memory and language is his poem 'Pasado en claro' (1975), a title which in its very ambiguity of translation from the Spanish to English suggests the multivalent connotations of Paz's view of memory. The translation of this poem as 'A Draft of Shadows',[29] however inaccurate it may be in literal terms, does extract from the original Spanish title the implication of the passage of memory from a shadowy draft to the clarity of a clean copy. With the equivocal meaning of 'pasado' as both the past and the passage, and with its closeness to the word 'pasos' or steps, the title suggests that the poet is capable through his acts of language to reproduce and rewrite a past clarified and lit up by an interior sun – which is the poetic imagination. Here it is not a question of an exterior sensory stimulus, as it was with Proust, but of an interior one provoked by 'the subsoil of language' ('el subsuelo del lenguaje') with words serving as the stimuli. Memory is built with words, whose shadows are the reflections of the past. Words are the interior eyes which trace the past and reproduce it for the poet in its pristine form. 'I am inside the eye', Paz writes, as he speaks of memory as insight. Paz writes about the capacity of the eyes to hear – creating a mixed metaphor for the act of poetry which combines image and sound. This recovery of the past demonstrably breaks down verb tense: 'Yo estoy en donde estuve':

> I am where I was:
> I walk behind the murmur,
> Footsteps within me, heard with my eyes,
> The murmur is in the mind, I am my footsteps . . .
> I am the shadow my words cast.[30]

In the very first and last stanzas of the poem, the poet speaks of 'pasos mentales', of mental footsteps which bridge letters to each other in the formation of words and their recreation of the past. 'Words glitter in the shadows', he writes. Words give him entrance into an interior world of memory. Memory is as much an invention as a retrieval. With his use of the word 'mental', Paz suggests a cerebral mechanism of memory which enacts transformations that function by way of additions and erasures. The present subsumes the past that is recalled.

With lines from Wordsworth's autobiographical poem *The Prelude* as its epitaph, Paz's poem is also a return to a childhood past presented through the eyes of a young boy. But rather than fabricating a narration that reconstructs the autobiographical past in chronological, linear sequence, Paz returns to particular fragments of his childhood scene in Mexico. Paz mentions a primeval garden and its ash tree, the sounds of the Mexican Aztec language, the school dictation, the plaza, the trees, the church, the arcade, the portal, the house inhabited by the elderly. Such images from the past become woven together through the act of language.

The metamorphosis of memory is specifically conveyed through the recollection of a natural object central to his childhood: the fig tree in his village of Mixcoac. Elsewhere Paz described the fig tree's germination: 'The fig tree, six months dressed in sonorous green, the other six a charred ruin of the summer sun.'[31] In this prose poem, he speaks of the fig tree's metamorphosis, creating an objective correlative of the memory process from the natural, physical world. Just as the fig tree passes without blossoms directly to its fruit, so does memory arise through a metamorphosis of images out of darkness by the transforming power of language. Again, sunlight transfigures the tree, analogous to language recreating the past scene.

The entire garden is a resource for memory. The poet must sift through the 'dead' material of the past presented as dried seeds, broken letters, scattered names. The poem itself sculpts and revives the errant sounds on a page of signs which retrieves the past. Mirrors and echoes suggest the reflective power of words to recreate the past. They are memories built with words.

For Paz, memory is not a stable object of retrieval, nor a static scene. In contrast to a writer like Proust who recaptures childhood scenes as tangible realities, Paz transforms such scenes into constructs of language. It is not a garden, but a garden of memory. It is not a patio, for example, but a patio of words:

> I am where I was:
> Within the indecisive walls
> Of that same patio of words.[32]

Like Nin, Paz recovers inner cities which are spaces, not places, within himself where his writing gives access to the past. Accordingly, Paz perceives language to be the receptacle for the memory retrieval in the mind. Memory for Paz is an invention of writing, an act of creation, where the only reality is language and its transforming power. Writing itself or 'escritura' illuminates the past, bringing it out of the shadows in illuminations which are reminiscent of Rimbaud:

> The sun, in my writing, drinks the shadows.
> Between the walls – not of stone,
> but raised by memory–[33]

Paz's favorite indigenous images of the salamander and the sunstone, and their respective associations of fire and light, further suggest the illuminating power of language to swallow up the darkness of apparent oblivion. Thereupon, a sense of timeless present is created in the retrieval of the past. Ultimately, language is the transforming agent for Paz. But Paz suggests how the memory process proceeds from darkness to light in two early poems 'Sun Stone' and 'Solo for Two Voices' from the collection *Salamandra* which set personal memory in the context of cosmic time marked by solar and lunar phenomena.

If the long poem 'Sun Stone'(1957), overtly makes its 584 free verses correspond to the revolution of the planet Venus, it also makes more subtle references to Paz's native Aztec cosmology, whose calendar begins with the year of the East and birth of the sun. Within such contexts of cyclical time, suggested by the calendar stone, Paz puts memory in timelessness. In what becomes a typical itinerary for memory in Paz's poetry, the poet takes himself on a journey through dark, labyrinthine passageways, 'limitless corridors of memory'[34] ('corredores sin fin de la memoria') as he enters fictional empty houses tracking shadows of the past. Along the way, he recovers the single memory of an individual moment 'el instante' which then goes through a process of expansion and germination. It is fascinating to see how Paz uses the metaphor of soil, designated in 'Pasado en claro' as subsoil of language, for the territory of the brain from which memories grow:

> The numinous moment shines, pierces itself
> and ripens inward, ripens and puts forth roots,
> it grows within me, it completely fills me
> lavishes out on me delirious branches . . . [35]

Memories are roots in the dark which grow into a tree, a symbol for the poet's imagination. Paz uses physical language to suggest the growth process of germination and ripening.

In the case of this poem, the darkness is underscored by the suggestion that it is memory perhaps from a dream, 'a moment/recovered tonight, standing against a dream'.[36] If the memory specifically involves an unforgettable moment of adolescent love, the female is the catalyst providing illumination, reinforced by Paz's subsequent reference to mythical females such as the water sprite Melusine, the legendary nymph of transformation. Yet another clue to the process of transformation with respect to the memory process is the allusion to the mercury circulating in his veins as the moment ripens:

> and in my veins its mercury circulates,
> the tree of the mind . . .
> the past is not the past, but it is here, now.[37]

In the physical world mercury is a catalyst, and the conversion is instantaneous, as in the change of verb tense from 'fue' (was) to 'está siendo' (is happening now).

Hence, in 'Sun Stone' memory involves catalytic change as Paz focuses upon the turning point of poetic instants which bring forth memory in the journey out of labyrinthine darkness. In this process, the forehead ('el frente'), as a symbol for the mind, is also scrutinized. At first it is described as being 'sightless' in the night-time. Eventually, however, as the memory emerges, the sun penetrates the forehead and succeeds in awakening the brain: 'The sun has forced an entrance through my forehead.'[38] Similarly, in 'Pasado en claro', the sun opens the forehead 'el sol abre mi frente'. In 'Sun Stone', water imagery, in terms of rivers, does not suggest a stream of consciousness, but a purification of the mind from dead language in the recovery process. The poem begins and ends with an evocation of a kind of timeless paradise setting of poplar trees, fountains, willows, rivers, which suggest eternal time and recurrence, under the aegis of what was called a 'timeless sun'. For Paz, memory awakens the mind and brings it into relations with the cosmos beyond the confines of earthbound time.

Paz's poem 'Solo for Two Voices' from the collection *Salamandra* connects such memory retrieval more specifically with acts of language. With its magical power of transformation, language itself is catalytic. Using the same metaphors as in 'Sun Stone', Paz calls memory 'a root in the dark',[39] but here language specifically is the agent that uncovers it. In the atmosphere of the winter solstice, when the sun is 'in exile' ('desterrado') at its farthest point south of the equator, and darkness reigns, memory emerges from the darkness of forgetting as poetic language prunes away dead words to recast letters which recreate the past. As in 'Pasado en claro' there is reference to the 'clean world' which emerges in memory. Like the Surrealists, Paz is intent on purifying language in a passage from opacity to transparency, resulting from verbal illumination. The critic Jason Wilson has invented the term 'mentalist poetics' to describe Paz's activity of the mind in language. Wilson gives an example: 'A metaphor of vertigo and the vision granted by the *instante poético* is provided by the notion of transparency.'[40] Such transparency is linked to the power of memory.

Certain common concrete images of the natural world can be gleaned from Paz's poetry to show his organic view of the memory process. There is the central symbol of the sun as well as the soil, the roots, the river, the tree – earthy elements suggesting the fertile terrain of the brain. Memory involves germination from dark environments and subsequent illumination. It involves catalytic transformation – what is, in fact, anticipatory of modern-day scientists' view of memory transmission by neurotransmitters.

It is also interesting that Paz's poems 'El balcón' and 'Vuelta' ('Return') pick up Baudelaire's image of the balcony as the site of memory retrieval but go on to internalize it. The image of the balcony acquires a mental concreteness, which spatializes the time factor in the workings of memory. Memory involves purviews from heights. In 'Vuelta' memory is a balcony over the void of an abyss as the poet has difficulty in retrieving the Mixcoac of twelve years before because of the intrusion of the present, crass modern scene. Earlier in the poem

'El balcón' the poet more successfully 'touches' the distant memories with his thoughts amidst the vertigoes surrounding the balcony. Paz writes:

> Elbows leaning on the balcony
> I see
> This distance that is so near[41]

For the Mexican poet and his Aztec tradition, time and space are fused, as he himself points out in essays on the Mexican character, *El laberinto de la soledad*. The French ethnologist Jacques Soustelle has explained this cosmology of ancient Mexicans: 'Each space is linked to a time or to time. Thus Mexican mentality does not know the abstract time and space but rather places and events.'[42] Moreover, rather than the linear sense of time in the Western world, a circular sense of time is experienced – that which readily applies to the labyrinthine passageways of the poet seeking traces of memory.

Nin, Borges and Paz, therefore, retrieve memories not as coherent pictures of the past but as verbal signifiers. Together they create a version of modernist memory which involves close focus rather than a narrative recall of linked events. For them, memory is neither integrative nor synthetic, as it was with previous writers. It is not substance to be recovered. Instead, it is a succession of desultory images, which are catalyzed into the density of metaphor and metonymy. Arising from layers of the fragmented personality, these word-images are a resource for appropriation by verbal art. Octavio Paz put it best when he said, 'Language and myth are vast metaphors of reality.'[43] For him and other modernists 'each word conceals a certain metaphorical charge that is ready to explode as soon as the secret mechanism is tripped'. By recapturing such resonant words of the past, these writers are able to recreate their memories.

For these writers language carries the memory traces. Those traces are registered for Nin as a 'groove' reached by the footsteps of language, as a selective noun like 'eternity' which designates the retrieval for Borges, and as the subsoil of language from which poetic metaphors grow for Paz. For Nin, childhood trauma impelled her to reject the exact and painful substance of memory on behalf of myth. For Borges, the memory process is the triage by which words survive as selected fragments that fertilize the imagination. For Paz, the memory germinates and is catalyzed in poetic images. All three Hispanic writers convey an earthy sense of memory, which germinates out of darkness through the poetic image into the mythic dimension. Their poetic language becomes the ultimate mediator and illuminator of a buried past recovered through the engrossing present of verbal art which approximates the memories on the written page.

8

The Almond and the Seahorse: Neuroscientific Perspectives

In the last decade of the twentieth century, designated by *Scientific American* as the century of the brain, special attention was paid to the role of the limbic system in the creation of long-term memory. Two particular sections of the brain were implicated: the amygdala and the hippocampus, seen by some to work hand in hand, moving from the emotional to the cognitive components of memory.[1] Notably, the distinctions between these two structures of the brain have exciting repercussions for understanding the literary material I have already displayed. I am using their juxtaposition as a metaphor to distinguish between forms of mental processing. That is to say, on the simplest level, two sorts of memory can be detected: the sensory-emotional one on the one hand, and the factually based cognitive kind, on the other. Both structures receive and integrate inputs from specialized sites of the cerebral cortex and are therefore intermediaries in the ultimate formation of memory. They are mediators in the circuit of memory, which involves encoding, storage and retrieval – that can be detected in both science and literature.

It is my intention here to provide a panoramic overview of main developments of memory research that can help inform the interpretation of literary texts and artistic works. Specifically, the juxtaposition of different approaches in scientific memory research, as here presented, helps illuminate the classification of the diverse memory events that have been discussed in this book. In turn, such literary works may also enhance the evidentiary base for refining the theories and perspectives which have developed to date in this nascent field. It is a strange fact, for example, that the only major recourse to the literary field by the scientists is the single madeleine incident of Proust, which has provided continuous debate over the functions of the amygdala and hippocampus.

135

The many more untapped, wide-ranging examples of memory events that this book has uncovered can be further assessed in terms of the ongoing scientific discussion of memory scrutinized in the current chapter.

Whereas the almond-shaped amygdala is seen in the immediate reception of emotion, the seahorse-shaped hippocampus has come to be known as the processing center which strengthens connections over time between incoming perceptions into consolidations that become memory. Furthermore these two structures seem to represent demarcations between unconscious automatic memory and conscious deliberate memory. Conspicuously, the evolutionarily older amygdala has been seen to store memory about emotional states, memory for motor and sensory experiences. As such it has been characterized by neuroscientists as implicit, nondeclarative memory. On the other hand, the adjacent and larger hippocampus harbors memory of facts and personal events, producing explicit, declarative memory. In fact, damage to the hippocampus has been found to cause amnesia in animals such as rats and monkeys. Such damage is known to impair explicit memory in humans; on the other hand, damage to the amygdala has no such effect. The neuroscientist Stuart Zola-Morgan, in experiments with animals, found in 1989 that lesions in the amygdala did not impair declarative memory, whereas lesions in the hippocampus did.[2] Furthermore, it appears that for the amygdala, stimuli produce the memory, whereas for the hippocampus, it is the context itself, the place or environment, that produces the memory. Along with such distinctions, however, there are necessary connections between the amygdala and the hippocampus which continue to be explored.

Autobiographical memory, what the psychologists and neuroscientists often call 'episodic memory', is associated with the hippocampus and takes its place at the top of the hierarchical divisions of memory systems. It has been defined as 'a memory of events personally lived and situated in their temporal and spatial context of acquisition'.[3] It is a conscious awareness of past happenings, to be distinguished from dreaming, imaging and problem solving. Furthermore, in this type of recall, 'retrieval is most effective when it occurs in the same context in which the information was acquired and in the presence of the same cues'.[4] That is to say, there is similarity between the context of encoding and conditions of retrieval, what some might call the 'engraphy' and the 'ecphory'. It was originally the Canadian neuropsychologist Endel Tulving who held this view and coined the term 'episodic memory' in 1972 in a paper which distinguished it from semantic memory or timeless knowledge shared with others.[5] Tulving, who went on to write an entire book on the subject,[6] contributed largely to this encoding specificity principle and the functional properties of what he designated as 'retrieval cues'.

This type of long-term episodic memory is characterized by a richness of phenomenological detail, a sense of reliving the experience, a sense of a travel through time, and a feeling of exact reproduction of the past. The setting or place as well as the emotional state would be included in such retrieval. In the terms of cognitive psychologists, like William F. Brewer, such 'personal memory' is described as a 'recollection of a particular episode from an individual's past' which 'frequently appears to be a "reliving" of the individual's phenomenal experience during that earlier moment. The contents almost always include reports of visual memory.'[7] Recall of the earlier mental experience is said to be included. Accordingly, Rousseau's and Wordsworth's meditations about childhood would fit into this category; Wordsworth went back to the particular place to retrieve the memory; Rousseau simply evoked a past mood generated by a particular setting or place. In Rousseau's case, it is the emotion which produces the memory in the encoding stage, and the memory which reproduces the emotion in the retrieval stage. The Romantic ethos of sincerity and authenticity attaches a belief value to those memories with the conviction that they are 'true' and veridical.

This widely accepted definition of episodic memory, however, tends to yield a rather narrow view of autobiographical memory. In fact, the scrutiny of a whole literary subgenre of fictional autobiography, referred to in some of the literary examples, suggests that this form of memory is more complex and broader than scientists might believe. It is telling, therefore, that the contemporary American psychologist Daniel Schacter calls attention to the notion of memory distortion as a natural and common vulnerability of personal memory, often observed in cases of frontal lobe damage. For example, he maintains that 'source memory', the ability to recall when and where an event transpired, may be easily impaired. This deficit may occur before reaching the structures of the medial temporal lobe. In Schacter's view, failures in source memory can lead to what he calls 'confabulation' or false recollections of events that did not in fact take place. Moreover, since the encoding process involves the subjective element of experience and draws on degrees of preexisting knowledge, it can introduce further distortion. It's common, after all, for two people to have entirely different experiences of the same event. Also, Schacter writes of the altering effects of present circumstances on past events: 'New memories are inevitably influenced by old memories, which opens the door to distortion as a relatively common occurrence'.[8] Even the way the past is probed or questioned can create distortions. Schacter thus focuses most of all on the contextual aspect of the retrieval environment as 'the distorting effects of present circumstances on past events'[9] – what constitutes an important variable in the acquisition of memory and its reconstruction of the past. From this perspective, Schacter's theories could offer a view of Rousseau and his Romantic imagination that is quite different from the idealistic premises of Rousseau's own era which involve subjectivity as a necessary component of retrieval. The scientific notion of confabulation also jars with Salvador Dalí's playful but defined notion of 'authentic false childhood memories' stemming from his dream-based surrealist imagination. Dalí, in remembering such memories that were construed by his childhood imagination, holds that they are real: 'The difference between false memories and true ones is the same as for jewels: it is always the false ones that look the most real, the most brilliant.'[10]

With a different perspective from Schacter's and without the supportive recourse to literary texts, the British neuroscientists Tim Shallice and Paul Burgess use the term 'confabulation' to designate a normal element of healthy autobiographical memory. These scientists go beyond the more common consideration of it as a clinical concern arising from frontal lobe lesions or 'source' amnesias due to aging. In concentrating on long-term memory, Shallice envisaged 'nested structures involving a number of processing domains'.[11] Since such stratifications could require in turn a multilevel process of retrieval, lapses in memory could then occur in normal subjects. Such superimpositions of memory with selective lapses are apparent in, for example, Faulkner's juxtaposition of memory sequences, Apollinaire's displacements of memory events, and Anaïs Nin's architectural layering of inner landscapes, as seen in the examples from literature. Moreover, it is interesting to observe that such gaps are often seized upon opportunistically by creative writers as material for artistic creation.

Also, more generally, conflations of memory have been recognized by some cognitive psychologists as giving rise to a variation of personal memory called 'generic memory'. For example, Brewer explains: 'Repeated exposure to a set of related experiences can give rise to a generic image of the experiences.'[12] Generic memory, therefore, lacks the specificity with respect to a precise time period or date in the past, and renders instead a conglomerate of repeated experiences. The best example would be repeated summer experiences resulting from a return to the same place, year after year. Virginia Woolf's *To the Lighthouse* would certainly fall into this category, as it transforms specific recall to levels of abstraction. This type of recollection can be distinguished from 'source memories' which refer to specific times and places for the memory events.

ˑ Woolf admitted, however, that outside of her art, she did retain specific memories which were 'sealed' by way of visual 'scene making'. This particular manner of encoding and storing visual memories could be especially pertinent to the work of the neuroscientist Alain Berthoz, who is keenly interested in the hippocampal functioning with respect to spatial memory and memory of place. In particular, he has been interested in visual memory acquired through the perception of visual objects or space in movement in cortical areas, from the frontal cortex deeper in the parietal cortex, which is a locale for what he terms 'topokinetic memory'. His article 'Parietal and Hippocampal Contribution to Topokinetic and Topographic Memory' implicates the neurons of the hippocampus as serving in the storage of such memories. Berthoz contends that this dynamic process is based on multisensory cues including a sense of movement or kinesthesia (added to the traditional five senses) and involving the connection of several brain structures. He notes that the left hippocampus is especially operative in memories of the relation between whole-body movements and the environment.[13] Elsewhere, in his book *Le Sens du mouvement* (1997) Berthoz had pointed to the intricate function of the hippocampus in processing a 'configurational memory of events and the temporal sequence in which these events occurred'.[14] Berthoz applauds the neuroscientist Edmund Rolls for considering this role of the hippocampus as is manifest in the reconstruction of memory from partial elements:

> For me, one of the most fascinating aspects of Rolls's theory is that he identified, in the neuronal structure of the hippocampal network, properties that enable it to recall an episode or a combination of sensations given only a portion of the information initially memorized.

In fact, the British neuroscientist Edmund Rolls presented in his paper 'A Theory of Hippocampal Function in Memory' (1997) the notion that a partial memory cue in the autoassociative network of the hippocampus can contribute to the formation of long-term episodic memories. Rolls posits that if such autoassociation can allow various elements of an episode, for example, its spatial context, the people present, what was seen, etc., to be stored as one memory event, then its recall from a fragment by way of back-projections from the hippocampus to the neocortex can occur:

> Later recall of that episode from the hippocampus in response to a partial cue can then lead to reinstatement of the activity in the neocortex that was originally present during the episode. The theory described here shows how the episodic memory could be stored in the hippocampus and later retrieved to the neocortex.[15]

Subsequently, in his book *The Brain and Emotion* (1999), Rolls went on to focus on the emotional component within this contextual aspect of memory storage and retrieval. He writes: 'It is suggested that whenever memories are stored, part of the context is stored with the memory.'[16] This phenomenon readily applies to Romantic memory, as has been seen. According to Rolls, another aspect of emotional processing concerns memory retrieval in that 'the recall of a memory occurs best in such networks when the input key to the memory is nearest to the input original pattern of activity which was stored. It thus follows that a memory of, for example, a happy episode is recalled best when in a happy mood state.'[17] Again, the locus for such contextual processing is thought to be in the associative neuronal networks of the hippocampus. In line with the approach of William James, more recently, Tulving and Rolls consider memory to be often dependent on emotional conditions at the time of retrieval.

An acute form of emotional recall is described by the catchy term 'flashbulb memory'[18] first introduced by the cognitive psychologists Roger Brown and James Kulik to designate a shocking, common external event that preserves the personal experience of it. The Kennedy assassination or, more recently, the Terrorist attack on the World Trade Center in New York City are clear examples. Discussion of such emotion-triggered memories has centered on the structure of the amygdala. In terms of literary examples, James Joyce's Christmas dinner scene proves to be a particularly poignant memory for the young artist because it relates to the death of the controversial Irish leader Charles Parnell.

The connection of emotion with memory has surfaced in another form in Joseph Ledoux's best seller *The Emotional Brain* (1996), which focused in particular on the amygdala as the receptor of the 'model emotion' of fear. This subject leads to studies about fear conditioning, which becomes particularly interesting to psychologists and psychoanalytical approaches to autobiographical literature, concentrating on traumas, childhood abuse, and the like. Although studies of such emotion can bring insight into the topic of the neural basis of memory, he has cautioned[19] about the general unreliabity of brain mapping and tracing in studies of localization since certain areas of the brain can be bypassed under certain conditions, as in the direct shortcut route from the sensory thalamus to the amygdala. As previously mentioned, both Woolf and Nin averred that memory can leave its trace by painful emotion.

Historically speaking, the phenomena of engrams have been pursued from the time of their discovery by the German biologist Richard Semon in 1904. It was he who coined the term for the cumulative encoding and storage of an enduring memory trace. Subsequently, the word was given prominence in the article 'In Search of the Engram' (1950) by the Harvard psychologist Karl Lashley. Ironically, what may not be fully acknowledged in the frequent citation of this article is that it actually provided more questions than answers in the search for the so-called engrams. As a behaviorist interested in the effects of brain damage on the ability to acquire habits, Lashley himself concentrated on the sensory areas of the cerebral cortex, refusing to delve into subcortical levels. He humbly declared that his experimentation 'has discovered nothing directly of the real nature of the engram'.[20] He challenged the previous studies of nineteenth-century clinical neurology that attempted to localize specific memory traces. For he argued that pathways of specific memory traces across the cortex were not identifiable. Influenced by Gestalt psychology, Lashley was suggesting that there were other factors in the detection of memory which included 'the pattern'[21] of energy on the sense organ, the factors of space and time, the combinative activity of neurons as in 'reverberatory circuits'. He declared that 'there is no great excess of cells which can be reserved as the seat of special memories'.[22] He also demonstrated that associative areas of the neocortex could not be considered to be static storehouses of memory and saw them rather as being 'concerned with modes of organization'.[23] Despite Lashley's conclusion that it is 'not possible to demonstrate the isolated localization of a memory trace', he seems responsible for spurring some future scientists on in search of sites for specific memory functions in considering the engram as a physical entity.

Interestingly, the 'literary' case of Proust proves the point about the intricacies of memory tracing. The famous Proustian paradigm of memory remains all the more complex since it is both autobiographical and stimulus-produced, dependent on the contingencies of the 'present' to evoke the past. In fact, Proust is the only writer seriously referred to by scientists in their discussions about the localization of engrams. At first, scientists envisaged engrams of the Proustian kind in the context of the amygdala for understandable reasons, given Proust's focus on sensory stimuli of memory and its inextricable link with emotion – notably the 'rush' of exquisite feelings. Such a localization was based on the established connections between the amygdala and emotion. The inspiration of Proust leads a neuroanatomist like Herbert P. Killackey to marvel at the morphological complexity of the neocortex – 'the extensive role of sensory imagery in the memory process, and, by extension the role of the neocortex toward which most sensory information is directed'.[24] Like others, this scientist refers unilaterally to the taste and smell of Proust's madeleine as suggestive of the fact that chemical senses play an important role in the memory process. The poet Baudelaire could also be brought into this discussion because of his keen olfactory sense which is a gateway to his memories; after all researchers have singled out the highly charged emotive aspect of the olfactory sensations due to their most direct route to the limbic system.

Subsequently, scientists like Larry Squire and Stuart Zola-Morgan laid the groundwork for placing the madeleine episode in the autoassociative network of the neurons of the hippocampus because of the role of this organ in the integration of the various perceptions once the initial trigger is called up. Their landmark paper 'The Medial Temporal Lobe Memory System' (1991) in the journal *Science* featured the hippocampus as the principal storage site relied upon and called upon by the neocortex in the evocation of long-term declarative memory.[25] Models of human and animal amnesia were used to detect the anatomical components of such coordinated memory function. In a later article 'Memory, Hippocampus and Brain Systems' (1995) Squire went on to develop his view of the hippocampus as part of the larger structure of the medial temporal lobe, which includes the entorhinal cortex, the parahippocampal cortex, and the perirhinal cortex. Specifically for declarative memory, he has concluded that the amygdala is excluded from this system. Squire's main goals have been to 'link particular brain regions and systems to various kinds of memory' and to locate 'where the synaptic changes occur that support different kinds of memory'.[26] Generations after Lashley, Squire considers this search for exact localization of memory sites as the challenge for neuroscience in the future. So, too, the jury is still out on the madeleine episode.

Whereas Proust has been connected to the study of engrams, poets like Baudelaire and Paz fall within the context of biochemical approaches to the study of memory. Their evocation of certain memories is conveyed as a chemical process, actually compared metaphorically to drug-induced states by Baudelaire and expressed by the catalytic power of poetic language by Octavio Paz. In neuroscience, the subject of tracing on the synaptic level has offered significant results for neuropharmacologists, who come to be known by *the* chemical enzyme they identify in the creation and the strengthening of neuronal circuits. The creation of synapses in any of the structures involves a chain reaction which connects signals through a junction from one neuron to another. The biochemical side of such transmissions has become spectacular with the focus on neurotransmitters which ultimately account for the synaptic transmissions by way of certain enzymes that are activated. Eric Kandel, who early on examined the activity of nerve cells in the hippocampus, has studied protein synthesis (that activates adenylyl cyclase) and gene expression required for changes in synaptic connectivity for the creation of long-term memory.[27] The molecular biologist Tim Tully, in dealing with the genetic etiology of memory, has most vividly referred to the protein CREB as a 'master switch' that, when turned on as a result of recurrent events, induces long-term memory.[28] Of course, in current and past studies, various neurotransmitters have been identified as memory enhancers. For example, acetylcholine for Jean-Pierre Changeux (subsequently interesting for those who study Alzheimer's Disease), serotonin for J.T. Goldberg and Antonio Damasio, dopamine for Arvid Carlsson and Jacques Glowinski, protein kinase A for Aryeh Routtenberg, caplain for Gary Lynch, syntaxin for Serge Laroche, glutamate for T.H. Brown and Joseph Ledoux. Moreover, it has been shown that varying doses can have positive or negative effects.

In neurotransmitter systems, hormonal influences have been studied in terms of modulations of memory: 'memory storage may normally be regulated by stress-related hormones that are released by emotionally arousing experiences'.[29] For example, James McGaugh, among others, has singled out norepinephrine to be a memory enhancer when injected into the amygdala.[30] It is also commonplace to cite the age-old adrenaline as a memory enhancer. Moreover, in this chemical context of memory, standard Freudian notions of repression of traumatic memories can be explained in terms of certain opiates such as enkephalins. As the neurobiologist Ted Abel and his colleagues have noted: 'A painful incident may lead to repression because endogenous opiates are released in response to the experience, and these in turn can interfere with the memory storing process.'[31] Anaïs Nin, with her metaphor of chemical compounds forming unconscious memories, comes to mind here.

The structural aspects of brain circuitry have also been studied in the hippocampus, where the strengthening of synapses can be detected. The fascinating process of the catalytic neurotransmitters is said to lead to the modification of the neurons' dendrites, making the neurons more susceptible to incoming information. The neurobiologist Gary Lynch has explored the structural changes in the hippocampal neurons. Throughout his research, he has continuously presented a neuroanatomical model of the combination networks of sensory inputs. His early, pathbreaking studies in the 1980s focused on a schema which pointed to the changes of the dendritic spines that are prompted by electrical signals and enzyme activity as the increased receptivity by neurotransmitters created new synapses for the rapid formation of memories.[32] His 1986 book *Synapses, Circuits and the Beginnings of Memory* probed the olfactory-hippocampal circuit in this respect. In his focus on the hippocampal region as a model for the study of the brain as a whole, he selected olfaction 'as a model for cortical combinatorial systems',[33] because the sense of smell is directly interconnected with various parts of the limbic system. As discussed, Baudelaire's poetry, marked by intense olfactory memories, gives further evidence for such directed synaptic formations.

Clearly, the field of brain research has become highly specialized and segmented. This is particularly true in the United States, where three major approaches can be discerned: the biochemical, the structural and the electrophysiological. Nevertheless, a few scientists have accompanied such physiological discussions with reflections about larger philosophical issues. A leading exemplar is Antonio Damasio, the biologist who has spoken about 'Descartes error', what he defines as the French philosopher's dualist notion positing for Western thought 'the abyssal separation between body and mind'.[34] Damasio has even contested his colleagues, the neuroscientists who go the other way and view the mind exclusively in terms of brain events without regard for its customary interaction with the coexisting social and physical environments. In his 1994 book Damasio objected to the notion of an intellect independent of emotion, and he attacked the Cartesian concept of a 'disembodied mind', the fallacious view that 'the suffering that comes from physical pain or emotional upheaval might exist separately from the body'.[35] With his study of what he calls the 'neurobiology of rationality', Damasio was at the vanguard of theorizing the biological link between memory and emotion.

The metaphysical issues raised by Damasio have been confronted more broadly by leading scientists in France where the Cartesian tradition is ingrained in the collective consciousness. Two prominent conferences took place in the 1990s focusing on Bergsonian legacy for neuroscience – which naturally brings larger issues into light.[36] I have witnessed first hand that a particularly intense, ongoing discussion has emerged among leading scientists at the prestigious Collège de France, the old forum for experimental psychology at the beginning of the last century. It is as if we have come full circle a century later. The implications of such debates for the study of memory are especially stimulating in view of the pragmatic studies which are overwhelming the field. The neuroscientist Alain Berthoz has become a mediating figure in such debates, having assembled a book *Leçons sur le corps, le cerveau et l'esprit* featuring some of the initiators of the cognitive sciences at the Collège de France who were concerned as well with the broader perspectives. Despite his own specializations, Berthoz has urged a synthetic approach which would take into consideration necessary interactions between the network of psychologies and the various physiological approaches to the nervous system. Berthoz's own statement 'il faut passer du cerveau à la pensée'[37] ['we must pass from the brain to thought'] highlights the challenge for a larger understanding of mental processes.

It is an interesting, basic fact that problematics surround the use and translation of the French word 'esprit', which in turn shapes the way the study of memory is discussed. I have called attention to the point that, despite the ambiguous meaning of the word, the poet Baudelaire had begun to connect 'l'esprit' to a physical brain or 'le cerveau' as concerns the stimulation of the senses, a very avant-garde notion for a writer of his time. Still, I find it very illuminating that some current-day scientists have become cautious about giving equivalents for the word 'esprit'.[38] A striking instance is found in a parenthesis in the original French version of Changeux's *L'Homme neuronal*, which is deleted in the official English language translation of the book, *Neuronal Man*:

Le débat sur le 'mind–body problem' (que les auteurs français hésitent à traduire: problème des relations de 'l'âme' et du corps!) n'existe que dans la mesure où l'on affirme que l'organisation fonctionnelle du système nerveux ne correspond pas à son organisation neurale.[39]

[The debate on the 'mind–body problem' (an expression that the French authors hesitate to translate: for them, it is the problem of the connections between the 'soul' and the body!) only exists when one affirms that the functional organization of the nervous system does not correspond to its neural organization.]

Changeux admits that he is reluctant to translate the word 'mind' into French, because the French word 'esprit' produces a confusion of meaning in that it carries along with it the repercussions of the notion of 'spirit' and thereby conjures up the old Bergsonian dualism of the body and the soul. So, Changeux goes so far as to even question the use of the word 'esprit': 'A quoi bon parler d'"Esprit"?';[40] ['What's the use of speaking of the mind?'].[41] In his view, as long as the so-called 'spiritual' is eradicated, reductive as it might appear, he posits that correlations can be made between mental and neuronal activity. Ultimately, Changeux vividly constructs a 'footbridge' or 'passerelle' between the two:

> ... to destroy the barriers that separate the neural from the mental and construct a bridge, however fragile, allowing us to cross from one to the other. ...[42]

And with panache, he proclaims: 'L'homme n'a dès lors plus rien à faire de l'"Esprit", il lui suffit d'être un Homme Neuronal';[43] ['Man no longer has any need of the "Esprit"; it is enough for him to be Neuronal Man'].

Changeux weaves his discussion of memory within his continued treatment of the mind/brain debate. He treats the subject within an extended interdisciplinary dialogue with the French philosopher Paul Ricoeur in their book *Ce qui nous fait penser: la nature et la règle* (1998). Changeux remains uncomfortable with Ricoeur's formulation of the physical brain as the 'substrate' of thought, or mental experience. In response, Changeux rather humbly presents his own neurobiological approach as admittedly reductive and inadequate for explaining fully the phenomenological mental experience that he describes as *'internal reflective processes'*.[44] But in also challenging the metaphysical legacy of Bergson, which treated thought ('pensée') as independent of the brain ('cerveau'), Changeux refutes Bergson's notion of memory:

> Bergson, in *Memory and Matter* (1896), had concluded that 'memory must be, in principle, a power absolutely independent of matter'. ... On this point, however, the great philosopher's intuition proved to be mistaken.[45]

In contrast, Changeux speaks of the scientifically established notion of the 'materialization' of memory traces. However, he has also pointed to the interconnections between different kinds of memory traces in the brain. For instance, he, like others, connects the emotional component of memory to the amygdala:

The neurosciences provide a definite basis for asserting a connection between the memorized cognitive representation, the knowledge trace, and the emotional trace associated with this knowledge, which appears to be located at the level of the various pathways that unite the frontal cortex with the limbic system, and most especially with a specialized nucleus, the amygdala.[46]

Previously, dismissing the idea of a unilateral localization of traces in either the hippocampus or the temporal lobe, he had envisaged 'the memory trace as spread throughout the cortex and maybe even through a large part of the rest of the brain'.[47]

Like Changeux, another outspoken French neuroscientist, Jean Delacour, has presented a model of the memory system which 'does not have a single anatomical location'.[48] In his view, the memory system involves the whole brain and consists of the interaction of three interacting structures: the association cortex (for motor and sensory activity), the limbic system (for arousal and excitability) and the prefrontal cortex (for deliberate behavior). Delacour takes a tempered approach to the subject of traces, viewing memory as being affected by the short life of individual neurons and their enzymes. He also emphasizes the variation in the accessibility of traces, based on conditions present at the moment of retrieval. For example, in differentiating the brain from a computer, he notes the possibility in human memory for interference by adjacent, competing memories. 'De façon générale, la mémoire vivante est beaucoup moins localisée que celle d'un ordinateur';[49] ['Generally, living memory is much less localized than that of a computer']. Eventually, however, he arrives at the conclusion that long-term memory in the adult depends on the *plasticity* of the nervous system, the capacity of the nerve tissues to form new connections, an 'exuberance' which naturally declines with age. Other scientists, however, are currently envisaging neuron renewal. Survival factors often known as trophic interactions are being explored in connection with synaptic pathway formation in the hippocampus during maturity. Ira B. Black speculates that tropic factors are affected by excitatory or inhibitory transmitters.[50] And Changeux has already argued that memory in later age is compensated for by a replacement of chemistry by geometry in the sedimentation and stratification of the synapses.

The topic of memory attrition brings attention to the phenomenon of 'oubli', or biological forgetting. Some recent researchers have studied the consolidation of memory in sleep, performed by the hippocampus.[51] Others have observed that the elimination of certain ordinary trivia can provide for acquisition of long-term memory. On the other hand, the redundancy resulting from the coexistence of several memory systems can account for the reversibility of forgetting. It is also true that forgetting can provide a compensation for surcharge which can arise from an overload of short-term memory. Early on, the studies of amnesia by Ribot had demonstrated this notion.[52] Over time, long blocks of forgetting can safeguard the original imprint intact rather than jeopardize it with interference. This returns us to Changeux's point that 'To learn is to stabilize preestablished synaptic combinations, and to eliminate the surplus.'[53] Without connecting his data to current scientific findings, the literary critic Harald Weinrich in his book *Lethe* does confront Bergson by interpreting Proust's involuntary memory as being indirectly connected to forgetting rather than to 'durée': 'das unwillkürliche Gedächtnis untertunnelt ein langes und tiefes Vergessen';[54] ['Unconscious memory progresses in subterranean fashion through a long and deep oblivion']. Weinrich's conclusion through the literary experience is that contrary to Freud, such forgetting is purgative and beneficial in its human and poetic form. In a strictly literary context, Weinrich is sensing the strengthening of memory through selectivity. The poets Mallarmé and Borges, as has been seen, have both provided additional data for the interaction between remembering and forgetting.

Just as forgetting can contribute to remembering, so, too, may the study of short-term memory shed light on long-term memory and layering of memories. Striking elucidations of these aspects of memory study can be drawn from the literary texts of Faulkner and Nin, and even from comments by Salvador Dalí, as shall be seen. Nin, in particular, demonstrates interactions between short-term and long-term memory. Initially, scientific researchers classified short-term and long-term as separate storage systems. Derived in part from William James's category of primary memory, Alan Baddeley first offered the model of working memory in 1974[55] to designate the temporary storage of information necessary for the performance, in the prefrontal cortex, of cognitive skills, including learning and reasoning. More recent research has been concerned with the interaction between different types of memory. Eric Kandel has compared synaptic plasticity in long-term and short-term memory and has discussed the process of consolidation which converts short-term into long-term memory. Also, Antonio Damasio has pointed out regions where emotion and working memory actually interact.[56] Changeux has averred that in actual practice, working memory solicits varieties of long-term memory but which are 'differentially activated when...called back up to the working compartment'.[57]

It was Tulving who in 1995 proposed a formal model of organization of memory in five systems: procedural, perceptual priming or cue based, semantic or factual memory not tied to language, primary or working memory, and episodic. Yet even with these categories, Tulving asserted that 'classification requires a multilevel approach'.[58] He went on to stress that such taxonomy should not be limited to neuro-anatomical analyses which seemed to stress cortical geography instead of functioning.

Such classification considers procedural memory and perceptual memory to be forms of unconscious memory, which has received insufficient scientific exploration. Since, for example, procedural memory has always been involved with habit, this automatism has demeaned the study of unconscious memory. Furthermore, the Freudian notion of repressed, traumatic memories remains predominant over other forms of unconscious memories. Nonetheless, those cognitive neuroscientists who have pursued the subject have realized the subtleties of unconscious memory beyond the well-known Freudian interpretation.

For example, some researchers who have been engaged in sleep research focusing on dream memory, have unwittingly called to mind the Surrealists with their interest in the peculiarities of dream states. The neuroscientist Jonathan Winson has hypothesized that the brain mechanism that underlies the unconscious is a normal associative process, however distorted it might appear; it is not a defense mechanism as Freud viewed it. In fact, in terms of evolution, it was the complete neural system prior to the advent of consciousness. Winson states:

> I find the unconscious a cohesive, continually active mental structure which takes note of life's experiences and reacts according to its own scheme of interpretation and responses. This reaction is reflected nightly in our dreams.[59]

Similarly, J. Allan Hobson and Robert Stickgold have pointed to physiological reasons for the chaotic imagery and bizarre discontinuity that is manifest in the intense dream phase known as Rapid Eye Movement (REM) sleep. They state:

> From our perspective, the presence in sleep of thoughts, images, and emotions is sufficient to characterize this sleep as altered consciousness rather than unconsciousness.[60]

Only in 1987 did the psychologist Daniel Schacter give a definition to the currently used term 'implicit memory', stating 'when previous experiences facilitate performance on a task that does not require conscious or intentional recollection of those experiences'.[61] More recently, his book *Searching for Memory*, has gone on to elaborate on distinctions between implicit and explicit memory that he had originally made; he states: 'while our sense of self and identity is highly dependent on explicit memory for past episodes and autobiographical facts, our personalities may be more closely tied to implicit memory processes'.[62] But he is left with an unresolved issue: 'We don't yet know whether differences between the hippocampus and the amygdala are implicated in the peculiar kinds of implicit emotional memory that has been observed in some psychogenic amnesia patients.'[63] Although Schacter finds the amygdala to be fully involved in mediating persisting emotional after-effects of unconscious memory, he also recognizes the role of the hippocampus in consolidating memories during sleep. By even mentioning Pierre Janet and his notion of dissociated memories of the unconscious mind and by reconsidering the inhibitory processes suggested by Freud as actually playing a significant role in memory (rather than in forgetting), Schacter seems to be reevaluating certain memory debates of the 1880s. It also appears as though Schacter were continuing the discussion of the collaboration between unconscious and conscious memory initiated by Hermann Ebbinghaus in that era.

Aside from speculations with respect to localization, implicit memory has perhaps been most discussed within the context of language. There is the widely disseminated work of Steven Pinker, who takes the study of memory in the direction of psycholinguistics. Notably, his book *The Language Instinct*, which considers the neural organization of language, has popularized the notion of the computational brain with the connectivity of neural microcircuitry. Despite what he calls the 'near consensus' that the left perisylvian area of the cerebral cortex is the locale for language,[64] he admits that language functions are actually 'hard to pin down in the brain'.[65]

More specifically, the psychologist Douglas L. Nelson has discussed experiments on what he calls 'target study words' and their 'set size effects', which implicitly draw in past associates in long-term memory. He writes:

> First, the presence of such effects indicates that previously acquired connections to related words in long-term memory can influence recall . . . Second, such effects indicate that unconsciously activated

information can affect memory for consciously experienced events.[66]

He goes on to say that such information previously acquired may never have even surfaced to the level of conscious awareness. In this manner, Nelson draws on automatic and implicit aspects of memory which can suddenly emerge. This implicit component in turn suggests a connectionist formulation. It also can be related to the linguistic approach to memory unwittingly used by such poets as André Breton and Octavio Paz who in their articulation of individual word images transpose clusters of connections provided by past associations into new contexts. Nelson's own PIER model of 1992 'assumes that cued recall is determined by *P*rocessing *I*mplicit and *E*xplicit *R*epresentations'.[67] He proceeded to consider ways of integrating the two kinds of memory. All along, he also offers a means of incorporating the processes of encoding and retrieval in the studies. But for him it is not a question of circumstances surrounding the encoding, as it is for Tulving. It is rather the closest associates of a word: words with a smaller set of associates have a recall advantage. Such associates can be activated automatically. Given such findings, Nelson suggests that the contributions of the unconscious memories are a resource to be probed by future scientists.

The study of memory thus figures in debates between what is called the symbolist and the connectionist approach. The symbolist models offer the traditional notion of memory permanently stored intact as representational, classified according to the category of memory, and retrieved in standard sequence. The connectionist models do not accept this fixed notion of memory storage, of a single memory trace. Instead, they suggest a more transitory evocation of memory, dependent upon a network of connections, involved in a patterned activity of the brain. The contingencies of the moment play a role in the interaction between a system and the environment, so that the actual functioning of the memory system produces the results. Implicit memory, with its wealth of hidden connections, seems to be better explained within this model. The psychologist James L. McClelland is known for having come up with a memory trace synthesis model to describe the reconstructive memory retrieval process which activates the connections among units:

It also involves contributions from background knowledge based on information acquired very gradually over the course of a lifetime of experience directly within the neocortical system. If these ideas have any validity, we cannot see remembering as recall, but as a synthesis of contributions from many different sources of information.[68]

Ultimately, this approach supports the notion of language as another trigger mechanism for memory – that words themselves can be stimuli that can prompt the assembling of memory traces distributed throughout the brain. It has been seen that poets and writers, especially of more modern times, have exploited the use of stimulus words in their art.

Despite the specificity attributed to certain regions of the brain for purposes of encoding and recuperating memory, therefore, most scientists would agree that a holistic approach to memory remains necessary. In light of advances in the study of the memory process made by the diverse factions of pharmacological studies, computer modeling, and neuroimaging approaches, scientists are admitting that increasing collaborative efforts are on the venue for the future. For one, the neurologist Marek-Marsel Mesulam has acknowledged 'the growing belief that explorations in the general areas of mind/brain/behavior are ripe for meaningful multidisciplinary approaches'.[69] As this book has demonstrated, the marking of the literary pathways can lead toward new frontiers of such consilience, with the recognition that literary writers provide beacons particularly into the dark corridors of unconscious memory yet to be explored.

Afterword. Images of the Artists: Dalí, Dominguez and Magritte

Three paintings of the twentieth century feature memory in an unforgettably striking way: Dalí's *The Persistence of Memory* (1931), Oscar Dominguez's *Memory of the Future* (1938) and Magritte's *La Mémoire* (1948). All three paintings are surrealist, containing visual presentations of memory and time through the intermediary of concrete objects and the art of juxtaposition which are germane to surrealist artistic technique. Moreover, with their visionary but concrete optic on the future, it is all the more intriguing, if not paradoxical, to extract from the artwork some final hypotheses regarding the memory process.

It is a known fact that modern art became closely involved in the early twentieth century with the formal depiction of concepts. Art critics from Roger Fry to Guillaume Apollinaire and Kazimir Malevich attested to this fact in terms of Post-Impressionism, Cubism and Futurism. In fact, in the years 1923–25, Malevich coined the apt term 'painterly science'.[1] But it was André Breton who, most specifically, demonstrated first in 1928 in *Le Surréalisme et la peinture* and later in his 1939 essay 'Des Tendances les plus récentes de la peinture surréaliste', that surrealist poetry and painting shared the same tenets and techniques. Following the first wave of Cubism, which probed the third dimension suggested by cubes, cones and pyramids, the so-called fourth dimension became the fashionable subject to be explored. However, as the art critic Linda Henderson has pointed out, few artists fully understood the true scientific non-Euclidean meaning of the term, which was actually first introduced by Herman Minkowski as the notion of 'space–time' in his 1908 paper.[2] Henderson makes the following distinction:

After the 1920s artistic interest in Einstein's space–time world was most often divorced from the earlier tradition of a spatial fourth dimension, which had begun to recede in the past.[3]

Einstein's relativity theory, which proliferated after 1920, most certainly attracted Dalí in his notion of soft, melted watches. These watches are presented in several paintings, the most famous of which bears memory in its title. In his piece 'Les Pleurs d'Héraclite', from his 1935 short volume *La Conquête de l'irrationnel*, Dalí comically envisages these watches as 'the Camembert of time and space'.[4] Given the physicist's notion of the relativity of time and the physical effect of the clock paradox which demonstrates the phenomenon of 'time dilation', memory also can persist beyond the confines of stationary clock time. Like other artists of his era, including such an ostensibly unrelated writer as William Faulkner, Dalí defies clock time through the use of memory. Yet the openness of surrealist art to multiple interpretations allows the artist-critic Marcel Jean to offer his own 'reading' of the painting biographically – what can be considered alongside the scientific interpretation of 'Einsteinian camembert'. Jean prefers to relate the watches to a possibly specific childhood memory. In *The History of Surrealist Painting*, Jean points out that the common childhood experience of showing one's tongue ('langue') to the doctor can be expressed in a play on words 'la montre molle', meaning 'shows it soft'.[5] The fact that Jean connects the painting to a childhood memory gives additional support to the idea that Dalí's view of personal memory figures within the framework of Einsteinian time.

But Dalí himself offers the most precise account of the genesis of the painting in his illuminating and entertaining autobiography *The Secret Life of Salvador Dalí*, published in English in 1942. Dali writes:

This picture represented a landscape near Port Lligat, whose rocks were lighted by a transparent and melancholy twilight; in the foreground an olive tree with its branches cut, and without leaves.[6]

He goes on to say that this landscape would serve as the setting for some idea which he subsequently saw as two soft watches, 'one of them hanging lamentably on the branch of the olive tree'. He does not refer to the third melted watch in the painting, which he places on what appears to be a fabricated surrealist dream object of a fishlike form lying on the beach. Dalí anecdotally relates that he had conceived this painting in faraway Paris, after a meal with strong Camembert – hence the unexpected, involuntary association. Dali had just returned to Paris after a glorious three-month stay with his wife Gala in Port Lligat, close to Cadaqués, where he had spent his childhood and early adolescence. It appears, then, that the painting imbibes these long-term memories of Dalí, revived, notably, by a recent short-term memory of a stay in his beloved region. The background of jagged rock formations especially evokes the actual landscape of Cadaqués connected to his childhood. As I have myself witnessed, there is nothing 'surreal' about those mountains on the Catalan coast so often present in Dalí's paintings, for they stand there in real life. Dalí himself describes the mountains as elementary rock formations coming down into the sea 'in a grandiose geological delirium'.[7]

This typical Dalinian landscape can be seen as a simulacrum of a psychic state. It materializes in the 'very corporeity of the granite'[8] the overwhelming and continuous and dominant presence of that child-hood memory set against malleable, passing time and demonstrating what Dalí termed the 'morphological aesthetics of the soft and the hard'. Dalí's autobiography confirms this persistence of long-term memory as he refers back to early ages of five and six in the very setting of Cadaqués and the neighboring town of Figueras where Dalí was born. He writes later that the intervening years of late adolescence and early adulthood become 'blotted out until they totally disappeared'[9] to give precedence to his early memories: 'From the moment of my arrival at Cadaqués I was assailed by a recrudescence of my childhood period.' Dalí admitted that such memories were often tinged with reverie and fantasy. His 'paranoiac-critical method' of voluntary hallucination of unexpected associations sets authentic memories in new contexts and allows for the persistence of memory through the power of the imagination.

Dalí's contemporary, the Caribbean painter Oscar Dominguez, used the trope of solidification in connection with memory, pursuing the artistic representation of memory in a more graphic way. If, as André Breton stated, Dominguez was one of the few artists who most seriously understood the Einsteinian space–time concept, it is in that context that he also positioned memory. In a footnote to his article 'Des Tendances les plus récentes de la peinture surréaliste' Breton cites Dominguez's practice of 'lithochronic surfaces' as opening up 'a window on the strange world of the fourth dimension, constituting a sort of solidification of time' ('une fenêtre sur le monde étrange de la qua-trième dimension, constituant une espèce de solidification du temps').[10] In a subsequent essay written by Dominguez entitled 'La Pétrification du temps' (1942), the artist himself pointedly defines what he means by 'lithochronic surfaces', which demonstrate for him in visual terms the solidification of time. As an artistic expression of movement forward in the spacetime context, Dominguez introduced a strange model of a succession of lions:

> Between the lion Lo, or lion at the moment $t = 0$, and the lion Lf or final lion, is located an infinity of African lions, of diverse aspects and forms.[11]

In tracing the 'enveloping surface', in terms of the 'enveloping super lion', he obtains the lithochronic surface, which demonstrates 'a movement to the solid state'.

Although as a rule mathematicians can do without visual demonstrations of their abstract theories, writers and artists need the concrete word or image to illustrate. From his writings, it would seem that Dominguez was strongly challenged by the visualization of space–time and that he sought to depict it in his paintings. It is most interesting to recognize that he also treated memory in this special geometric context.

A close examination of the 'Memory of the Future' painting shows it to be richly provocative with the typical surrealist technique of multiple associations and apparent contradiction. The very title of the painting calls to mind the frontispiece of Breton's essay 'Introduction au discours sur le peu de réalité' with its enigmatic phrase 'Le Souvenir du Futur'.[12] In the painting, the craterlike grooves, from a scientific standpoint strongly suggest the presence of matter. Such awareness of masses in turn reflects very specifically Einstein's General Theory of Relativity, (1916) which stated that gravitating masses curve the surrounding space time. The presence of this relativity-specific geodesics, a scientific term which, in fact, Dominguez uses rather loosely in his essay, positions memory in the curvilinear context vividly represented by the black grooves of the painting. The physicist John Archibald Wheeler has formulated Einstein's conception of gravity into a catchy expression 'mass grips spacetime, telling it how to curve'.[13] Demonstrably, memory is visibly connected to the marked dimension of depth in the painting. Furthermore, it is placed within three time zones: the past represented by the clouds in the background, the typewriter and its sprout of words as the present central object, and the future suggested by the stark surrealist craters on the other side of the crevice.

It would seem that the typewriter, a machine for writing in the days before the computer, is being regarded as a mediator for the memory

1. Oscar Dominguez, *Memory of the Future* (1938).

2. René Magritte, *La Mémoire* (1948).

process employed by the literary writer to project the memories of the past into the future. Curiously and probably unintentionally, there is a faint suggestion of neurons or configuration of synapses in the 'sprouting' from the typewriter which itself is also the only quasi 'human element' in this cosmic painting. Its presence fits the standard surrealist practice of the juxtaposition of distant realities – the manmade machine and the supernatural setting of a twilight zone which actually intensifies the natural décor. The layers of white along the cliffs suggest paper sheets, the surface for the written word which preserves memory and projects it into the future. Obviously, the surrealist connection between the memory and the subconscious is also incarnate in this painting. The geological landscape once again suggests the stratification of memory, evoked as well in literature, as has been seen, for example, in Anaïs Nin's or Octavio Paz's imagery of memory-grooves.

In contrast to Dominguez and Dalí and their intellectual images of memory, the Belgian artist Magritte, who often painted parts of human bodies, offers an interestingly biological and emotional expression of memory in *La Mémoire*. First of all, the painting recalls the age-old blood trope for memory that Homer had introduced. In Book XI of *The Odyssey*, the dead, who are naturally sunk in the oblivion of Hades, are awakened to their memories when they drink the sacrificial dark blood (*haima kelainon*) of memory given to them by Odysseus who is seeking to recover certain facts of the past. For ancient Homer, too, memory thus seems to have been conceived as a biological phenomenon. Memory was the lifeline for consciousness, the inner river. But in addition, the modern painter seems to be focusing on the storage of memory. Obsessed by his own concept of the blood-blotched brow, Magritte produced four versions of the painting with the same title in the years 1938–54. Each painting presents a classical, marble head of a woman with a bloodstain covering one temple. It visualizes the notion of an emotional brain, the blood suggesting painful, traumatic memories, which emerge despite the curtain of forgetfulness, pronounced as it is in the painting. The dripping blood also links pain to the creative process, which is here represented by memory. The brain, like a sculptured piece of art, retains the memory. In fact, does not the piece of art reflect the brain's capacity for the storage of memory? The substitution in the versions of 1948 and 1954 of a sphere for the apple, denaturalizes the presentation and suggests instead the physical factors of mass and gravity; once again an artist is moving the expression of memory into the fourth dimension. Overall, by juxtaposing various spatial forms such as the plaster head and the sphere, which might be present in a sculptor's studio, Magritte seems to be linking the artistic and the scientific, the concrete with the abstract. He is thereby suggesting the ultimate permanence of memory solidified and stored by the brain's recourse to artistic objects.

Definitively, through the haunting and repeated image of the painting *La Mémoire*, Magritte blatantly presents the enduring process of memory fixed in stone. According to the terms set up in this book, simply speaking, Dalí and Dominguez, with their intellectual images of memory suggesting the hippocampus, were 'seahorse' artists, whereas Magritte was more of an 'almond' painter, his images springing from the emotional context of the amygdala. Together, these artists presented startling images which actually offer yet another touchstone in the study of memory. Dalí 'melts' the watches of passing time to underscore by contrast the persistence of memory. In all three paintings, artistic objects imply the power of the human imagination to retain and recreate memory. Dalí with his unidentifiable 'dream object' lying on the sand, Dominguez with his typewriter, and Magritte with his sculptured head feature the supremely human factor of art as a distinctive elucidator of the memory process. For the artist and the literary writer alike, the powers of image-making and language, with which the human brain is endowed, are the ultimate means for capturing and sustaining memory.

Notes

Introduction

1. This vast topic is slowly gaining recognition as evidenced by two recent books which address the subject of memory in literature in a general manner: Jean-Ives Tadié's *Le Sens de la mémoire* (1999) and James Olney's *Memory and Narrative* (1998). Tadié, in his treatment of French texts exclusively, does not offer concrete in-depth analyses of the actual workings of memory in those texts. Olney links the expression of memory to the fiction of narrativity in three selected authors without recourse to any scientific data concerning the memory process. A prior study by John E. Jackson, *Mémoire et création poétique* (1992) had already been concerned with links between the memory process and its fictionalization in literature.

1 Memory in the Era of Dynamic Psychology: Nineteenth-Century Backgrounds

1. Théodule Ribot, *Les Maladies de la mémoire* (1881; Paris: Félix Alcan, 1888), p. 1.
2. Ibid., p. 3.
3. Alfred Binet, *Introduction à la psychologie expérimentale* (Paris: Félix Alcan, 1894), p. 69. Binet had begun his investigations under the influence of British associationism with the publication of his first article 'De la Fusion des sensations' in the *Revue philosophique* (1880), 10: 284–94. There he considered the possibility of memory as exact replication of the past through the association of similar ideas or sensations, the tactile, for example. Dismissing this early point of view and going beyond initial investigations of elementary psychological life in primitive life forms, he went on to tackle more complex material. His subsequent writings included studies of two strata of consciousness in dual personalities and a later book *L'Etude expérimentale de l'intelligence* (1922) in which memory was viewed as a faculty.
4. Hermann Ebbinghaus, *Memory: a Contribution to Experimental Psychology*, trans. Henry A. Ruger and Clara E. Bussenius (New York: Dover Publications, 1964), p. 19.
5. William James, 'Frederic Myers' Service to Psychology' in *Essays in Psychical Research* (Cambridge, Mass.: Harvard University Press, 1986), p. 198.
6. Letter of 15 février 1905 of Henri Bergson to William James in R.M. Moise-Bastide (ed.), *Ecrits et paroles* (Paris: Presses Universitaires, 1957). Bergson wrote that the subconscious was an integral part of consciousness, '*interwoven with it* et non pas *underlying it*'.
7. Henri Bergson, *Oeuvres* (Paris: Presses Universitaires de France, 1963), p. 161.
8. Pete A.Y. Gunter, 'Bergson, Images and Neuronal Man' in *Bergson et les neurosciences: Actes du Colloque international de neuro-philosophie* (Lille: Les Empêcheurs de penser en rond, 1997), p. 124. This colloquium and a conference entitled *Bergson et les mémoires* (1 October 1997, Department of Cognitive

Sciences at the Université Victor Segalen at Bordeaux) have dealt with Bergson's scientific legacy. For example, B. Andrieu has stated: 'L'avantage actuel du modèle bergsonien des deux mémoires (l'une localisée, l'autre non localisable) se trouve dans la description neuropsychologiques des systèmes mnésiques qui fonctionnent en parallèle' (*Cerveau et mémoires* [Paris: Editions Osiris, 1998], p. 67). R. Jaffard has found important contributions in Bergson toward understanding animal memory: 'Certaines thèses developpées par Bergson dans *Matière et mémoire* éclairent d'une façon remarquable les données les plus actuelles issues de l'expérimentation animale' (*Cerveau et mémoires*, p. 94). See also Pete Gunter's book *Bergson and the Evolution of Physics* (Knoxville: University of Tennessee Press, 1969).

9. Henri Bergson, *Matter and Memory*, trans. Nancy Margaret Paul and W. Scott Palmer (New York: Zone, 1991), p. 83. When the French text is not given in my text, this English translation is being used.
10. Henri Bergson, *Matter and Memory*, p. 88.
11. Bergson, *Matière et mémoire*, in *Oeuvres*, p. 233.
12. Bergson, *Matter and Memory*, p. 152.
13. Ibid., p. 139.
14. Bergson, 'L'Ame et le corps' in Bergson *et al.*, *Le Matérialisme actuel* (Paris: Flammarion, 1913), p. 42.
15. Ibid., p. 43.
16. Ibid., p. 38.
17. Bergson, *Matter and Memory*, p. 154.
18. See Bergson, *L'Evolution créatrice* (1907; Paris: Presses Universitaires de Paris, 1962), p. 4. Bergson writes: 'la mémoire...n'est pas une faculté de classer des souvenirs dans un tiroir ou de les inscrire sur un registre'; 'Memory...is not a faculty of arranging recollections in a drawer or inscribing them in a register.' As shall be seen, the metaphor of the register would pertain to Rousseau's view; that of the drawer would pertain to Baudelaire. Both are here dismissed by Bergson.
19. Bergson, *Matter and Memory*, p. 128.
20. Bergson, *Durée et simultanéité: à propos de la théorie d'Einstein* (Paris: Félix Alcan, 1922), p. 62.
21. Ibid., p. 61.
22. This painting (whose original French title is 'Une Leçon clinique à la Salpêtrière), now hanging in the former Faculté de Médecine in Paris (Université de Paris V – now René Descartes), depicts Charcot demonstrating a case of a hysterical woman to his colleagues at the Salpêtrière hospital.
23. See Notes to Breton, *Oeuvres complètes*, Vol. 1., ed. Marguerite Bonnet (Paris: Gallimard, 1988), p. 1730.
24. Pierre Janet, *L'Automatisme psychologique* (1889; Paris: Félix Alcan, 1973), p. 15.
25. Ibid., p. 218.
26. See Pierre Janet, 'Les Actes inconscients et la mémoire pendant le somnambulisme', *Revue philosophique*, 25 (1888): 238–79.
27. Pierre Janet, *L'Automatisme psychologique*, p. 119.
28. Ibid., p. 13.
29. Ibid., p. 107.
30. Frederic W.H. Myers, *Human Personality and Its Survival of Bodily Death*, edited and abridged by Leopold H. Myers (London: Longmans, Green & Company, 1918). The quotations in the paragraph are from pp. 99–100 of the text.

31. Ibid., p. 137.
32. Pierre Janet, *De l'Angoisse à l'extase*, Vol. 1 (Paris: Alcan, 1926), pp. 286–7.
33. Janet, *L'Evolution de la mémoire* (Paris: A. Chahine, 1928), p. 190.
34. See Malebranche, *De la Recherche de la vérité*, ed. Pierre Janet (Paris: Alcan, 1886).
35. See this discussion of Bergson by Janet in *L'Evolution de la mémoire et de la notion du temps*, p. 196.
36. Sigmund Freud, 'Childhood Memories and Screen Memories', *The Standard Edition of the Complete Psychological Works of Sigmund Freud*, Vol. 6 (1901; London: Hogarth Press, 1960), p. 43.
37. Ibid.
38. See Carl Jung 'Experimental Observations on the Faculty of Memory' (orig. German 1905; *Collected Works*, Vol. 2: 272–87. Jung sought to demonstrate Freud's theory through experimental investigations with reactions by hysterical patients to stimulus-words.
39. Sigmund Freud, 'Notiz über den "Wunderblock"', *Internationale Zeitschrift für Psychoanalyse*, 11 (I), 1–5. GW, XIV. For a French translation of this article, see *Résultats, idées, problèmes*, vol. II (1921–38), 3rd Edition, Paris: Presses Universitaires de France, 1922.
40. As cited by Jean-Pierre Changeux, *Neuronal Man*, p. 274.
41. William James, *Principles of Psychology*, Vol. 1 (1890; New York: Dover Publications, 1950), p. 655.
42. Ibid., p. 646.
43. Ibid., p. 646.
44. Ibid., p. 655.
45. Ibid., p. 239.
46. Ibid., p. 654.
47. James, p. 239.
48. For three decades from the 1880s on, James was engaged in a dialogue with the founders of the Society for Psychical Research who he believed were bringing advances to the field of psychological science. See James, *Essays in Psychical Research* (Cambridge, Mass: Harvard UP, 1986). In particular he gave much praise to Myers, who along with Binet and Janet in France were exploring 'a new conception of our mental possibilities', p. 188.
49. Ibid., p. 204.
50. James' review of Frederic W.H. Myers' posthumous book, *Human Personality and its Survival of Bodily Death* in William James, *Essays in Psychical Research*, pp. 206–7.
51. Interestingly, James' own 'Notes on Automatic Writing' of 1889 had been cited by Janet in his Preface to the Second Edition of *L'Automatisme psychologique* of 1894, p. 27. James also had cited Janet in the last pages of the first volume of *Principles of Psychology*.

2 Rousseau and the Romantics: Autobiographical Memory and Emotion

1. *The Confessions of Jean-Jacques Rousseau*, trans. J.M. Cohen (1781; Harmondsworth: Penguin, 1953), p. 19. Henceforth, unless otherwise indicated, citations

from this translation of the work will be included parenthetically in the text. Where the original French is cited followed by my own translation for purposes of greater accuracy, reference will be to the Pléiade edition, *Oeuvres complètes de Jean-Jacques Rousseau,* vol. 1.

2. Among those who believe in the general accuracy of Rousseau's account are his biographer John Morley and the Pléiade editor Bernard Gagnebin. Morley writes: 'Other people wrote polite histories of their outer lives, amply coloured with romantic decorations . . . Though, as has been pointed out already, the *Confessions* abound in small inaccuracies of date, hardly to be avoided by an oldish man in reference to the facts of his boyhood, whether a Rousseau or a Goethe, yet their substantial truthfulness is made more evident with every addition to our materials for testing them' (Morley, *Rousseau* [London: Chapman & Hall, 1873], 2: 302). Gagnebin states: 'Les documents d'archives confirment en général les dires de Rousseau quant aux faits, moins nettement quant aux dates' (Jean-Jacques Rousseau, *Oeuvres complètes,* Pléiade edition, ed. Bernard Gagnebin and Marcel Raymond [Paris: Gallimard, 1959], 1: 1229n). On the other hand, more recently James Olney alludes to what he calls Rousseau's 'narrative memory', questioning its actual veracity: 'The effect of memory in Rousseau . . . or the effect of memory-and-imagination, is to transform the singular event of history into the always-occurring event of the as-if world of fiction and of autobiographical narrative memory' (Olney, *Memory and Narrative*, p. 195).

3. Jean-Jacques Rousseau, *The Reveries of a Solitary Walker*, trans. Charles E. Butterworth (New York: New York University Press, 1979), p. 54.

4. Jean-Jacques Rousseau, *Les Rêveries du promeneur solitaire*, ed. S. De Sacy (Paris: Le Livre de Poche, 1965), p. 83.

5. William Wordsworth, *Selected Poems*, ed. John O. Hayden (Harmondsworth, UK: Penguin, 1994). All subsequent citations from Wordsworth's poetry are from this edition.

6. Wordsworth, *Selected Poems*, pp. 449–50. The subsequent quotation, also from the Preface to *Lyrical Ballads*, is on p. 446.

7. See also, for example, Leconte de Lisle's 'Souvenir' and Théophile Gautier's 'Le Château du souvenir'.

8. Alphonse de Lamartine, *Oeuvres poétiques complètes* (Paris: Gallimard, 1963), p. 39. The English translations of Lamartine's poems are my own.

9. Alphonse de Lamartine, *Graziella, Raphaël* (Paris: Editions Garniers Frères, 1955), p. 133.

10. Lamartine, *Raphaël*, p. 309.

11. Lamartine, *Oeuvres poétiques complètes*, p. 28.

12. See Commentary to the poem 'Souvenir' in Lamartine, *Méditations poétiques* (Paris: Editions Garniers Frères, 1956), p. 229.

13. Lamartine, *Oeuvres poétiques complètes*, p. 1239.

14. See Paul de Musset, *The Biography of Alfred de Musset*, trans. Harriet W. Preston (Boston: Roberts Brothers, 1877), p. 223.

15. Alfred de Musset, *Poésies complètes*. Pléiade edition. (Paris: Gallimard, 1957), pp. 404–9. The English translation of Musset's poem 'Souvenir' is my own.

16. Victor Hugo, *Oeuvres poétiques*, vol. 1, Pléiade edition (Paris: Gallimard, 1964), pp. 1093–8.

17. As formulated by James L. McGaugh, 'Emotional Activation, Neuromodulatory Systems and Memory' in Daniel L. Schacter (ed.), *Memory Distortion* (Cambridge, Mass: Harvard UP, 1995), p. 256.

3   Baudelaire, Rimbaud and 'Le Cerveau': Sensory Pathways to Memory

1. Arthur Rimbaud, 'Lettre à Georges Izambard' 13 May 1871, *Oeuvres complètes*, p. 249.
2. Charles Baudelaire, 'Etudes sur Poe, II', *Oeuvres complètes*, vol. 2, p. 315.
3. See Erik Kandel, *Principles of Neural Science*, p. 625.
4. *The Flowers of Evil, Paris Spleen*, trans. William H. Crosby (New York: Brockport, 1991), p. 77. For Baudelaire, whose poetry has been poorly translated for the most part, I have chosen the rather free translation of William H. Crosby. Otherwise, where not indicated, the translations are my own.
5. *The Flowers of Evil*, p. 56. The next French line of verse is from p. 58.
6. Crosby, p. 369. The next quotation is on the same page.
7. Crosby, p. 81.
8. Baudelaire, 'Le Peintre de la vie moderne', *Oeuvres complètes*, vol. 2, p. 698.
9. Crosby, p. 96. The next quotation is on the same page.
10. Baudelaire, 'L'Art mnémonique' in 'Le Peintre de la vie moderne', *Oeuvres complètes*, vol. 2, p. 698.
11. Crosby, p. 138.
12. Crosby, p. 137.
13. Crosby, p. 153.
14. See Edgar Allan Poe's 'The Philosophy of Composition' (1846), which describes the composition of his poem 'The Raven'.
15. Baudelaire, *Oeuvres complètes*, vol. 1, p. 45.
16. Wallace Fowlie, *Rimbaud* (New York: New Directions, 1946), p. 16.
17. Rimbaud, *Complete Works*, trans. Wallace Fowlie, p. 125.
18. Ibid., p. 121.
19. See Mallarmé's poem 'Brise Marine' in *Oeuvres complètes*, p. 38.
20. Mallarmé, *Oeuvres complètes*, p. 51.
21. Mallarmé, 'Variations sur un sujet' in *Oeuvres complètes*, p. 368.
22. See Harald Weinrich, *Lethe*, p. 176.
23. Mallarmé, *Oeuvres complètes*, p. 67.
24. Ibid., p. 45.
25. Ibid., p. 286.
26. Huysmans, *Against Nature*, trans. Robert Baldick (New York: Penguin Classics, 1959), p. 84. The next quotation is on the same page.
27. Ibid., p. 85.
28. Ibid., p. 25.
29. Ibid., p. 101.
30. Ibid., p. 110.
31. Ibid., p. 60.
32. Ibid., p. 174.
33. Ibid., p. 84.
34. Huysmans, *A Rebours* (Paris: Gallimard, 1977), p. 218.

4   Proust and the Engram: The Trigger of the Senses

1. See my last chapter, 'The Almond and the Seahorse' (pp. 135–52), for discussion of Lashley's seminal paper.
2. Proust, *A La Recherche du temps perdu*, Pléiade edition (Paris: Gallimard, 1987), vol. 3, p. 456.
3. Proust, *A la Recherche*, vol. 1, p. 46.
4. See Nicolas Malebranche, *The Search after Truth*, trans. Thomas M. Lennon (Columbus, Ohio: Ohio UP, 1980), Book II, ch. 3, 'Memory', pp. 106–7.
5. See Richard Semon, *Mnemic Psychology* (1909, German original; London: George Allen & Unwin, 1923), p. 154.
6. Pierre Janet, *L'Evolution de la mémoire*, p. 190. See also my chapter 1, p. 17. Janet's edition of Malebranche is *De la Recherche de la vérité* (Paris: Alcan, 1886).
7. See Samuel Beckett, *Marcel Proust*, New York: Grove Press, 1931.
8. See Gilles Deleuze, *Proust and Signs*, trans. Richard Howard (1964; New York: George Braziller, 1972).
9. See this discussion in my last chapter. In his book, *Leçons sur le corps, le cerveau et l'esprit* (1999), Alain Berthoz asked whether the understanding of the 'mystery' of the Proustian engram was not within our reach: 'Le mystère de la madeleine de Proust serait-il à notre portée?' (p. 372).
10. Brissand succeeded Charcot at the Salpêtrière in 1893. Solliers was recommended to Proust by Brissand after the death of Proust's mother in 1905, an overwhelmingly painful event which aggravated Proust's nervous disorders. An informative exposition on Marcel Proust at the Bibliothèque Nationale in the Fall 1999, which I attended, included showcases of these doctors' works.
11. Adrien Proust, *L'Hygiène du neurasthénique* (Paris: Masson, 1897), p. 76.
12. Ibid.
13. Théophile Ribot, *Les Maladies de la mémoire*, p. 157.
14. Proust, *A la Recherche*, vol. 1, p. 182.
15. See Joyce N. Megay, *Bergson and Proust* (Paris: Vrin, 1976).
16. The first personal contact between Proust and Bergson was in 1892, when Proust was the best man (*garçon d'honneur*) at the marriage of his cousin Louise Neuburger with Bergson. Apparently, that social event gave no impetus at that time for a dialogue. It has been said that despite such family connections, the differences in personality between Bergson and Proust kept them apart. It is known, however, that Proust attended some of Bergson's classes at the Sorbonne (1891–93) and Bergson's inaugural lecture at the Collège de France (1900), but that lecture was on the subject of causality.
17. See 'La Méthode de Sainte-Beuve' in *Contre Sainte-Beuve* (Paris: Gallimard, 1971), pp. 221–2. Proust writes: 'Un livre est le produit d'un autre moi que celui que nous manifestons dans nos habitudes, dans la société, dans nos vices; ['A book is the product of another self than the one which we show in our habits, in society, in our vices'].
18. See note 16 in Chapter 1.
19. Bergson, *Oeuvres*, p. 295.
20. Bergson, 'Mémoire et reconnaissance', in *Revue philosophique* (March 1896), 41: 233.

21. Proust, *A la Recherche*, vol. 4, p. 451.
22. Proust, *Swann's Way*, in *Remembrance of Things Past*, trans. C.K. Moncrieff and Terence Kilmartin (New York: Random House, 1981), vol. 1, p. 203. The subsequent citations from *Remembrance of Things Past* are from this translation of Proust.
23. Proust, *Remembrance*, vol. 1, p. 47.
24. Proust, *A la Recherche*, vol. 1, p. 7.
25. Proust, *Remembrance*, vol. 3, p. 716.
26. Proust, *Remembrance*, vol. 1, p. 6.
27. Proust, *A la Recherche*, vol. 1, p. 184.
28. Proust, *Contre Sainte-Beuve* (Paris: Gallimard, 1954), in 'Collection Idées'; see Preface, p. 55.
29. Proust, *A la Recherche*, vol. 1, p. 43.
30. Proust, *Remembrance*, vol. 1, p. 51.
31. Ibid., p. 46.
32. Jean Delacour, 'Proust's Contribution to the Psychology of Memory', *Theory and Psychology* (2001), 11: 255–71.
33. This early version of 1912 known as 'Le Souvenir involontaire', Dactylographie corrigée (Paris, Bibliothèque Nationale, Department of Manuscripts) Reliquat Proust, was subsequently rejected. In fact, this document had a different arrangement of memory events from the 1913 corrected galley proofs, submitted to Grasset and accepted for publication. The latter, known to most readers, became the definitive version of *Du côté de chez Swann*, published on 8 November 1913. See *A La Recherche du temps perdu*, Placards Corrigés 11 June 1913. Bibliothèque Nationale, Department of Manuscripts, Paris, France.
34. Proust, *Remembrance*, vol. 1, p. 47.
35. Ibid., p. 50.
36. Proust, *A la Recherche*, vol. 1, p. 41.
37. Proust, *A la Recherche*, vol. 4, p. 462.
38. Ibid., p. 466.
39. Proust, *Remembrance*, vol. 3, p. 924.
40. Ibid., p. 921.
41. Proust, *Contre Sainte-Beuve*, Pléiade edition (Paris: Gallimard, 1971), p. 211.
42. Proust, *A la Recherche*, vol. 3, p. 153.
43. Proust, *Remembrance*, vol. 2, p. 783.
44. Proust, *A la Recherche*, vol. 3, p. 154.
45. Proust, *Remembrance*, vol. 2, p. 783.
46. Proust, *A la Recherche*, vol. 3, pp. 154–6.
47. Ibid., p. 154.
48. Ibid., p. 153.
49. Ibid., p. 156.
50. Proust, *Remembrance*, vol. 2, pp. 787–8.
51. Proust, *A la Recherche*, vol. 4, p. 453.
52. Proust, *Remembrance*, vol. 3, p. 908.
53. Proust, *A la Recherche*, vol. 4, p. 445.
54. Proust, *Remembrance*, vol. 3, p. 899.
55. Proust, *A la Recherche*, vol. 4, p. 446.
56. Ibid., p. 447.

57. Proust, *Remembrance*, vol. 3, p. 901.
58. Ibid., p. 909.
59. Proust, *A la Recherche*, vol. 4, p. 452.
60. Proust, *Remembrance*, vol. 3, p. 907. The following quotations in this paragraph are all from the same page.

5   Woolf, Joyce and Faulkner: Associative Memory

1. William James, *Principles of Psychology*, vol. 1, p. 239. The next quotation is on the same page.
2. Jean-Paul Sartre, 'On *The Sound and Fury*; Time in the Work of Faulkner', *Literary and Philosophical Essays*, trans. Annette Michaelson (London: Rider, 1955), pp. 79–87.
3. Virginia Woolf, 'A Sketch of the Past' in Jeanne Schulkind (ed.), *Moments of Being* (New York: Harcourt Brace, 1976), p. 98. The next quotation is on the same page.
4. Ibid., p. 122. The next citation is on the same page.
5. Ibid., p. 81.
6. Ibid., p. 122.
7. Ibid.
8. Woolf, *Moments of Being*, p. 81.
9. Ibid., p. 67.
10. Virginia Woolf, *To the Lighthouse* (New York: Harcourt Brace, 1981), p. 172. The next quotation is on the same page.
11. Ibid., p. 147.
12. Ibid., p. 192.
13. Endel Tulving, *Elements of Episodic Memory* (New York: Oxford University Press, 1983), p. 160.
14. Woolf, *To the Lighthouse*, p. 172.
15. Entry of 30 August 1923, in *The Diary of Virginia Woolf*, vol. 2, p. 263. The next quotation, from the entry of 15 October 1923, is on p. 272.
16. Virginia Woolf, *Mrs Dalloway* (New York: Harcourt Brace, 1981), p. 3.
17. Ibid., p. 6.
18. Ibid., p. 41.
19. Ibid., pp. 42–3.
20. Endel Tulving, *Elements of Episodic Memory*, p. 171.
21. James Joyce, *A Portrait of the Artist as a Young Man*, ed. R.B. Kershner (Boston: Bedford Books of St. Martin's Press, 1993), p. 67.
22. Joyce, *A Portrait*, p. 89. The next quotation is from the same page.
23. Ibid., p. 143.
24. Ibid., p. 153.
25. William James, *Principles of Psychology*, p. 655.
26. James Joyce, *Dubliners* (New York: Viking Penguin, 1976), p. 203. The next quotation is from the same page.
27. Ibid., p. 218. The next quote is on p. 223.
28. Ibid., p. 40.
29. 1932 interview with Henry Nash Smith in *The Lion in the Garden: Interviews with William Faulkner*, ed. James B. Menucthe (New York: Random House, 1968), pp. 30–1.

30. 1952 Interview with Lois Bouvard in *The Lion in the Garden*, p. 70.
31. Interview in Japan, 5 August 1955, 'Colloquies at Nagano Seminar', in *The Lion in the Garden*, pp. 147–8.
32. Faulkner, *The Sound and the Fury* (New York: Norton, 1994), p. 5.
33. Ibid., p. 48.
34. Ibid., p. 51.
35. Ibid., p. 54. The next quotation is on the same page.
36. William Faulkner, *As I Lay Dying* (New York: Vintage, 1987), p. 9.

6   Apollinaire, Breton and the Surrealists: Automatism and Aleatory Memory

1. André Breton, *Oeuvres complètes* (Paris: Gallimard, 1988), vol. 1, p. 317.
2. Title of Introduction to *Le Révolver à cheveux blancs*. *Oeuvres complètes* (Paris: Gallimard, 1992), vol. 2, p. 49.
3. Guillaume Apollinaire, *Oeuvres poétiques* (Paris: Gallimard, 1956), p. 148.
4. Ibid., p. 45.
5. Ibid., p. 248.
6. See the Afterword of this book.
7. Apollinaire, *Oeuvres en prose* (Paris: Gallimard, 1977), p. 343.
8. Apollinaire, *Oeuvres poétiques*, pp. 39–40.
9. Ibid., pp. 41–2.
10. Apollinaire, 'Simultanéisme-Librettisme', in *Les Soireés de Paris*, no. 25 (15 June 1914), pp. 322–5.
11. André Breton, *Oeuvres complètes* (Paris: Gallimard, 1988), vol. 1, p. 340.
12. Pierre Janet, *L'Automatisme psychologique* (1889; Paris: Alcan, 1973), p. 15.
13. André Breton, *Oeuvres complètes*, vol. 1, p. 948.
14. Ibid., p. 950.
15. See Philippe Soupault, *Vingt mille et un jours* (Paris: P. Belfond, 1980), p. 64.
16. Breton, 'Le Message automatique', in *Oeuvres complètes*, vol. 2, p. 386. (Breton approvingly quoted René Sudre's statement 'Ecriture inconsciente sera une expression plus juste'; ['Unconscious writing will be a more accurate expression']). See Breton, *Oeuvres Complètes*, vol. 2, p. 1540, n. 3.
17. Jean Starobinski, 'Freud, Breton, Myers', in *La Relation critique* (Paris: Gallimard, 1970), p. 332.
18. André Breton, 'Le Message automatique', *Oeuvres complètes*, vol. 2, p. 379.
19. Breton, *Oeuvres complètes*, vol. 1, p. 328.
20. See André Breton, 'Carnet 1920–1921', in *Oeuvres complètes*, vol. 1, p. 620.
21. Ibid.
22. Ibid., p. 618.
23. Ibid., p. 619.
24. Ibid.
25. This article first appeared in the journal *Littérature* on 1 November 1922. The citation is from Breton, *Oeuvres complètes*, vol. 1, p. 274.
26. Ibid.
27. Anna Balakian, *André Breton* (New York: Oxford UP, 1971), p. 65.
28. Breton, *Oeuvres complètes*, vol. 1, p. 317.
29. Breton, 'Lettre aux Voyantes', in *Oeuvres complètes*, vol. 1, p. 908.

30. Frontispiece to Breton, *Introduction au discours sur le peu de réalité* (Paris: Librairie Gallimard, 1927).
31. Breton, 'Les Champs magnétiques' in *Oeuvres complètes*, vol. 1, p. 58.
32. Breton, ibid., vol. 1, p. 64.
33. The original French of this little known text reads: 'Une mémoire la première sans doute et celle qui fait fleurir les astres, ouvrir les mains. Ceux qui la sollicitent sont grands. Mais le jardin des persécutions ferme ses portes sur eux et ils demeurent traqués par les thons de la mer, par les forts de la Halle, par les hosties à pattes d'araignées. Cette mémoire flatte ses servantes comme un grand seigneur pervers. La chambre à coucher est divisée par les parfums, parfum du Sud, Etoile de Nubie, collerettes d'enfant disparu . . . Cette mémoire apaisée, meurtrie, ouvragée comme une grille de fer, cède quelquefois la place à une boulette de poison. Le trolley qui avance dans les bois.' *Poisson soluble II* (2), in *Oeuvres complètes*, vol. 1, p. 515.
34. Breton, *Oeuvres complètes*, vol. 1, p. 516.
35. Ibid.
36. Jean-Pierre Cauvin, 'The Poethics of André Breton', in Cauvin (ed.), *Poems of André Breton* (Austin, Texas: U of Texas Press, 1982), p. xxii.
37. J. Allan Hobson and Robert Stickgold, 'The Conscious State Paradigm: a Neurocognitive Approach to Waking, Sleeping and Dreaming' in Michael S. Gazzaniga (ed.), *The Cognitive Neurosciences*, p. 1387.
38. Robert Desnos, 'Confession d'un enfant du siècle', in *Oeuvres* (Paris: Gallimard, 1999), p. 302.
39. Louis Aragon, *Le Mouvement perpétuel* (Paris: Gallimard, 1970), p. 66. The next quote, from the poem 'Sommeil de plomb', is on the same page.

7   Nin, Borges and Paz: Labyrinthine Passageways of Mind and Language

1. *The Seminar of Jacques Lacan*, Book III, trans. Russell Grigg (New York: W.W. Norton, 1993), p. 152. The full citation of Lacan's metaphor for memory is the following: 'However, it's made up of messages, it's a succession of little signs of plus or minus, which file in one after the other and go round and round like the little electric lights on the Place de l'Opéra that go on and off.'
2. Entry of August 1936 in *The Diary of Anaïs Nin*, vol. II, p. 112.
3. Nin, *The Novel of the Future*, p. 42.
4. Catherine Broderick, 'Cities of Her Own Invention: Urban Iconology in *Cities of the Interior* in Suzanne Nalbantian (ed.), *Anaïs Nin: Literary Perspectives* (London: Macmillan Press (now Palgrave Macmillan), 1997), p. 37.
5. Nin, *Seduction of the Minotaur* in *Cities of the Interior*, p. 543.
6. Ibid., p. 486.
7. Ibid., pp. 549–50.
8. Ibid., p. 531.
9. Ibid.
10. Ibid., p. 535.
11. Ibid., p. 536.
12. Ibid., p. 565.

13. Nin, *Cities of the Interior*, p. 567.
14. Ibid., p. 478.
15. Ibid., p. 487.
16. Nin, *Under a Glass Bell* (New York: Gemor Press, 1944), p. 63.
17. Nin, *Winter of Artifice* (Chicago: Swallow Press, 1948), p. 96.
18. Borges, *Selected Poems*, ed. Alexander Coleman (New York: Viking, 1999), p. 70.
19. Jorge Luis Borges, *Selected Poems*, edited and translated by Alexander Coleman, p. 133. The next quotation is on p. 135.
20. Borges, *Selected Non-Fictions*, p. 324.
21. Ibid., p. 325.
22. Ibid., p. 326.
23. Borges, *Selected Non-Fictions*, p. 4. The article with its Spanish title 'La Naderia de la Personalidad' was published only once in the original in *Inquisiciones* (Buenos Aires: Editorial Proa, 1925). The citation of the Spanish words from this article are from that original edition.
24. See Pliny, Book 7, Section 24 of *Natural History* (Cambridge: Harvard UP, 1947).
25. Borges, *Collected Fictions*, trans. Andrew Hurley (New York: Viking, 1988), p. 135. The next quotation is on the same page.
26. Carter Wheelock, *The Mythmaker* (Austin: University of Texas Press, 1969), p. 21.
27. *Borges at Eighty: Conversations*, ed. Willis Barnstone (Bloomington: Indiana University Press, 1982), p. 20.
28. Ibid., p. 21.
29. See Octavio Paz, *A Draft of Shadows*, trans. Eliot Weinberger (New York: New Directions, 1972).
30. Paz, *A Draft of Shadows*, p. 155.
31. Octavio Paz, *Aguila o Sol?/ Eagle or Sun?*, trans. Eliot Weinberger (New York: New Directions, 1976), p. 103.
32. Paz, *A Draft of Shadows*, p. 129.
33. Ibid., p. 151.
34. Paz, *Configurations*, p. 7.
35. Ibid., p. 13.
36. Ibid., p. 11.
37. Ibid., p. 13.
38. Ibid., p. 33.
39. Ibid., p. 47.
40. Jason Wilson, *Octavio Paz: a Study of his Poetics* (London: Cambridge UP, 1979), p. 75.
41. Paz, *Configurations*, p. 89.
42. Jacques Soustelle, *La Pensée cosmologique des anciens mexicains* (Paris: Hermann & Cie, 1940), p. 58. The original French reads: 'chaque espace est lié à un temps ou à des temps. Ainsi la mentalité mexicaine ne connaît pas l'espace et le temps abstraits, mais des sites et des événements.'
43. Paz, *The Bow and the Lyre*, p. 24. The next quote is on p. 27.

8   The Almond and the Seahorse: Neuroscientific Perspectives

1. In the early 1990s, these structures were highlighted by the appellation of a journal, *The Hippocampus*, first published in 1991, and a volume

The Amygdala: Neurobiological Aspects of Emotion, Memory, and Mental Dysfunction, edited by John P. Aggleton, appearing in 1992 (New York: Wiley-Liss).

2. See Zola-Morgan, S., L.R. Squire and D.G. Amaral, 'Lesions of the amygdala that spare adjacent cortical regions do not impair memory', *Journal of Neuroscience* (1989), 9: 1922–36.

3. Definition from Francis Eustache's seminar 'Neuroanatomie fonctionnelle comparée de la mémoire de travail et de la mémoire épisodique', 27 March 2000, Collège de France, Paris, France.

4. Eric Kandel, *Principles of Neural Science*, p. 1238.

5. See Endel Tulving, 'Episodic and Semantic Memory', in E. Tulving and W. Donaldson, (eds), *Organization of Memory* (New York: Academic Press, 1972), pp. 381–403.

6. Endel Tulving, *Elements of Episodic Memory* (Oxford: Clarendon Press, 1983).

7. William F. Brewer, 'What is Autobiographical Memory?', in David C. Rubin (ed.), *Autobiographical Memory* (Cambridge: Cambridge UP, 1986), p. 34.

8. Daniel L. Schacter, *Searching for Memory* (New York: Basic Books, 1996), p. 104.

9. Ibid., p. 105.

10. Salvador Dalí, *The Secret Life of Salvador Dalí*, p. 38.

11. Paul W. Burgess and Tim Shallice, 'Confabulation and the Control of Recollection' in *Memory*, 1996. vol. 4, p. 367.

12. William F. Brewer, 'What is Autobiographical Memory?' in Rubin (ed.), *Autobiographical Memory*, p. 30.

13. See Alain Berthoz, 'Parietal and Hippocampal Contribution to Topokinetic and Topographic Memory' (1999), in N. Burgess *et al.* (eds), *The Hippocampal and Parietal Foundations of Spatial Cognition* (Oxford: Oxford UP, 1999), p. 398.

14. Alain Berthoz, *The Brain's Sense of Movement*, trans. Giselle Weiss (Cambridge, Mass: Harvard UP, 2000), p. 130. The next quotation is on the same page.

15. Edmund T. Rolls, 'A Theory of Hippocampal Function in Memory', *Hippocampus* (1996), 6: 601–20.

16. Edmund T. Rolls, *The Brain and Emotion* (Oxford: Oxford UP, 1999), p. 144.

17. Ibid.

18. R. Brown and J. Kulik, 'Flashbulb Memories', *Cognition* (1977), 5: 73–99.

19. Ledoux emphasized this point in a lecture entitled 'Les Emotions' given at the conference 'Journée de neuropsychologie J.L. Signoret' at the Salpêtrière Hospital in Paris, France, on 15 November 1999.

20. Karl S. Lashley, 'In Search of the Engram', in Frank A. Beach, Donald Hebb *et al.* (eds), *The Neuropsychology of Lashley: Selected Papers* (New York: McGraw Hill, 1960), pp. 500–1.

21. Ibid., p. 492.

22. Ibid., p. 502.

23. Ibid., p. 501. The next quote is on the same page.

24. Herbert P. Killackey, 'Morphology and Memory', in Gary Lynch (ed.), *Synapses, Circuits and the Beginnings of Memory* (Cambridge, Mass: MIT Press, 1986), p. 119.

25. See Larry R. Squire and Stuart Zola-Morgan, 'The Medial Temporal Lobe Memory System', *Science*, 253 (20 September 1991), 1380–6.

26. Larry R. Squire and Barbara J. Knowlton, 'Memory, Hippocampus and Brain Systems', in Michael S. Gazzaniga (ed.), *The Cognitive Neurosciences* (Cambridge, Mass: MIT Press, 1995), p. 832.

27. See Eric Kandel, *Principles of Neural Science*, p. 1272.
28. See Tim Tully, 'Regulation of Gene Expression and its Role in Long-term Memory and Synaptic Plasticity', *Proceedings of the National Academy of Science USA*, 94 (April 1997): 4239–41. See also John B. Connolly and Tim Tully, 'You Must Remember This: Finding the Master Switch for Long-term Memory', *The Sciences*, June 1996, pp. 37–42.
29. James L. McGaugh, 'Emotional Activation, Neuromodulatory Systems, and Memory', in Schacter, *Memory Distortion*, p. 257.
30. James McGaugh, 'Involvement of Hormonal and Neuromodulatory Systems in the Regulation of Memory Storage', *Annual Review of Neuroscience* (1989), 12: 255–87.
31. Ted Abel *et al.*, 'Steps toward a Molecular Definition of Memory Consolidation' in Schacter, *Memory Distortion*, p. 318.
32. This approach was given popular recognition by George Johnson's article 'Memory: Learning How It Works' in *The New York Times Magazine* (9 August 1987), featuring Lynch and his calpain hypothesis.
33. Gary Lynch, *Synapses, Circuits, and the Beginnings of Memory* (Cambridge, Mass: MIT Press, 1986), p. 57.
34. Antonio Damasio, *Descartes' Error: Emotion, Reason and the Human Brain* (New York: Putnam, 1994), p. 249.
35. Ibid., p. 250.
36. A conference 'Bergson et les mémoires' took place at the Department of Cognitive Sciences at the Université Victor Ségalen in Bordeaux, France on 1 October 1997. An earlier colloquium on 'Bergson et les neurosciences' was also held in France in 1995, under the direction of Philippe Gallois and Gérard Forzy.
37. Alain Berthoz, *Leçons sur le corps, le cerveau et l'esprit* (Paris: Editions Odile Jacob, 1999), p. 19.
38. The French word 'esprit' has often been mishandled in translation of literary texts as well. For example, in the case of Baudelaire's famous poem 'Correspondances': 'Qui chantent les transports de l'esprit et des sens', there was the notion of the fusion of mind and body. Several translators, such as Joanna Richardson, have mistranslated 'esprit' as soul (Penguin edition). My own early book *The Symbol of the Soul from Hölderlin to Yeats* made it very clear that the concept of 'soul' was dying out in the mid-nineteenth century, being gradually replaced by the material self.
39. Jean-Pierre Changeux, *L'Homme neuronal* (Paris: Librairie Arthème Fayard, 1983), p. 364. The translation from the French is my own, in order to give the important parenthesis that was deleted in the English language translation.
40. Ibid.
41. Nonetheless, more recently in the 1990s certain scientists have revived this debate at conferences in France regarding Bergson's legacy for science.
42. Jean-Pierre Changeux, *Neuronal Man*, trans. Laurence Garey (Princeton NJ: Princeton UP, 1985), p. 168.
43. Changeux, *L'Homme neuronal*, p. 227.
44. Changeux and Ricoeur, *What Makes Us Think*, trans. M.B. DeBoivse (Princeton: Princeton UP, 2000), p. 47.
45. Ibid., p. 141. As Changeux indicates, the citation from Bergson is from *Matière et mémoire* (Paris: PUF, 1991). Changeux's criticism of Bergson is

found on p. 163 of the original French version of Changeux's and Ricoeur's book, *Ce qui nous fait penser: la nature et la règle* (Paris: Editions Odile Jacob, 1998).

46. Changeux, Ricoeur, *What Makes us Think*, p. 141.
47. Changeux, *Neuronal Man*, p. 167. In light of his Darwinian notion of epigenesis, in more recent times Changeux has provocatively provided a hypothesis regarding the mental mechanism of the child, which suggests his ultimate view of the variability and development of memory across an individual's lifetime. Curiously, Changeux's description of the possibility of aleatory mental combinations in the early encoding of memory seems attuned to aspects of the surrealists' view of memory in their intentional mimicking of the childhood state of mind.
48. Jean Delacour, 'The Memory System and Brain Organization: From Animal to Human Studies', in L.G. Nilsson and H.J. Markowitsch (eds), *Cognitive Neuroscience of Memory* (Göttingen: Hogrefe & Huber, 1999), p. 259.
49. Jean Delacour, *Apprentissage et mémoire: une approche neurobiologique* (Paris: Masson, 1987), p. 210.
50. See Ira B. Black, 'Trophic Interactions and Brain Plasticity', in Michael S. Gazzaniga (ed.), *The Cognitive Neurosciences* (Cambridge, Mass: MIT Press, 1995), p. 15.
51. See Pietro Badia, 'Memories in Sleep: Old and New', in Richard R. Bootzin, John F. Kihlstrom and Daniel L Schacter (eds), *Sleep and Cognition* (Washington, DC: American Psychological Association, 1990).
52. See Ribot, *Les Maladies de la mémoire*.
53. Changeux, *Neuronal Man*, p. 249.
54. Harald Weinrich, *Lethe*, p. 192.
55. A.D. Baddeley and G.J. Hitch, 'Working Memory' in G.H. Bower (ed.), *Recent Advances in Learning and Motivation*, vol. 8, pp. 47–90, New York: Academic Press.
56. See Damasio, *Descartes' Error*, p. 71. Damasio considers this region of interaction to be the anterior cingulate cortex in the limbic system. Through the study of the neurotransmitter serotonin, he has also pointed out 'the system connection between ventromedial prefrontal cortices and amygdala', pp. 77, 184. Although Damasio does not specifically deal with the subject of memory in this book, he does suggest connections between the decision-making capacity of the prefrontal cortex and somatic states which constitute a kind of memory which can influence the reasoning mechanism of the brain.
57. Changeux and Ricoeur, *What Makes Us Think*, p. 139. Changeux elaborates: 'Objects of knowledge called up to the working compartment are also recruited from the regions of the cortex where long-term memories are stored: visual areas for concrete images; motor areas for actions on the world; specialized parts of the temporal areas for the recognition of faces, animals, and artifacts, including tools and instruments; a group of areas distributed over the cortex and converging in the frontal cortex for "abstract" concepts.'
58. Endel Tulving, 'Concepts of Human Memory' in Larry Squire *et al.*, *Memory: Organization and Locus of Change* (New York: Oxford University Press, 1991), p. 14.
59. Jonathan Winson, *Brain and Psyche*, p. 245.

60. Michael S. Gazzaniga (ed.), *The Cognitive Neurosciences*, p. 1378.
61. Daniel Schacter, 'Implicit Memory: History and Current Status', in *Journal of Experimental Psychology* (1987), p. 501.
62. Daniel Schacter, *Searching for Memory*, p. 233.
63. Ibid., p. 232.
64. See Steven Pinker, 'Introduction' to *Language*, in Michael S. Gazzaniga (ed.), *The Cognitive Neurosciences*, p. 852.
65. Steven Pinker, *The Language Instinct*, p. 323.
66. D.L. Nelson, 'Implicit Memory', in Peter E. Morris (ed.), *Theoretical Aspects of Memory* (London and New York: Methuen, 1994), p. 157.
67. See D.L. Nelson and T.A. Schreiber, 'Processing Implicit and Explicit Representations', in *Psychological Review* (1992), 99: 322–48.
68. James L. McClelland 'Constructive Memory and Memory Distortions: a Parallel-Distributed Processing Approach', in Daniel L. Schacter (ed.), *Memory Distortion*, p. 88. Although the memory trace synthesis model was introduced in 1981, it bears sustained validity.
69. Schacter (ed.), *Memory Distortion*, p. 384.

Afterword. Images of the Artists: Dalí, Dominguez and Magritte

1. From Kazimir Malevich, 'Non-Objectivity', as quoted by Linda D. Henderson, *The Fourth Dimension and Non-Euclidean Geometry in Modern Art* (Princeton: Princeton UP, 1983), p. 292.
2. See Herman Minkowski, 'Space and Time', in J.J.C. Smart (ed.), *Problems of Space and Time* (New York: Macmillan Co, 1964), pp. 297–312.
3. Henderson, p. 336.
4. Salvador Dalí, 'Les Pleurs d'Héraclite', in *La Conquête de l'irrationnel* (Paris: Editions Surréalistes, 1935), p. 25.
5. See Marcel Jean, *The History of Surrealist Painting*, trans. Simon Watson Taylor (1959; London: George Weidenfeld & Nicolson, 1960), p. 218.
6. Salvador Dalí, *The Secret Life of Salvador Dali*, trans. Haakon M. Chevalier (New York: Dover, 1993), p. 317. The next quotation is on the same page.
7. Ibid., p. 304.
8. Ibid., p. 304. The next quotation is on the same page.
9. Ibid., p. 219. The next quotation is on the same page.
10. André Breton, *Le Surréalisme et la peinture* (New York: Brentano's, 1945), p. 152, n. 1.
11. Oscar Dominguez, 'The Petrification of Time', trans. Lucy R. Lippard in *Surrealists on Art* (Englewood Cliffs, NJ: Prentice Hall, 1970), p. 109. The next citations from this text are on the same page.
12. See my discussion of this article in Chapter 6.
13. John Archibald Wheeler, *A Journey into Gravity and Spacetime* (New York: Scientific American Library, 1999), p. 12.

Bibliography

1. Scientific works on memory, the brain, and related fields

Aggleton, John P. (ed.). *The Amygdala: Neurobiological Aspects of Emotion, Memory, and Mental Dysfunction*, New York: Wiley-Liss, 1992.

Andreasen, Nancy C. *Brave New Brain: Conquering Mental Illness in the Age of the Genome*, New York: Oxford University Press, 2001.

Babinski, Joseph. *Exposé des travaux scientifiques du Dr. Joseph Babinski*, Paris: Masson, 1913.

—— and J. Froment. *Hystérie-pithiatisme et troubles nerveux d'ordre réflexe en neurologie de guerre*, Paris: Masson and Cie, 1917.

Beach, Frank A. (ed.). *The Neuropsychology of Lashley: Selected Papers*, New York: McGraw Hill, 1960.

Bergson, Henri. *Durée et Simultanéité*, 1922; Paris: Quadridge, 1998.

——. *Ecrits et paroles*. Rassemblées par R.M. Moise-Bastide, Paris: Presses Universitaires, 1957.

——. *L'Evolution créatrice*, 1907; Paris: Presses Universitaires de Paris, 1962.

——. *Matter and Memory*, 1908; New York: Zone, 1991.

——. 'Mémoire et reconnaissance', *Revue philosophique*, Vol. 41 (1896), 225–48.

——. *Oeuvres*, Paris: Presses Universitaires de France, 1963.

——, H. Poincaré and C. Gide (eds). *Le Matérialisme actuel*, Paris: Flammarion, 1913.

Bergson et les neurosciences: Actes du colloque international de neuro-philosophie, Lille: Les Empêcheurs de penser en rond, 1997.

Berthoz, Alain (ed.). *Leçons sur le corps, le cerveau et l'esprit*, Paris: Editions Odile Jacob, 1999.

——. *The Brain's Sense of Movement*. (1997; orig. French), trans. Giselle Weiss, 1997; Cambridge, Mass.: Harvard UP, 2000.

Binet, Alfred. *The Experimental Psychology of Alfred Binet: Selected Papers*, ed. Robert H. Pollack and Margaret W. Brenner, New York: Springer, 1969.

——. *Introduction à la psychologie expérimentale*, Paris: Félix Alcan, 1894.

——. *L'Etude expérimentale de l'intelligence*, Paris: Alfred Costes, 1922.

Bootzin, Richard R., John F. Kihlstrom and Daniel L. Schacter (eds). *Sleep and Cognition*, Washington, DC: American Psychological Association, 1990.

Bower, Gordon H. *Psychology of Learning and Motivation: Advances in Research and Theory*, New York: Academic Press, 1979.

Brissand, Edouard. *L'Hygiène des asthmatiques*, Paris: Masson, 1896.

Brown, R. and J. Kulik. 'Flashbulb Memories', *Cognition*, 5 (1977): 73–99.

Burgess, N., K.J. Jeffery and J. O'Keefe (eds), *The Hippocampal and Parietal Foundation of Spatial Cognition*, New York: Oxford UP, 1999.

Burgess, Paul W. and Tim Shallice. 'Confabulation and the Control of Recollection', *Memory*, 4 (1996).

Changeux, Jean-Pierre and Paul Ricoeur. *Ce qui nous fait penser: la nature et la règle*, Paris: Odèle Jacob, 1998.

——. *L'Homme neuronal*, Paris: Librairie Arthème Fayard, 1983. English edition: *Neuronal Man*, trans. Lawrence Gary, Princeton: Princeton UP, 1985.

—— and Paul Ricoeur. *What Makes Us Think?*, trans. of *Ce qui nous fait penser: la nature et la règle* by M.B. DeBevoise, 1998; Princeton, NJ: Princeton UP, 2000.

Charcot, Jean-Martin. *Charcot the Clinician: The Tuesday Lessons*, trans. Christopher G. Goetz, 1889; New York: Raven Press, 1982.

Connolly, John B. and Tim Tully. 'You Must Remember This: Finding the Master Switch of Long-term Memory', *The Sciences*, May–June 1996, pp. 37–42.

Damasio, Antonio R. *Descartes' Error: Emotion, Reason, and the Human Brain*, New York: G.P. Putnam's Sons, 1994.

——. *The Feeling of What Happens*, New York: Harcourt Brace, 1999.

Delacour, Jean. *Apprentissage et mémoire: une approche neurobiologique*, Paris: Masson, 1987.

——. 'Proust's Contribution to the Psychology of Memory: the 'Réminiscence' from the Standpoint of Cognitive Science', *Theory & Psychology* (2001) 11: 255–71

Ebbinghaus, Hermann. *Memory: A Contribution to Experimental Psychology*, New York: Dover, 1964.

Ellenberger, Henri F. *The Discovery of the Unconscious: The History and Evolution of Dynamic Psychology*, New York: Basic, 1970.

Freud, Sigmund. *The Standard Edition of the Complete Psychological Works of Sigmund Freud*, Vol. 6, 1901; London: Hogarth Press, 1960.

Friedman, Alan J. and Carol C. Donley, *Einstein as Myth and Muse*, Cambridge: Cambridge UP, 1985.

Gazzaniga, Michael S. *et al.* (eds). *The Cognitive Neurosciences*, Cambridge, Mass.: MIT Press, 1995.

Gunter, P.A.Y. (ed.). *Bergson and the Evolution of Physics*, Knoxville: University of Tennessee Press, 1969.

Hartmann, Eduard von. *Philosophy of the Unconscious: Speculative Results according to the Inductive Method of Physical Science*, 1931; London: Routledge & Kegan Paul, 1950.

Henderson, Linda Dalrymple. *The Fourth Dimension and Non-Euclidean Geometry in Modern Art*, Princeton: Princeton UP, 1983.

Jaffard, E., B. Andrieu and B. Claverie. *Cerveau et mémoires: Bergson, Ribot et neuropsychologie*, Paris: Editions Osiris, 1998.

James, William. *Essays in Psychical Research*, Cambridge, Mass.: Harvard UP, 1986.

——. *Principles of Psychology*, 2 vols, 1890; New York: Dover, 1950.

Janet, Pierre. *De l'Angoisse à l'extase*, Paris: Alcan, 1926.

——. *L'Automatisme psychologique*, 1889; Paris: Editions Odile Jacob, 1998.

——. 'Les Actes inconscients et la mémoire pendant le somnambulisme', *Revue philosophique*, Vol. 25 (1888), 238–79.

——. *L'Evolution de la mémoire et de la notion du temps*, Paris: A. Chahine, 1928.

Johnson, George. 'Memory: Learning How It Works', *The New York Times Magazine*, 9 August 1987.

Jung, Carl. *The Collected Works of C.G. Jung*, Vol. 2, Princeton: Princeton UP, 1973.

Kandel, Eric J., Thomas M. Jessell and James H. Schwartz (eds). *Principles of Neural Science*, 1991; New York: McGraw-Hill, 2000.

Lacan, Jacques. *The Seminar of Jacques Lacan. Book II. The Ego in Freud's Theory and in the Technique of Psychoanalysis*, 1978 French; trans. Sylvana Tomaselli, New York: W.W. Norton, 1991.

——. *The Seminar of Jacques Lacan. Book III. The Psychoses, 1955–1956*; 1981 French; trans. Russell Grigg, New York: W.W. Norton, 1993.

Lashley, Karl S. *The Neuropsychology of Lashley: Selected Papers*, ed. Frank A. Beach, Donald Hebb *et al.*, 1950 New York: McGraw Hill, 1960.

Lynch, Gary. *Synapses, Circuits, and the Beginnings of Memory*, Cambridge, Mass.: MIT UP, 1986.

McGaugh, James L., Gary Lynch and Norman W. Weinberger (eds). *Brain and Memory: Modulation and Mediation of Neuroplasticity*, New York: Oxford UP, 1995.

Morris, Peter E. and Michael Gruneberg (eds). *Theoretical Aspects of Memory*, London: Routledge, 1994.

Myers, Frederic W.H. *Human Personality and its Survival of Bodily Death*, ed. and abr. by Leopold H. Myers, London: Longmans, Green & Co., 1918.

Nilsson, L.G. and H.J. Markowitsch (eds). *Cognitive Neuroscience of Memory*, Göttingen: Hogrefe & Huber, 1999.

Pinker, Steven. *How the Mind Works*, New York: W.W. Norton, 1997.

——. *The Language Instinct: How the Mind Creates Language*, 1994; New York: HarperPerennial, 1995.

Proust, Adrien, *L'Hygiène du neurasthénique*, Paris: Masson, 1897.

Regnard, Bourneville and P. *Iconographie photographique de la Salpêtrière: Service de Charcot*, Paris: V. Adrien Delahaye & Co., 1877.

Ribot, Théodule. *Les Maladies de la mémoire*, 1881; Paris: Félix Alcan, 1881.

Rolls, Edmund T. *The Brain and Emotion*, Oxford: Oxford UP, 1999.

——. 'A Theory of Hippocampal Function in Memory', *Hippocampus* 6 (1996): 601–20.

Rubin, David S. (ed.). *Autobiographical Memory*, Cambridge: Cambridge UP, 1986.

Schacter, Daniel L. (ed.). *Memory Distortion: How Minds, Brains, and Societies Reconstruct the Past*, Cambridge, Mass.: Harvard UP, 1995.

——. *Searching for Memory: The Brain, the Mind, and the Past*, New York: Basic, 1996.

Semon, Richard. *Mnemic Psychology*, London: George Allen & Unwin, 1923.

Shallice, Tim and Elizabeth K. Warrington. 'Independent Functioning of Verbal Memory Stores: A Neuropsychological Study', *Quarterly Journal of Experimental Psychology*, 22 (1970): 261–73.

Smart, J.J.C. (ed.), *Problems of Space and Time*, 1964; New York: Macmillan (now Palgrave Macmillan), 1973.

Soustelle, Jacques. *La Pensée cosmologique des anciens mexicains*, Paris: Hermann & Cie, 1940.

Squire, Larry J. *et al.*, (eds). *Memory: Organization and Locus of Change*, New York: Oxford UP, 1991.

Tully, Tim. 'Regulation of Gene Expression and Its Role in Long-term Memory and Synaptic Plasticity', *Proceedings of the National Academy of Sciences*, Vol. 94 (April 1997), 4239–41.

Tulving, Endel. *Elements of Episodic Memory*, New York: Oxford UP, 1983.

—— and W. Donaldson (eds). *Organization of Memory*, New York: Academic Press, 1972.

Winson, Jonathan. *Brain and Psyche: The Biology of the Unconscious*, Garden City, NY: Anchor, 1985.

2. Literary and critical works

Apollinaire, Guillaume. *L'Esprit nouveau et les poètes*, 1917; Paris: J. Haumont, 1946.
——. *Oeuvres en prose*, Paris: Gallimard, 1977.
——. *Oeuvres poétiques*, Paris: Gallimard, 1956.
Aragon, Louis. *Le Mouvement perpétuel*, Paris: Gallimard, 1970.
Balakian, Anna. *André Breton*, New York: Oxford UP, 1971.
Barnstone, Willis (ed.). *Borges at Eighty: Conversations*, Bloomington: Indiana UP, 1982.
Baudelaire, Charles. *Oeuvres complètes*, Vols 1 and 2, Paris: Gallimard, 1976.
——. *The Flowers of Evil and Paris Spleen*, trans. William H. Crosby; Brockport, NY: BOA Editions, 1991.
Beckett, Samuel. *Proust*, New York: Grove Press, 1931.
Borges, Jorge Luis. *Collected Fictions*, ed. Andrew Hurley. New York: Viking, 1998.
——. *Selected Non-fictions*, ed. Eliot Weinberger, New York: Viking, 1999.
——. *Selected Poems*, ed. Alexander Coleman, New York: Viking, 1999.
Breton, André. *Le Surréalisme et la peinture*, New York: Brentano's, 1945.
——. *Oeuvres complètes*, Paris: Gallimard, Vol. I (1988); Vol. II (1992).
——. *Poems of André Breton*, ed. Jean-Pierre Cauvin, Austin: University of Texas Press, 1982.
——and Philippe Soupault. *Les Champs magnétiques: le manuscrit original facsimile et transcription*, Paris: Lachenal & Ritter, 1988.
Breunig, Leroy C. *Guillaume Apollinaire*, New York: Columbia UP, 1969.
Carter, William C. *Marcel Proust. A Life*, New Haven and London: Yale UP, 2000.
Chiles, Francis. *Octavio Paz: The Mythic Dimension*, New York: Peter Lang, 1987.
Dalí, Salvador. *La Conquête de l'irrationnel*, Paris: Editions Surréaliste, 1935.
——. *The Secret Life of Salvador Dalí*, New York: Dover Publications, 1993.
Deleuze, Gilles. *Proust and Signs*, trans. Richard Howard, 1964; New York: George Braziller, 1972.
Desnos, Robert. *Oeuvres*, Paris: Gallimard, 1999.
Faulkner, William. *As I Lay Dying*, 1930; New York: Vintage, 1987.
——. *The Portable Faulkner*, ed. Malcolm Cowley, 1946; New York: Penguin, 1977.
——. *The Sound and the Fury*, ed. David Minter, 1929; New York: W.W. Norton, 1994.
Fein, John M. *Toward Octavio Paz: A Reading of His Major Poems, 1957–1976*, Lexington, KY: The UP of Kentucky, 1986.
Fowlie, Wallace. *Rimbaud*, New York: New Directions, 1946.
Hugo, Victor. *Oeuvres poétiques*, Paris: Gallimard, 1964.
Huysmans, Joris-Karl. *Against Nature*, trans. Robert Baldick, 1884; New York: Penguin, 1959.
——. *A Rebours*, 1884; Paris: Gallimard, 1977.
Jackson, John E. *Mémoire et création poétique*, Paris: Mercure de France, 1992.
Jean, Marcel. *The History of Surrealist Painting*, trans. Simon Watson Taylor, 1959; New York: Grove, 1960.
Joyce, James. *A Portrait of the Artist as a Young Man*, ed. R.B. Kershner. 1914–15; Boston: Bedford Books of St. Martin's Press, 1993.
——. *Dubliners*, ed. Robert Scholes, 1914; New York: Viking Penguin, 1976.
Lamartine, Alphonse-Marie-Louis de. *Graziella, Raphaël*, Paris: Editions Garniers Frères, 1955.

——. *Méditations poétiques*, ed. Jean des Cognets, Paris: Editions Garnier Frères, 1956.

——. *Oeuvres poétiques complètes de Lamartine*, Paris: Pléiade, 1963.

Lippard, Lucy. *Surrealists on Art*, Englewood Cliffs, NJ: Prentice-Hall, 1970.

Malebranche, Nicolas. *De la Recherche de la vérité*, ed. Pierre Janet, Paris: Alcan, 1886. Translated as: *The Search after Truth* (trans. Thomas M. Lennon and Paul J. Olscamp); *Elucidations of the Search after Truth* (trans. Thomas M. Lennon); *Philosophical Commentary* (trans. Thomas M. Lennon), Columbus: Ohio State University Press, 1980.

Mallarmé, Stéphane. *Oeuvres complètes*, Paris: Gallimard, 1945.

Megay, Joyce N. *Bergson and Proust*, Paris: Vrin, 1976.

Menucthe, James B. (ed.). *The Lion in the Garden: Interviews with William Faulkner*, New York: Random House, 1968.

Merrell, Floyd. *Unthinking Thinking: Jorge Luis Borges, Mathematics, and the New Physics*, West Lafayette, IN: Purdue UP, 1991.

Morley, John. *Rousseau*, London: Chapman and Hall, 1873.

Musset, Alfred de. *Poésies complètes*, Paris: Gallimard, 1957.

Musset, Paul de. *The Biography of Alfred de Musset*, trans. Harriet W. Preston; Boston: Roberts Brothers, 1873.

Nalbantian, Suzanne. *Aesthetic Autobiography: From Life to Art in Marcel Proust, James Joyce, Virginia Woolf and Anaïs Nin*, London: Macmillan (now Palgrave Macmillan), 1994.

—— (ed.). *Anaïs Nin: Literary Perspectives*, London: Macmillan (now Palgrave Macmillan), 1997.

Nin, Anaïs. *Cities of the Interior*, 1959; Chicago: Swallow Press, 1974.

——. *The Novel of the Future*, London: Macmillan (now Palgrave Macmillan), 1968.

——. *Under a Glass Bell*, New York: Gemor Press, 1944.

——. *Winter of Artifice: Three Novelettes*, 1945; Chicago: Swallow Press, 1948.

Olney, James. *Memory and Narrative: The Weave of Life-Writing*, Chicago: University of Chicago Press, 1999.

Paz, Octavio. *Aguila o Sol?/Eagle or Sun?*, trans. Eliot Weinberger; New York: New Directions, 1976.

——. *Alternating Current*, trans. Helen R. Lane, 1967; New York: Viking, 1973.

——. *The Bow and the Lyre*, trans. Ruth L.C. Simms, Austin: University of Texas Press, 1973.

——. *Configurations*, trans. G. Aroul *et al.*, New York: New Directions, 1971.

——. *A Draft of Shadow and Other Poems*, ed. and trans. Eliot Weinberger, Elizabeth Bishop and Mark Strand, New York: New Directions, 1972.

Proust, Marcel. *A la Recherche du temps perdu*, Paris: Gallimard, Vol. I (1987); Vol. II (1988); Vol. III (1988); Vol. IV (1989).

——. *Contre Sainte-Beuve*, Paris: Gallimard, 1954.

——. *Le Carnet de 1908*, ed. Philip Kolb, Paris: Gallimard, 1976.

——. *Remembrance of Things Past*, 3 vols, New York: Random House, 1981.

——. *Swann's Way*, trans. C.K. Scott-Moncrieff and Terence Kilmartin, New York: Vintage, 1981.

Reck, Andrew J. *Introduction to William James: An Essay and Selected Texts*, Bloomington: Indiana University Press, 1967.

Rimbaud, Arthur. *Oeuvres complètes*, Paris: Gallimard, 1972.

Rousseau, Jean-Jacques. *Confessions*, trans. J.M. Cohen, 1781; New York: Penguin, 1953.

——. *Les Rêveries du promeneur solitaire*, ed. S. De Sacy, Paris: Le Livre de Poche, 1965.

——. *Oeuvres complètes*, ed. Bernard Gagnebin and Marcel Raymond, Paris: Gallimard, 1959.

——. *The Reveries of the Solitary Walker*, trans. Charles E. Butterworth, New York: New York University Press, 1979.

Sartre, Jean-Paul. *Literary and Philosophical Essays*, trans. Annette Michaelson; London: Rider, 1955.

Soupault, Philippe. *Vingt mille et un jours : entretiens avec Serge Fauchereau*, Paris: P. Belfond, 1980.

Soustelle, Jacques. *La Pensée cosmologique des anciens mexicaines*, Paris: Hermann & Cie, 1940.

Starobinski, Jean. *La Relation critique: l'oeil vivant II*, Paris: Gallimard, 1970.

Tadié, Jean-Yves and Marc. *Le Sens de la mémoire*, Paris: Gallimard, 1999.

Weinrich, Harald and Steven Rendall. *Léthé: art et critique de l'oubli*, 1997; Paris: Fayard, 1999.

Wheeler, John Archibald. *A Journey into Gravity and Spacetime*, New York: Scientific American Library, 1990.

Wheelock, Carter. *The Mythmaker: A Study of Motif and Symbol in the Short Stories of Jorge Luis Borges*, Austin: University of Texas Press, 1969.

Wilson, Jason. *Octavio Paz: A Study of His Poetics*, Cambridge: Cambridge UP, 1979.

Woolf, Virginia. *Moments of Being: Unpublished Autobiographical Writings*, New York and London: Harcourt Brace Jovanovich, 1976.

——. *Mrs. Dalloway*, 1925; New York and London: Harcourt Brace Jovanovich, 1981.

——. *To the Lighthouse*, 1927; New York: Harcourt Brace Jovanovich, 1955.

Wordsworth, William. *Selected Poems*, ed. John O. Hayden, Harmondsworth, UK: Penguin, 1994.

Index